NYC Schools Under Bloomberg and Klein:
What Parents, Teachers, and Policymakers Need to Know

NYC Schools Under Bloomberg and Klein:

What Parents, Teachers, and Policymakers Need to Know

Essays by:

Diane Ravitch • Deborah Meier

Deycy Avitia • David C. Bloomfield • James F. Brennan

Hazel N. Dukes • Leonie Haimson • Emily Horowitz

Jennifer L. Jennings • Steve Koss • Maisie McAdoo

Udi Ofer • Aaron M. Pallas • Steven Sanders

Sol Stern • Patrick J. Sullivan • Andrew Wolf

Lulu

New York, 2009

Published in association with

Class Size Matters

124 Waverly Place

New York, NY 10011

www.classsizematters.org

Published 2009

Designed by Be Rivera

ISBN 978-0-557-07437-2

C◯NTENTS

Contributors

Deycy Avitia
is the Coordinator of Education Advocacy for the New York Immigration Coalition (NYIC). She oversees the English language learner (ELL) Education Taskforce and the Equity Monitoring Project for Immigrant and Refugee Education (EMPIRE). She serves on Community Board 11 in East Harlem and the board of directors of New Immigrant Community Empowerment (NICE) and Violence Intervention Program (VIP), a Latina organization dedicated to ending violence in the lives of women. She is also a founding member of Art for Change. She holds an Ed.M. in Education Policy and Management from Harvard Graduate School of Education, where she also served as a research assistant for the Harvard Civil Rights Project.

David C. Bloomfield
is Professor of Educational Leadership, Law & Policy at Brooklyn College, CUNY, and the CUNY Graduate Center. He is an elected parent member of the Citywide Council on High Schools, 2004–present, and served as its president from 2006 to 2007. He was former General Counsel for the New York City Board of Education and is the author of *American Public Education Law.*

James F. Brennan
represents the 44th New York State Assembly District in Brooklyn. He is the Chair of the New York State Assembly Committee on Cities and is the senior member of the Education Committee, having served on it throughout his twenty-five years in the Assembly.

Hazel N. Dukes
is the president of the NAACP New York State Conference and a long-time civil rights activist.

Leonie Haimson
is the founder and executive director of Class Size Matters.

Emily Horowitz
is a professor of Sociology and Criminal Justice at St. Francis College in Brooklyn. She completed her Ph.D. at Yale University in 2002. She served on the Community Education Council in Manhattan's District 6 from 2006 to 2008.

Jennifer L. Jennings
is a doctoral candidate in sociology a Columbia University, who will join the Department of Sociology at New York University in fall, 2009. She will spend her first two years on leave at Harvard University as a Robert Wood Johnson Health and Society post-doctoral scholar. She wrote a blog under the name "Eduwonkette" that is archived at www.edweek.org.

Steve Koss
is a public school parent and former mathematics teacher in the New York City public schools, and in in China. He has been a member of the District 2 Community Education Council and a Parents' Association president.

Maisie McAdoo
is a writer and researcher for the United Federation of Teachers.

Deborah Meier

spent more than four decades working in public education as a teacher, writer, and advocate. In 1974 she founded Central Park East (a K-6 public school) and in 1985, Central Park East Secondary School. From 1992 to 1996, she co-directed the Coalition Campus Project, which successfully redesigned two large, failing New York City public high schools and created a dozen new small public schools. She was an advisor to New York City's Annenberg Challenge and Senior Fellow at the Annenberg Institute at Brown University from 1995 to 1997. From 1997 to 2005 she was the founder and principal of the Mission Hill School, a K-8 school in the Boston Pilot Network. She is currently a senior scholar at New York University's Steinhardt School of Education and serves on the board of The Coalition of Essential Schools. She is the author of many books and articles on education reform.

Udi Ofer

is the Advocacy Director at the New York Civil Liberties Union. Ofer is responsible for supervising the NYCLU's work to end the overpolicing of New York City schools. He drafted the Student Safety Act, which would provide for oversight and accountability of police practices in New York City schools.

Aaron M. Pallas

is Professor of Sociology and Education at Teachers College, Columbia University. He has also taught at Johns Hopkins University, Michigan State University, and Northwestern University, and served as a statistician at the National Center for Education Statistics in the U.S. Department of Education. He is a Fellow of the American Educational Research Association and a member of the Sociological Research Association.

Diane Ravitch

is Research Professor of Education at New York University, and author of many books on the history of education, including *The Great School Wars: A History of the New York City Public Schools*. She is a senior fellow at the Brookings Institution in Washington, D.C. She was an Assistant Secretary of Education under the first Bush Administration and was later appointed twice by President Clinton to the National Assessment Governing Board, on which she served from 1998 to 2004.

Steven Sanders

represented the 74th District of the New York State Assembly from 1978 to 2005. He served on the Education Committee for the duration of his tenure and chaired it from 1995 to 2005. He is currently a partner in CraneSanders, a government consulting firm.

Sol Stern

is the author of *Breaking Free: Public School Lessons and the Imperative of School Choice* and a Contributing Editor of *City Journal*.

Patrick J. Sullivan

is the Manhattan member of the Panel for Educational Policy, appointed by Manhattan Borough President Scott M. Stringer in June, 2007. His two sons attend public school in Manhattan.

Andrew Wolf

wrote a column that frequently touched on educational topics for the New York Sun for six and a half years. He has been involved in community journalism for thirty-five years and is editor and publisher of the *Riverdale Review* and the *Bronx Press* newspapers.

Introduction

- Diane Ravitch

In 2002, the New York State Legislature enacted legislation giving control of the New York City public schools to Mayor Michael Bloomberg. At the time, the mayor promised that the legislation would inaugurate an era of accountability, transparency, and effectiveness. Since then, the New York City public schools have experienced sweeping, radical change in every aspect of their operation, from their structure to their budget to curriculum and instruction to the ways in which schools are evaluated.

The purpose of this volume is to appraise the changes initiated during these years. The contributors to this collection of essays are united in our concern for the children who attend the public schools and the well-being of the public school system. We are also united in our desire to see these reforms fully discussed and debated. We believe that the necessary debate has not occurred. These essays attempt to make such a debate possible by setting forth a broader range of views than the public customarily encounters in the media.

The proponents of mayoral control have been very successful in bringing their views to the public. They rely on an extensive and sophisticated media enterprise. The New York City Department of Education now employs a public-relations staff of at least a dozen professionals, compared to only three in 2002. The mayor's office also has a large public relations department to call attention to his accomplishments. These considerable media assets are enhanced by the Fund for Public Schools, chaired by Chancellor Joel Klein. The Fund is a non-profit organization that was founded to improve the services in our public schools, but has spent millions of dollars on publicity campaigns to promote the record of the Bloomberg/Klein administration. The Fund's advertisements have appeared in subway cars and stations, in bus-stop shelters, and on television and radio. The members of the board of the Fund for Public Schools are leading figures in the city's media and financial elite. They include Caroline Kennedy and Mort Zuckerman (the publisher of the *Daily News*), and Wendi Murdoch (wife of the publisher of the *New York Post*). The editorial boards of those publications have been staunch advocates for the Department of Education, not only echoing its press releases and applauding its policies, but, when called upon, ready to challenge anyone who questions the Department of Education's achievements.

The legislation that granted control to the mayor in June 2002 brought an end to a governance system intended to promote school decentralization. The legislature established the decentralized system in 1969, in response to angry protests in minority communities. The system from 1969 to 2002 was governed by a Board of Education that had seven members: five appointed by the five borough presidents and only two by the mayor. The 1969 legislation also established community school districts, each with an elected local board and its own superintendent. The local boards controlled the elementary and junior high schools, while the central board maintained supervision over the high schools. The central board also selected the city's chancellor of schools and had oversight of the budget and education policy.

The era of decentralization was actually an anomaly in the city's history of school governance. From 1873 to 1969, the customary form of school governance was mayoral control; during that time, the mayor appointed every single member of the central Board of Education. That board, in turn, chose the superintendent of schools, oversaw the budget, and approved the superintendent's policies. Under mayoral control during those years, the mayor decided how much money the schools got from the city budget, but otherwise left the daily management of the schools to the board and its chosen leader.

When Mayor Bloomberg took control of the public schools in 2002, that tradition —in which the mayor relied on and respected the professional judgment of educators—-was abandoned, and the city embarked on a form of intrusive and authoritarian mayoral control unprecedented in the city's history. The mayor selected a non-educator, attorney Joel Klein, as his chancellor of schools, and the two of them launched a sweeping effort to remake the school system from top to bottom. Over the next several years, everything that happened in the schools would be redesigned, overhauled, reorganized, and reorganized again.

The law required the preservation of the city's thirty-two community school districts, but the mayor and chancellor acted as if they did not exist. The law anticipated that there would continue to be a Board of Education with real (though diminished) authority, with a majority of its members appointed by the mayor. The mayor renamed it the Panel on Education Policy and fired two of his own appointees when they disagreed with him, effectively turning the body into a rubber stamp. Under mayoral control, public involvement in the schools was curtailed, and there were no meaningful checks and balances to offset the mayor's power. The mayor and the chancellor regularly made decisions of great consequence to students, families, schools, and communities without public hearings, public discussion, or public review.

Klein spent the first several months of his tenure meeting with consultants and committees. In January 2003, the mayor and the chancellor revealed their program, which they called "Children First." It involved a comprehensive reorganization of the school system. Instead of the thirty-two local school districts described in the law, there would be ten regions, each headed by a regional superintendent. Under each regional superintendent would be local instructional supervisors, each of whom would monitor implementation of the new programs in a dozen or so schools. The mayor's plan imposed a citywide instructional program in reading and mathematics. Every school would have literacy coaches and math coaches, to make sure that the mandated programs were correctly and precisely taught. They created an organization called the Leadership Academy, to train new principals. They implemented their program with the opening of school in the fall of 2003.

In 2007, Chancellor Klein launched yet another major reorganization, this time eliminating the regions he and the mayor had earlier created and promulgating a new idea called "empowerment." Supervision was removed, and schools were told either to declare themselves to be "autonomous" schools in the "empowerment zone" or to affiliate with a support organization that could help them but neither evaluate nor supervise them. Hundreds of new and inexperienced principals were left to figure out what to do on their own. A majority of principals have retired or been replaced since the beginning of the Bloomberg/Klein era.

New initiatives, unmentioned when "Children First" began in 2003, eventually took precedence over the original agenda. One was the department's commitment to small schools, especially small high schools. Over the course of the past seven years, most of the city's large high schools have been closed and reopened as collections of small schools. That these schools share space in the same building has predictably created logistical problems and competition for facilities. The primary funder of the small high schools was the Gates Foundation. In late 2008, the Gates Foundation announced that it was curtailing support for small high schools because its own research showed that students in these schools were not making as much progress in reading or mathematics as their peers in large high schools. But New York City's Department of Education forged ahead, insisting that its small high schools were successful and closing down large high schools despite protests by parents, teachers, and students.

Another new priority that was not mentioned as part of the original "Children First" plan was charter schools. The chancellor and the mayor lobbied hard to get the legislature to allow the city to increase the number of its charters from fifty to one hundred. They embraced charter schools and regularly boasted of their test scores and successes. This was strange because charter schools are not run by the New York City Department of Education. It is like the president of Macy's telling customers to shop at Bloomingdale's. In their enthusiasm for charters, the mayor and chancellor overlooked the fact that charters accept only students who apply in a lottery, which guarantees them a more motivated student body than the regular public school in the same neighborhood, which must accept all students; charters are allowed to cap their enrollment and class size at any level they wish; and charters set their own disciplinary policies, which enable them to remove students who are disruptive or low-performing. The students ousted from charters then return to the regular public schools.

Then there was the Department of Education's accountability initiative, which first appeared in 2007, in which schools received a report card (so-called Progress Reports), summarized by a single letter grade. The mayor and chancellor called this the centerpiece of their reform effort and warned that they would close down schools that got an F. The grade of each school was based mainly on one-year changes in standardized test scores, with greater weight given to progress than to performance. A small part of the grade consisted of ratings by teachers and parents, a measurement of questionable validity since the respondents knew that they were casting a ballot on the survival of their school. There were many strange anomalies, in which very low-performing schools received an A or B for their progress, while very high-performing schools received failing grades. In many cases, the city's grades conflicted with the schools' rating by the state. The grading system focused the city's principals and teachers on test preparation, since test scores became the measure of whether a school would be praised or damned, and whether the principal and teachers would get a bonus and merit pay.

The mayor pledged to parents and elected officials that he would expand access to gifted and talented programs in underserved areas. But after the Department of Education based its new admissions policy solely on the results of standardized tests that were not designed for this purpose and decreed that there would be a strict cutoff at the ninetieth percentile, the number of minority children admitted to gifted programs dropped sharply. In several primarily Black and Hispanic districts, so few children were admitted to gifted programs that gifted classes had to be suspended. Nearly 40 percent of the students who reached the cutoff score lived in the city's four most affluent districts. Education researchers could have predicted this result, and did, because children in relatively affluent homes have greater access to advantages (pre-Kindergarten, lessons, educational toys, play groups, etc.) than children in poor homes. Any high-stakes test, especially when administered to young children, will reflect those disparities in economic opportunity.

Over the past seven years, the mayor and chancellor asserted that their reforms were a national model. Their story has been told and celebrated in national magazines and has even gained international attention. Indeed, New York City won the Broad Prize as the most improved urban district in 2007.

Yet the authors of these essays are not persuaded. We know that the city's budget for education has increased by nearly 80 percent, according to the chancellor, but we have not seen the increased spending reflected in smaller classes nor improved programs. Instead, we have seen more money spent on testing and test preparation and bonuses for higher test scores. We are not persuaded that a school system focused solely on producing higher test scores is necessarily an improved school system, especially since the soaring state test scores were not confirmed by the independent tests administered by the federal government in 2007. Many scholars have challenged the methods by which the Department of Education measures its own success.

The essays collected in this volume review different aspects of the "Children First" reforms.

Leonie Haimson, founder of Class Size Matters, presents a brief history of the "Children First" initiative. Haimson is a New York City public school parent and a creator of the New York City Public School Parents blog.

I have analyzed New York City's performance on the federal testing program called the National Assessment of Educational Progress [NAEP]. I am a historian of education at New York University, and I was a member of the National Assessment Governing Board—which oversees NAEP—from 1997 to 2004.

Jennifer L. Jennings and Aaron M. Pallas have analyzed evidence about the achievement gap in New York City public schools over the past seven years. The achievement gap is the term that describes the disparity in scores between White and Asian students on the one hand, and Black and Hispanic students on the other. Pallas is on the faculty at Teachers College, Columbia University.

Leonie Haimson analyzes the record of the Bloomberg/Klein administration in regard to class size.

David Bloomfield reviews the implementation of small schools policy in the New York City public schools. Bloomfield is a professor at Brooklyn College and a former president of the Citywide Council on High Schools.

Emily Horowitz writes about persistent overcrowding in the New York City public schools. She is a sociologist at St. Francis College in Brooklyn.

Patrick Sullivan considers the status and functioning of the Panel on Education Policy, the body that replaced the Board of Education during the Bloomberg administration. He points out that the term "Panel on Education Policy" was not written into the law of 2002. Sullivan is a member of the Panel, appointed by Manhattan Borough President Scott Stringer.

Jennifer L. Jennings and Leonie Haimson have analyzed graduation and discharge rates. Jennings is a sociologist at New York University specializing in education.

Steve Koss reviews the results of state test scores and the phenomenon of score inflation. Koss is a former New York City public high school teacher and is a public school parent leader.

Hazel Dukes, of the NAACP, considers whether the Bloomberg/Klein administration policies have truly advanced equity in the school system.

Aaron M. Pallas and Jennifer L. Jennings evaluate the Bloomberg/Klein administration's program for grading schools.

James Brennan, a member of the New York State Assembly from Brooklyn, offers an overview of state test scores before and after the current era of mayoral control. Assemblymember Brennan is a member of that body's Committee on Education.

Sol Stern of the Manhattan Institute and Andrew Wolf report on cheating as a response to pressure on principals and teachers to produce ever higher test scores. Stern is a senior fellow at the Manhattan Institute; Wolf is a journalist who wrote many columns on education for the *New York Sun*.

Udi Ofer, of the New York Civil Liberties Union, considers the status of students' civil rights in the current era.

Maisie McAdoo, a writer and researcher for the United Federation of Teachers, examines the condition and progress of special education today in the school system.

Deycy Avitia, of the New York Immigration Coalition, writes about progress among English Language Learners [ELLs] during the Bloomberg/Klein Administration.

Sol Stern explores the reading curriculum mandated by the Bloomberg/ Klein administration in 2003. Stern, as noted above, is a fellow of the Manhattan Institute and has written extensively for *City Journal* on New York City education issues.

Steven Sanders explains the intentions of the governance law that established mayoral control in 2002. Sanders was chairman of the New York State Assembly's Committee on Education when the law was drafted.

Deborah Meier writes about what has come of the hopes and dreams of school reformers of the last few decades. A former teacher and principal, Meier was the founding principal of the Central Park East school in Manhattan and the founding principal of the Mission Hill School in Boston.

These essays are our effort to ignite a genuine debate and dialogue about the future of the New York City public school system.

Let the debate begin!

"Children First":
A Short History

- Leonie Haimson

In June of 2002, the New York State Legislature gave unprecedented powers to a newly elected Mayor, Michael Bloomberg, to run the New York City public school system. He was granted the authority to appoint both a majority of Board of Education members and the schools chancellor. This would be the first time in the 160-year history of the city's schools that the mayor rather than the board appointed the educational leader of the school system. On July 29, Bloomberg announced the selection of Joel Klein as chancellor.

Joel Klein was a former anti-trust attorney and assistant attorney general who more recently had worked for a year and a half as a corporate executive at Bertelsmann AG, an international media corporation. The day before the press conference in which Klein's appointment was announced, the financially troubled company disclosed that its chief executive, Mr. Klein's superior, was resigning.[1]

At the press conference, held at Tweed Courthouse, the new headquarters of the renamed Department of Education (DOE), Bloomberg called Klein "a visionary." Klein had little experience in education, aside from a brief period teaching math in Queens during a leave of absence from law school in the late 1960s. He had never served on the board of an educational institution nor had shown any interest in public education as a private citizen. *The New York Times* reported that Bloomberg had made the decision to appoint Klein quickly:

> With the city's Board of Education abolished, replaced by an advisory committee with no real authority, Mr. Bloomberg moved secretly, consulting with few, to find a chancellor who could take over the system before the start of the school year . . . Although a news release on Mr. Klein described him as possessing "considerable experience in the field of education," this experience seems to have been limited to studying education for a bit and teaching math to sixth graders at a public school in Long Island City briefly, before he entered the Army Reserve . . . They travel in similar social circles. Mr. Bloomberg called Mr. Klein "a friend," a term he extends to just about anyone he has ever shared dinner with . . . The business backgrounds of both men infected their locution yesterday. They took turns referring to education as a "product" and things like "systems analysis" to evaluate problem schools.[2]

Within a few days, Klein obtained a waiver from the New York State Commissioner of Education to become Chancellor despite his lack of formal education credentials.[3] After a brief search, Klein announced several top appointments, including Diana Lam as deputy chancellor for teaching and learning. Lam had a controversial track record as superintendent in Providence, Rhode Island, San Antonio, Texas, and elsewhere.[4] Within nineteen months, Lam had resigned, amidst allegations that she had defied conflict-of-interest rules by trying to secure a job for her husband in the school system.[5]

On October 3, 2002, Klein announced the beginning of his overhaul of the schools, called "Children First," supported by a $4 million grant from the Broad and Robertson Foundations and a team of management consultants from McKinsey and Company. The DOE described "Children First" in the following terms:

> The goal of Children First is to create a system of outstanding schools where effective teaching and learning is a reality for every teacher and child . . . .Children First will involve listening to parents, teachers, principals, superintendents, students, community-based organizations, corporations, foundations, institutions of higher education, faith-based organizations, and public officials.[6]

The public engagement process consisted of five focus-group meetings with parents and educators, and a survey posted on the DOE website. At the same time, Klein quickly assembled ten working groups to address all aspects of the school system, from curriculum to staffing and organizational structure, whose members were kept secret until a series of Freedom of Information Act requests were filed. Although DOE officials had repeatedly claimed there were public school parents and working classroom teachers in these groups, when the FOIL was finally responded to, it was clear that there were none.[7]

On Martin Luther King, Jr., Day in January 2003, Mayor Bloomberg and Chancellor Klein announced the major components of the first phase of "Children First," including a standardized curriculum for all but two hundred relatively high-performing elementary schools. The curriculum would consist primarily of "Everyday Math" and the "Balanced Literacy" approach to reading, supplemented by the *Month by Month Phonics* reading program. They also announced that literacy and mathematics coaches would be assigned to every school, to train teachers in these programs and enforce certain pedagogical procedures in a highly centralized, micro-managed approach to instruction.

Immediately, there was criticism of the choice of curricula—especially *Month by Month Phonics,* which, according to a letter written by a group of reading specialists, is "woefully inadequate," "lacks the ingredients of a systematic phonics program," "lacks a research base," and "puts beginning readers at risk of failure in learning to read."[8] The constructivist mathematics program,

"Everyday Math," was opposed by a group of mathematicians and scientists from several New York City universities, who pointed out that it had twice failed California's rigorous textbook adoption process and gave insufficient attention to developing fluency in arithmetic, basic operations, and computation.[9]

Like future phases of the department's reorganizations, the formulation of these policies took place with little public scrutiny. These working groups produced no reports, held no hearings, and, when the initial set of policy changes was announced, produced no written document that could provide a convincing rationale or explanation for any of their decisions. Bas Braams, a professor of mathematics and scholar of mathematics education at New York University, commented at the time:

> The New York City schools system is the size of that of a small country. I find it remarkable that the NYC DOE would select a mandated core curriculum through a process in which there is apparently no proper documentation of the considerations that went into that choice . . . There appears to be no clear record of the Department's priorities, no record of any comparative evaluation of candidate curricula, and no record of the expert testimony and opinion upon which you relied.[10]

Arbitrariness also characterized the decision to exempt two hundred schools from the mandated curricula: few noticed that there was almost no overlap between these schools and a list of those that had made the most improvements over the last four years compiled by the State Education Department just a few months before. Indeed, many of the schools that had made the most improvements in mathematics and/or English had to switch to the new curricula despite their progress.

The first phase of "Children First" also involved a radical reorganization of the school system's structure. Although the state law required the preservation of thirty-two community school districts, district offices were dissolved and replaced by ten regional offices and six "regional operating centers" to provide back-office services. Schools were deprived of their entire traditional structure of support—and parents lost their primary avenue of appeal when their children were not receiving adequate services or they were confronted with problems that their principals could not resolve. Several state legislators sued to force the city to restore the district structure, followed by two consent decrees, both of which the DOE essentially ignored.

Then, in 2006, the ten regions were dissolved and the thirty-two districts restored, but in name only. Instead, district superintendents were drafted into an expanded "accountability" initiative, becoming "Senior Achievement Facilitators," commanded to spend at least 90 percent of their time coaching schools outside their districts on how to analyze test score data. Principals were mandated to allocate funds from their budgets to obtain services formerly provided at no cost by the districts from hastily assembled "School Support Organizations," some internal to the DOE and others external: private organizations called "Partnership Support Organizations." The six "Regional Operating Centers" were further centralized into "Integrated Service Centers," one for each borough.

DOE officials justified the reorganizations, which were highly disruptive, as reducing the cost of the bureaucracy. But much of the apparent savings was achieved by shifting costs to individual schools and new organizational structures. Meanwhile, overall spending on education rose substantially, from $12.5 billion annually in 2002 to $21 billion in 2009. Teacher salaries were increased by 43 percent, while hundreds of millions of dollars were also expended on no-bid contracts, consultants, and other controversial initiatives.

The expanded accountability office spent $80 million on a supercomputer called ARIS to crunch test scores, and new "data inquiry teams" were established in every school to analyze this data. A system of "Progress Reports" was instituted, in which each school received a grade based largely on one-year changes in test scores. In addition, schools received "Quality Reviews," produced by teams of outside consultants, and large-scale incentive programs were established to pay students, teachers, and principals for improved results on standardized tests. In 2008, the budget of the accountability initiative had grown to at least $130 million per year, with another $26 million spent on new interim assessments, standardized tests given to students, every four to six weeks.[11]

The administration repeatedly claimed that as a result of its reorganizations, $200 million had been cut from the bureaucracy and redirected to the classroom. An analysis by the Educational Priorities Panel, however, found that during the first two years, there had been huge cuts to vital services, resulting in a full year in which many special education students were deprived of mandated services and/or referrals.[12]

In 2005, the city comptroller released a letter to the mayor, calling into question the claims that the current administration had directed additional spending to the classroom. He found that the head count of the central administration at Tweed had increased, and that New York City schools had suffered a net loss of over two thousand teachers in two years. The comptroller also observed that DOE had made independent analysis of its finances increasingly difficult: "DOE fiscal reporting practices have become markedly less transparent since the Department's restructuring . . . DOE has misapplied certain units of appropriation to report expenditures, commencing with FY 2004, in a way that makes it difficult, if not impossible, to track its use of public funds."[13]

A more recent analysis found that the headcount at Tweed continued to multiply. In June 2002, there were 1,719 officials employed by the central administration; as of November 2008, there were 2,442, an increase of 40 percent. The accountability office had also grown—from thirteen to eighty-nine employees—an increase of nearly 600 percent.[14]

The DOE public relations staff expanded as well, from five in 2002 to twenty-three in 2008—an increase over 400 percent.[15] Salaries of top bureaucrats at Tweed had also risen. By 2007, twenty-two DOE officials earned more than $180,000 a year, more than commissioners of any city agency, compared to only two in 2004.[16]

In addition, no-bid contracts routinely bypassed the city comptroller's office or any form of public review.[17] In 2000, during the previous administration, the school system had signed seven no-bid contracts worth a total of $693,000. In 2005 alone, DOE paid $120 million in no-bid contracts, nearly twenty times that amount, including a $17 million contract with Alvarez and Marsal under which seven consultants were paid more than $1 million each. Their expert advice led to thousands of city children left shivering on the curb in the middle of winter, unable to get to school because their bus service had been eliminated.[18] Between January 2006 and August 2008, an internal DOE committee approved 120 no-bid contracts, while denying only one: a $2.2 million deal with the New Teacher Center in California that was approved the following month for an even higher price tag of $2.8 million.[19]

Spending on contracts overall rose sharply—with 944 contracts approved in 2008, at a total cost of $1.9 billion.[20] According to an analysis from the city comptroller's office, one out of every five contracts in fiscal years 2007 and 2008 exceeded its estimated cost by at least 25 percent—revealing "troubling patterns of mismanagement." If these expenditures had been more accurately predicted, considerable cost savings could have been achieved through negotiation: "As a result, taxpayer money continues to be squandered through an opaque process that does not take advantage of the competitive marketplace."[21]

In 2005, the state passed a new audit law for all school boards, to deter corruption, fraud, and waste of taxpayer funds. By January 2006, all school boards throughout the state were directed to form committees to review their internal audits. Yet more than two years later, there was no evidence that DOE had ever established such a committee.[22] As many officials pointed out, including the city comptroller, the DOE refused "to adopt a set of formal procurement rules similar to those followed by every other City agency," and instead "exploited a gray area in the law—one that allows it to treat itself as a state agency whenever it is convenient to do so and then as a city agency when it is likewise convenient."[23]

The DOE claims exemption from many laws in addition to those governing financial transparency. Its official position is that since the mayor, and, through him, the chancellor, receive their authority directly from the state, no city law can restrict their actions. Accordingly, the administration refused to comply with the Dignity in All Schools Act, approved in 2004, prohibiting the bullying of gay and minority students and mandating training to prevent such incidents;[24] ignored cell phone legislation passed in 2007, requiring that students be allowed to carry cell phones to and from schools;[25] and violated mandatory recycling regulations, required of all other city businesses, residences, and agencies.[26]

At the same time, top management at Tweed became increasingly dominated by attorneys, consultants, and former corporate executives. A 2008 *Daily News* article about the personal wealth of some top Tweed officials briefly appeared online before it was stripped from the web and never appeared in the paper. In it a DOE spokesperson assured the reporter "that other top DOE officials were not multimillionaires and that two of the chancellor's roughly 20 senior advisers were life-long educators."[27]

As the administration became increasingly focused on the business of squeezing out better math and reading scores on standardized exams, there was a decline in attention paid to science, art, and and other subjects that were not tested. In 2007, Chancellor Klein eliminated Project Arts, a decade-old, $67.5 million program that provided the sole source of dedicated funding for arts education, saying that principals should be allowed to spend money however they saw fit.[28]

As of the 2007–2008 school year, only 8 percent of elementary schools complied with state requirements for instruction in visual arts, dance, theater, and music. Schools spent less on arts than the previous year, with a 63 percent decline in dollars for supplies and equipment, and 30 percent had no arts specialists whatsoever—up from 20 percent the year before—meaning that several hundred thousand students attended schools without a single certified arts teacher.[29]

At the same time, the administration expressed scant interest in improving classroom conditions by alleviating overcrowding or reducing class size. New York City classes remained the largest in the state by far, with little decrease in size over the course of the previous six years, despite receiving nearly a billion dollars in state aid and an equal amount of federal aid provided to the city specifically for class size reduction. The administration offered lots of excuses but no convincing rationale for their refusal to provide smaller classes, even after an audit by the state comptroller in 2006 and a State Education Department monitoring report in 2008, both of which found that the city had misused millions of state dollars dedicated to this purpose.[30] In a 2008 poll, 86 percent of New York City principals said they were unable to provide a quality education because of excessive class sizes in their schools.[31] According to DOE's own surveys, class size remained the top concern of public school parents, but the mayor attempted to obscure this clear result by lumping together several other categories to make it look as though other issues were of greater importance to parents.[32]

Despite the fact that a real estate development boom throughout the city had created thousands of units of new housing between 2005 and 2009, the administration appeared unconcerned about where all the additional students generated by development would attend school. Three separate reports were produced in the spring and fall of 2008, from the city comptroller, the Manhattan borough president, and a consortium of advocacy and parent groups and unions, all pointing out that the city's capital planning process for school construction was broken and would not create the additional seats necessary to prevent even worse overcrowding and higher class sizes in years to come.[33] Yet the DOE ignored these warnings—and produced a new five-year capital plan in November 2008 that would cut back on school construction even further, reducing the number of new seats by 60 percent, meaning the city would invest a smaller share of its total capital spending in school construction and repair than in any time in the previous ten years.[34]

While the proposed five-year capital plan called for the construction of only 25,000 new seats, the administration planned to provide one hundred thousand seats for charter school students by 2012.[35] This intention, if carried out, will necessitate closing more than one hundred zoned neighborhood schools. In the spring of 2008, the administration attempted to close several zoned schools in community school districts and replace them with charter schools that are not obligated to admit neighborhood children. The chancellor made this decision unilaterally, without the approval of the Community District Education Councils (CECs), the local parent boards whose assent to any change in zoning was one of the few powers specifically granted them by state law. This prompted a lawsuit, which temporarily halted the closures of the zoned schools.[36]

The marginalization of parents and the disregard of their views was a pervasive feature of the administration's policies from the outset of the Bloomberg administration. In 2004, Debra Eng, a parent leader from Brooklyn, wrote:

> Never has an administration been so unreceptive to parents and parent organizations, despite all the hype by the "Department of Education" to the contrary . . . Without consultation, radical changes were made to the regulations governing everything from class trips, zoning, PA/PTA's and President Councils, to deciding what beverages will be sold in every school building and what snacks are appropriate for our children to eat, right down to the "cookie cutter" methodology of how to teach all children . . .

> Cuts to school budgets, more students in the classrooms, seasoned administrators and teachers leaving the system either through retirement, often earlier than they had planned, or finding employment outside the New York City Public School system, and a top heavy and bloated aristocracy at Tweed and the Regions... We cannot even get a copy of a budget to show us where all the "savings" are in this new reorganization, and we understand that ...our elected officials cannot get this information as well.[37]

This open disregard for parents worsened over time. In the fall of 2007, the chancellor rewrote the regulations governing School Leadership Teams (SLTs), composed of half parents and half staff, eliminating their authority to approve comprehensive education plans and school-based budgets. The regulations, as well as the unilateral way in which they were revised, were subsequently ruled illegal by the State Commissioner of Education.[38] The DOE also opened and closed many schools without consulting CECs, as required by state law.[39]

The administration's insistence on ignoring the views of parents and community members has gone hand-in-hand with an accelerating attack on the whole notion of the neighborhood public school—which often anchors communities, particularly in low-income neighborhoods. The DOE's much-vaunted small-school initiative, subsidized by private money, flooded comprehensive neighborhood high schools with the high-needs students that the small schools had been allowed to exclude—including high percentages of English Language Learners and students with disabilities. In the few new high schools built, the administration refused to allow preference for admissions to neighborhood children.[40] When the DOE centralized admissions for elementary schools, which had previously been controlled by the individual districts, families of pre-Kindergarten students were obliged to re-apply to Kindergarten at their schools.[41] In the spring of 2009, the administration put hundreds of Kindergarten students on waiting lists for their zoned neighborhood schools.[42] These policies appeared designed to undermine the support of neighborhood residents—and their elected officials—for their local public schools, further easing the administration's plans to charterize and privatize the system.

The chancellor continually promoted the success of charter schools, which were given space in public school buildings, causing a loss of classrooms for the traditional public schools that were forced to share their space. Yet these charter schools were provided with the ability to cap enrollment and class size at low levels—a privilege not accorded traditional public schools, who were essentially denied this opportunity by the administration's refusal to use the state funds that had been allocated for class size reduction according to their intended function.[43] The chancellor's unrestrained praise for charter schools and his comparative contempt for traditional public schools was bizarre in light of the fact that he had been put in charge of improving the public schools; if charter schools were indeed more successful, that surely resulted from his own failure of leadership.

These policies, and the widening inequities that have resulted, have led to profound dissatisfaction among many parents and educators alike. A 2008 survey by the United Federation of Teachers revealed that 85 percent of New York City public school teachers believe that Chancellor Klein and the Department of Education had failed to provide them with the resources and supports they need to succeed. Similarly, 85 percent said that the chancellor's emphasis on testing had failed to improve education in their schools.[44] In a Quinnipiac poll taken in March 2009,

New York City public school parents disapproved of Mayor Bloomberg's handling of education by 54 to 41 percent.[45] The year before, in another poll, over 70 percent of parents identified class size reduction as the most important reform, and over 80 percent said that problems of overcrowding and/or excessive class sizes had remained the same or worsened over the last few years.[46] A majority of parents felt that the overwhelming emphasis on standardized testing had caused too much stress for their children, and many said that the school system was being run like a business rather than an educational enterprise. They also believed that the DOE had mismanaged finances and had embarked on too many confusing reorganizations.

Yet in a little noted interview in December 2003, Klein explained that the policies he pursued were intended to produce "creative confusion." As he said, "By doing the reorganization and actually causing some creative confusion in the system, it does make it harder for people to just rock back . . . I think in eight years you can expect the system will make adjustments."[47]

In this interview, he mentioned Jack Welch, former head of General Electric, who espoused a variant of this idea called "creative destruction," which calls for divesting companies and subsidiaries and acquiring new ones, on a rapid scale, with the hope that this will lead to higher profits. A few years earlier, Welch had said of his management philosophy: "A small company can only afford to make one or two bets or they go out of business. But we can afford to make lots more mistakes, and, in fact, we have to throw more things at the walls. The big companies that get into trouble are those that try to manage their size instead of experiment with it."[48]

Sure enough, early on, Klein invited Jack Welch to lecture to high-level administrators at Tweed. Carmen Fariña, at the time a regional superintendent but soon to replace Diana Lam as deputy chancellor, later commented: "Jack Welch said one thing that really struck me . . . You can't allow an organization to grow complacent. When you find those kinds of organizations, you have to tear them apart and create chaos. That chaos creates a sense of urgency, and that sense of urgency will ultimately bring (about) improvement."[49] This management style might have worked for GE shareholders, but it seems a particularly heedless approach when children's lives are at stake.

The ideological underpinnings of "Children First"—the enthusiasm for privatization and market mechanisms, the obsession with data, even when much of it was statistically unreliable—was accompanied by a tendency on the part of the mayor and the chancellor to continually shift blame onto incompetent administrators, lazy teachers, uninvolved parents, and the "culture of excuses" rather than accept the increased accountability that mayoral control was supposed to bring.[50] Though the mayor and chancellor have been in office for more than six years, with nearly complete authority over our schools, they remain fond of disparaging critics as defenders of the status quo.[51] With decentralization has come a further evasion of responsibility, as the success or failure of each individual school is left up to its principal and teachers. Indeed, Bloomberg and Klein insist on holding everyone accountable except themselves.

Rather than help our public schools improve by alleviating overcrowding or reducing class size, the administration has been eager to close schools down as rapidly as possible and put new ones, including charters, in their place. The history of "Children First" has shown that even autocrats can always find a way of blaming someone else. New York City children, alas, have been the first to be left behind by "Children First."

NOTES

1. Karla Scoon Reid, "Former Justice Official To Head N.Y.C. Schools," *Education Week,* August 7, 2002.

2. Jennifer Steinhauer, "The New Schools Chancellor: Overview; Bloomberg picks a lawyer to run New York Schools," *New York Times,* July 30, 2002.

3. Karen W. Arenson, "State Clears Mayor's Choice of Businessman for Schools Chief," *New York Times,* August 2, 2002.

4. Tamar Lewin, "Educator Has Accomplishments and Enemies," *New York Times,* August 31, 2002.

5. David M. Herszenhorn and Elissa Gootman, "Top Deputy Resigns Schools Post Over Effort to Get Husband a Job," *New York Times,* March 9, 2004.

6. DOE web site. Quoted in Bas Braams, "Predictions for Chancellor Joel Klein's Children First Initiative," November 26, 2002, and January 5, 2003, http://www.math.nyu.edu/mfdd/braams/links/cf-pundit.html.

7. The FOIL requests were made by Bas Braams, New York University Professor of Mathematics, NYC HOLD, December 15 and December 27, 2002. See Bas Braams, "The NYC Department of Education 'Children First' Working Groups (Two Requests Under the Freedom of Information Law or Act)," updated March 26, 2003, http://www.math.nyu.edu/mfdd/braams/links/foia-02.html.

8. See James Traub, "New York's New Approach," *New York Times,* August 3, 2003; Sol Stern, "Tragedy Looms for Gotham's School Reform," *City Journal,* Autumn 2003; Abby Goodnough, "Schools Chancellor Stands by His Choice of Reading Program," *New York Times,* February 26, 2003. Letter from Linnea Ehri, Bruce McCandliss, Dolores Perin, Hollis Scarborough, Sally Shaywitz, Joanna Williams, and Joanna Uhry to Joel Klein, February 4, 2003, http://www.nrrf.org/phonics _nyc-2-4-03.htm.

9. Bas Braams, "Klein's Math Problems," *New York Sun,* February 6, 2003.

10. Email from Bas Braams to Diana Lam, March 19, 2003.

11. Jennifer Medina, "Cost of Tracking Schools Is Said to Be $130 Million," *New York Times,* November 14, 2008. This estimate, from the Independent Budget Office, does not include the salaries and administrative costs of the district superintendents, now serving 90 percent of their time outside their districts to train schools in test score analysis. See "The School Accountability Initiative: Totaling the Cost," Independent Budget Office Fiscal Brief, November 2008.

12. "Adding up the Numbers: The Education Budget under Mayoral Control," Educational Priorities Panel, Bulletin #2, January 20. 2006, http://www.edpriorities. org/Info/CityBudget/Bulletin_2Jan06.pdf.

13. Comptroller William C. Thompson, letter to Michael Bloomberg, February 7, 2005, http://www.comptroller.nyc.gov/press/pdfs/PR05-02-017-letter-to-bloomberg.pdf. See also Elissa Gootman, "On How Much City Schools Cut Bureaucracy, a Rebuttal," *New York Times,* February 8, 2005, and Kathleen Lucadamo, "Ed Dept. Savings Called Shell Game," *Daily News,* February 8, 2005.

14. See "In NYC, Tis the Season for Sacrifice," Eduwonkette, May 27, 2008, http://blogs.edweek.org/edweek/eduwonkette/2008/05/in_nyc_tis_the_season _for_sacr_1.html.

15. Data from a file provided by the New York City Council Council Finance Division, dated March 1, 2009. See also Leonie Haimson, "Growing the Bureaucracy: But Guess Which Office at Tweed Has Actually Shrunk?," NYC Public School Parent blog, February 24, 2009, http://nycpublicschoolparents. blogspot.com/search?q=%22growing+the+bureaucracy.

16. Erin Einhorn, "18 Ed Dept. Bigs Making at Least 190G," *Daily News,* December 18, 2007; Erin Einhorn, "Educrat pay hits 180G+ for 29," *Daily News,* November 14, 2006.

17. "State Lawmakers Consider Limiting Mayor's Control Of Schools Budget," NY 1, May 12, 2004.

18. Elissa Gootman and David M. Herszenhorn, "Consultants Draw Fire In Bus Woes," *New York Times,* February 3, 2007.

19. See Angela Montefinise, "Ed. Dept. 'No bid' mess," *New York Post,* August 10, 2008.

20. Montefinise, "Ed. Dept. 'No bid' mess."

21. Comptroller William Thompson, letter to Joel Klein, April 1, 2009, http: //www. comptroller.nyc.gov/press/pdfs/04-01-09_doe-letter.pdf. See also Javier C. Hernandez, "Study Finds Vast Overspending by Education Dept.," New York Times City Room blog, April 1, 2009. Other contracts that were supposedly competitively bid have raised doubts. In July 2008, theLeadership Academy, a principal-training institute established with private funds by Chancellor Klein in 2003, won a supposedly competitive five-year, $50 million contract from the DOE to train principals, only a few months after Klein resigned as head of its board. The Academy continued to be housed in a DOE building in Long Island City, while its staff continued to have email addresses that identify them as DOE employees. Yet the Leadership Academy claims somehow to be independent, which allows it to be "off-budget" and even less fiscally transparent than the DOE *New York Sun,* June 30, 2008. See also Gail Robinson, "Public Schools, Private Money," Gotham Gazette, April 2, 2009, http://www.gotham gazette.com/blogs/wonkster/2009/04/02/public-schools-private-money/). Even more recently, the company Accenture won a $1.6 million contract that was

supposedly competitively bid, despite the fact that its bid was four times higher than that of the lowest bidder—and included payments of up to $315 an hour for the services of an entry-level project manager. "That's the highest rate I've ever heard in my life," a losing bidder told the *Post.* "There appears to be no integrity there and obviously there's no oversight" (Yoav Gonen, "Ed. Bigs Nix Low Bidders," *New York Post,* March 2, 2009).

22. See NYSSCPA newsletter, "Legislature Passes School Reform Bills" (July 2005). For more on the requirements of this law, see http://www.emsc.nysed.gov/ mgtserv/fiscal_accountability_legislation. Deborah Cunningham of NYSED confirmed to the author in an email correspondence that DOE had not certified that it was in compliance as of February 1, 2008.

23. Testimony by William C. Thompson, Jr., New York City Comptroller, during City Council hearings by the Committee on Education on governance of the New York City School District, February 6, 2009.

24. Leonie Haimson, "Mayor: Anti Harassment Measure 'Illegal' and 'Silly,'" NYC Public School Parent blog, June 5, 2007.

25. Yoav Gonen, "Students Hung up on Cellphone Rules," *New York Post,* January 2, 2008).

26. Angela Montefinise and Susannah Cahalan, "Il'litter'ate Schools Flunk Their Recycling," *New York Post,* October 28, 2007; Amy Zimmer, "School Recycling Scores Low Grade," *Metro NY,* June 3, 2008; Liz Goodwin, "On Earth Day, Schools Criticized for Lagging on Recycling," Gotham Schools, April 22, 2009, http://gothamschools.org/2009/04/22/on-earth-day-schools-criticized-for-lagging-on-recycling.

27. Leonie Haimson, "We Got the Story that Tweed Tried to Kill!," NYC Public School Parent blog, October 30, 2008, http://nycpublicschoolparents .blogspot. com/search?q=we+got+the+story+tweed, and Elizabeth Green, "The Daily News Story That Got Killed in the Night," Gotham Schools, October 30, 2008, http://gothamschools.org/2008/10/30/the-daily-news-story-that-got-killed-in-the-night/.

28. David Andreatta, "Ed. Dept. Gives Arts Program Culture $ock," *New York Post,* February 22, 2007.

29. "Annual Arts in Schools Report: 2007–2008," New York City Department of Education, October 2008. See also Richard Kessler, Executive Director, Center For Arts Education, "Statement on the Release of the New York City Department of Education Annual Arts in Schools Report 2007-2008," October 15, 2008,http://www.cae-nyc.org/pages/wp-content/uploads/ 2008/10/cae-statement -on-arts-in-schools-report-2007-2008.pdf; Yoav Gonen, "Schools in Art Failure," *New York Post,* October 16, 2008; and testimony by Kira Streets, Director of Public Engagement, Center For Arts Education, during hearings of the New York State Assembly Standing Committee on Education, February 6, 2009.

30. "New York City Department of Education Administration of the Early Grade Class Size Reduction Program," Report #2005–N–2003, New York State Office of the State Comptroller, March 15, 2006, http://www.osc.state.ny.us/audits/allaudits /093006 /05n3.pdf, and Deputy Commissioner Johanna Duncan-Poitier, New York State Education Department, "Contracts for Excellence–Monitoring Report," September 8, 2008, http://www.regents.nysed.gov/meetings/2008 Meetings/September 2008/0908emscd4.htm.

31. This survey, sponsored by the New York City Council, drew responses from over one third of all public school principals. See Emily Horowitz and Leonie Haimson, "How Crowded Are Our Schools? New Results from a Survey of NYC Public School Principals," October 3, 2008, www.classsizematters.org /principal_survey_report_10.08_final.pdf.

32. During the 2006–2007 and 2007–2008 school years, 23 and 24 percent of parents, respectively, chose reducing class size as their first choice among ten educational priorities. See "Learning Environment Survey 2006–2007" and "Learning Environment Survey 2007–2008," New York City Department of Education, http://schools.nyc.gov/NR/rdonlyres/F3D9A118-C51E-4E23-841C-2003 DB5B24C87DC/40757/les2008citywide.pdf. For more on the Mayor's attempt to obscure these results, see Elissa Gootman, "Survey Reveals Student Attitudes, Parental Goals and Teacher Mistrust," *New York Times*, September 7, 2007.

33. Office of the NYC Comptroller, "Growing Pains: Reforming Department of Education Capital Planning to Keep Pace with NYC's Residential Construction," May 9, 2008, http://www.comptroller.nyc.gov/bureaus/opm/reports/05-09-08_ growing_ pains.pdf; Office of Manhattan Borough President Scott M. Stringer, "Crowded Out: School Construction Fails to Keep up with Manhattan Building Boom," April 2008, http://mbpo.org/uploads/SCHOOLSREPORT.pdf; and Manhattan Borough President's Task Force on School Overcrowding, Class Size Matters, the United Federation of Teachers, and The Center for Arts Education, "A Better Capital Plan," October 2008, www.classsizematters.org/A_Better_ Capital_Plan_ final_final.pdf.

34. See also the chapter in this volume on school overcrowding by Emily Horowitz.

35. Carl Campanile and Yoav Gonen, "Ambitious Course: City Plans for 100,000 Charter Kids," *New York Post,* April 10, 2009.

36. Javier C. Hernandez, "Suit Challenges City Plan to Replace Three Schools," *New York Times,* March 25, 2009; Philissa Cramer and Elizabeth Green, "DOE dropping school closure plan that drew UFT, parent lawsuit," Gotham Schools, April 2, 2009; Javier C. Hernandez, "City Backs Down on a Plan to Replace Three Public Schools With Charters," *New York Times,* April 2, 2009. The chancellor said he would nevertheless force charter schools into these buildings, to share space with the existing schools. He also sent letters to all the parents at the schools he had intended to close, urging them to send their children elsewhere outside of their zone, or to apply to charter schools—essentially attempting to force the school to close through a mass exodus. See, for example, Chancellor Joel Klein, "Letter to parents at PS 150," April 3, 2009; http://schools.nyc.gov/NR/rdonlyres/49CA0485-E4A7-4390-AFDA-CB7291FB846B/58224/150_ April3_ Final_English.pdf.

37. Quoted in testimony by Leonie Haimson, during Manhattan Borough President hearings, "The Reorganization of the NYC Department of Education One Year Later: Are We Better Off Now?," September 7, 2004, www.classsizematters.org /testimonyMBP.doc.

38. Elizabeth Lazarowitz, "School Official Says Bloomberg Gave Too Much Power to Principals," Daily News, January 6, 2009; Philissa Cramer, "Under Law, DOE Not Always the Decider, State Ed Official Rules," Gotham Schools, January 7, 2009, http://gothamschools.org/2009/01/07/under-law-doe-not-always-the-decider-state-ed-official-rules/; Dorothy Callaci, "State Rules that DOE Was Wrong to Sideline School Leadership Teams," New York Teacher, January 22, 2009.

39. Juan Gonzalez, "Mayor Bloomberg and Joel Klein Determined to Keep Parents Seen, Not Heard," *Daily News,* February 25, 2009.

40. For example, in Sunset Park, where the community had battled to get a high school built for forty years, the DOE refused to allow any preference in admissions for neighborhood students. See Michèle De Meglio "Inside New Sunset Pk High School," *Brooklyn Courier,* February 12, 2009, and Ivette Feliciano, "Brooklyn Neighborhood Gets Long-awaited High School," December 12, 2007, http://ivettefeliciano.wordpress.com/category/stories-for-print. In May 2009, the DOE announced that Sunset Park High School would have to share its building with a charter school as well.

41. Phillissa Cramer, "Details on the Pre-K Proposal: No More Variances, No More Principal Discretion," Inside Schools, January 31, 2008, http://inside schools. blogspot.com/2008/01/details-on-pre-k-proposal-no-more.html andElissa Gootman, "From Pre-K to Kindergarten, a 2nd Lottery," New York Times Cityroom blog, January 23, 2009.

42. Elissa Gootman, "Children Face Rejection by Neighborhood Schools in Manhattan," *New York Times*, March 23, 2009; Julie Shapiro, "Tweed Unlikely for Village Students," *Downtown Express,* April 10, 2009; Beth Fertig, "More Are Applying to Public Kindergarten," WNYC radio, April 13, 2009; Rachel Monahan, "City Struggling to Find Room in Kindergarten for 3,000 kids—Even with Bigger Classrooms," *Daily News,* April 17, 2009; Hazel Sanchez, "NYC Kindergarten Crunch Overcrowding Schools," WCBS News, April 17, 2009; Yoav Gonen, "No Slots for Tots This Fall," *New York Post,* April 17, 2009.

43. See chapter on class size in this volume.

44. "Teachers Want Chancellor Klein to Do a Better Job," *New York Teacher,* June 26, 2008.

45. "Voters Say Mayor Mike Is Cold As His Approval Chills, Quinnipiac University New York City Poll Finds; He's A Fat Cat, But Still The Top Cat In Mayor's Race," Quinnipiac Institute, March 24, 2009.

46. The results included a statistically representative telephone survey of over six hundred public-school parents and an on-line survey of more than one thousand parents. See "The Independent Survey: Views of New York City Parents and Public School Leaders on Class Size, Testing, and Mayoral Control," Class Size Matters (February 2008), http://www.classsizematters.org/parent_survey_report_FINAL.pdf.

47. "Klein: I Can Overhaul the Schools—Just Give Me 8 Years," *Staten Island Advance,* December 7, 2003.

48. Quoted in Richard Foster, "The Welch Legacy: Creative Destruction," *Wall Street Journal,* May 1, 2002, reprinted at http://www.mckinsey.com/aboutus/mckinsey news/pressarchive/managersjournal_destruction.asp. Foster wrote, "What Mr. Welch recognized is that destroying one's own businesses–or knowing when to let go of them and move in a different direction–is a far surer way to generate value and outperform the market than to buckle down and try to protect what you've built, regardless of how grand…. Mr. Welch's greatest contribution to GE employees and shareholders has been to … attack first, defend when necessary." Foster was a senior partner at McKinsey & Company. McKinsey had a central role as consultants in redesigning the school system in the first phase of "ChildrenFirst. "Many McKinsey's employees, long on management theory and short on educational experience, were subsequently hired by DOE and contin-ue to play a role at Tweed to this day. See David M. Herszenhorn, "Not So Long Out of School, Yet Running The System," *New York Times,* March 25, 2004.

49. Mike France, "Can Business Save New York City Schools?," *Business Week,* June 9, 2003.

50. Joel Klein, "Stop Making Excuses, Start Holding Educators Accountable," *Daily News,* April 16, 2009.

51. See for example, "New York City Schools Chancellor Talks Reform in Park City," *Bridgeport (Conn.) News,* October 17, 2008.

Student Achievement in New York City: The NAEP Results

- Diane Ravitch

On November 15, 2007, the federal government released the scores of eleven urban districts that had participated in the National Assessment of Educational Progress (NAEP).[1] The news was not good for New York City, whose leadership had been proclaiming "historic gains" on state tests for the previous two years.

The assessments showed that from 2003 to 2007—the first four years of the "Children First" reforms—there were no significant gains for New York City students in three of the four areas tested: fourth-grade reading, eighth-grade reading, and eighth-grade mathematics. There were no significant gains in these grades and subjects for African American students, White students, Hispanic students, Asian students, or lower income students.

As the front-page of the *New York Times* read: "Little Progress for City Schools on National Test: Racial Gap Continues; Contrast with Results Seen on State Exams Under Bloomberg."[2] The story laid out the unexpected results, which "paint a generally stagnant picture for the city" in every subject other than fourth-grade mathematics. Jennifer Medina noted that Mayor Bloomberg had "trumpeted improving state test scores as evidence that the city is setting the pace for urban school reform," but the federal scores "suggest that the city's gains are limited." In fact, she pointed out, the most significant increase in fourth-grade reading scores occurred in 2002, "before Mr. Bloomberg took control." While the state scores showed a sharp upward trend, the national scores for eighth-graders were almost completely flat (slightly up in math, slightly down in reading).

The results reported by NAEP were startling, but no less surprising was the response of the Department of Education to the NAEP data. In the *New York Times* article, Chancellor Klein said that "he saw plenty of good news in the federal scores," though there were no gains in any grade or subject other than fourth-grade mathematics. The Department issued a press release on November 15 headed, "New York City Public School Students Make Gains on 2007 National Assessment of Educational Progress (NAEP) Tests." The first sentence said, "New York City students made impressive gains on the 2007 National Assessment of Educational Progress (NAEP) tests, with particularly significant progress achieved by 4th graders in mathematics compared to their peers in other cities and by Black 4th-grade students in both reading and math."[3]

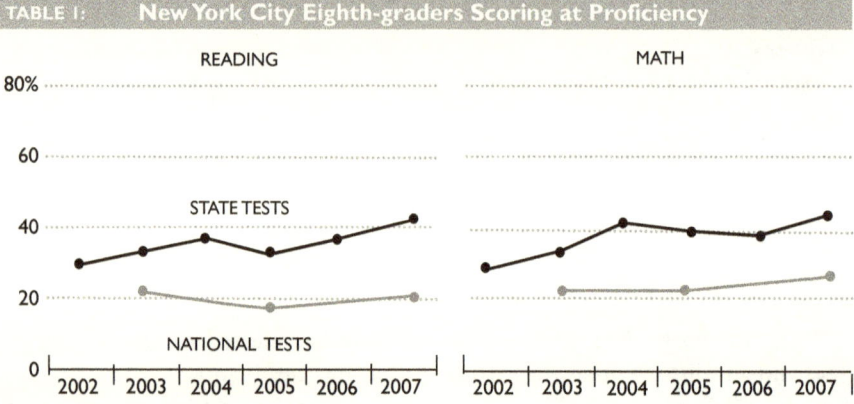

READING

MATH

80%

60

40

STATE TESTS

20

NATIONAL TESTS

0

2002 2003 2004 2005 2006 2007   2002 2003 2004 2005 2006 2007

Source: The New York Times

This statement was an exercise in denial. The findings of the NAEP assessment were unequivocal. With the exception of fourth-grade math, they were certainly not "impressive," by any measure.

In its reports to the public, NAEP displays both scale scores and achievement levels. The scale scores are a numerical average, while the achievement levels array student performance under the headings Advanced, Proficient, Basic, and Below basic. Whichever metric was used, New York City's gains were modest at best. In fourth-grade reading, New York City saw no significant change from 2003 to 2007. The only significant improvement occurred between the first assessment in 2002 and the next one in 2003, before the Bloomberg-Klein reforms were implemented. Students took the 2003 assessment in the spring of 2003; the Bloomberg-Klein education reforms were not installed until September 2003. There was "no significant change" in the achievement gap between the city and the state between 2003 and 2007. There was no significant change from 2003 or 2005 for lower income, Black, White, Hispanic, or Asian students. Neither was there any significant change in the overall percentage of students who scored at or above Basic or at or above Proficient as compared to 2003.

In eighth-grade reading, the results were depressingly similar. There was "no significant change" in the gap between city students and those in the state and "no significant change" for lower income students, White students, Black students, Hispanic students, and Asian students when compared to 2003 or 2005. There was "no significant change" in the percentage of students who scored at or above Basic or Proficient as compared to 2003 or 2005. Furthermore, the gap between eighth-grade students and the nation's students was very large; 41 percent of New York City's eighth-graders were reading "Below basic," as compared to 27 percent in the nation as a whole.

Fourth-grade mathematics was the only bright spot for New York City. Here students had a significantly higher score than in previous assessments. The gap narrowed between the city and the state. Lower income students had a higher average score compared to previous assessments. The scores for White students, Black students, Hispanic students, and Asian students were higher compared to 2003, but there was no significant change when compared to 2005. There was a significant increase in the percentage of students at or above Basic compared to 2003 and 2005 and a significant increase in the percentage of students at or above Proficient.

Yet a few days later, testing experts interviewed by Elizabeth Green of *The New York Sun* questioned the validity of the gains in fourth-grade mathematics: "So many New York City students received extra time and other accommodations on a respected national test this year that several testing experts are saying the results should be considered invalid."[4] Green reported that the accommodations rate—the proportion of students who got extra time or extra help—had soared, for this grade and subject, from 12 percent in 2003 to 25 percent in 2007. No other city tested by NAEP had an accommodations rate this large. Even Los Angeles, where 48 percent of the students were classified as English Language Learners, gave accommodations to only 8 percent of its students on the fourth-grade math test.

In eighth-grade mathematics, the scores were flat, despite the fact that New York City also gave accommodations to a larger percentage of its students (19 percent) than any other city tested; no other city even came close (the highest rate elsewhere—in Boston, Charlotte, and Chicago—was 12 percent). In this grade, the scores were "not significantly different" from 2003 and 2005. There was "no significant change" in the gap between the city and the state. Lower income students showed a higher average score than in 2003, but no change since 2005. There was "no significant change" in the average scores of Black students, White students, Hispanic students, or Asian students compared to previous assessments. There was "no significant change" in the proportion of students who scored at or above Basic, and no significant change in those who scored at or above Proficient, compared to 2003 and 2005.

When asked about the disparity between the state scores, which were on a steady upward trajectory, and the NAEP scores, which were mostly flat, spokesmen for the New York City Department of Education praised the state exams and belittled the National Assessment of Educational Progress. They said that the state tests all students, but the national assessment tests only a sample of students. They said that New York City's students prepare for the state tests, but don't prepare for the national assessments. They found many reasons to explain why the city's scores were rising on state tests but stagnant on the national exams.

But none of their reasons was persuasive. Of course, NAEP samples student performance, as it has for forty years. Its samples are statistically valid. Moreover, NAEP includes a much wider range of questions and tests each child with a few of them, making the assessment less vulnerable to score inflation than state exams, which offer a more limited number of questions to every child.[5] If students in New York City were actually improving in reading and mathematics, they should be able to demonstrate their prowess by accurately responding to a wide range of questions without specific test preparation. If they are unable to respond because they have not been prepared for a specific question, this reveals they have not mastered the necessary skills for high school, college, or the work place. As Harvard Professor Daniel Koretz has pointed out, when students have practiced repeatedly and intensively for a specific set of questions on an exam, that exam's results become less valid.[6] The point of NAEP is that it is an audit test, a test without high-stakes consequences that is intended to measure the state of student learning. As an audit test, its results are far more reliable and meaningful than any state tests. State tests with high stakes for students, teachers, administrators, and schools become corrupted when there are repetitive test-preparation activities that inflate scores and reduce the validity of the tests.

Indeed, NAEP is considered the gold standard of the testing industry.[7] In NAEP's four decades of existence, the federal government has invested tens of millions of dollars in improving its technical quality. There have been complaints over the years that NAEP's standards are too rigorous. But unlike state tests, NAEP produces consistent results from one test administration to the next, because its sampling techniques are accurate and the pool of students tested is not toyed with. By contrast, New York State tests have shown dramatic gains, which NAEP does not confirm. Those gains may be due to the exclusion of low-performing students or changes in the rigor of the test or changes in the "cut score" (the passing mark). No one can prepare for NAEP because no one knows in advance which students will be tested or what will be on the test. NAEP's difficulty level is stable over time because of the care exercised in field-testing the items. These are some of the reasons why Congress mandated that NAEP should serve as a common yardstick with which to monitor the progress of states and the accuracy of state test scores.

The National Assessment of Educational Progress (NAEP) was never intended to establish a national test or a national curriculum, but to serve as a gauge of student achievement across the nation. It was launched on the recommendation of the nation's leading education scholars in the mid-1960s. After a period of study and planning, the first national assessments were administered in 1969. NAEP periodically tests student performance in reading, mathematics, science, writing, history, the arts, civics, and economics. In response to the No Child Left Behind legislation, NAEP now tests reading and mathematics in every state every other year.

In its early years, NAEP reported results for the nation and regions, but not for states, school districts, schools, or individual students, to avoid any erosion of state and local control of the curriculum. In 1990, at the request of governors, Congress authorized state-level reporting of results. In 2002, Congress authorized urban district reporting for cities that volunteered to be assessed, after receiving a request by the Council of the Great City Schools. Six urban districts—including New York City—were assessed in 2002; ten in 2003; and eleven in 2005 and 2007. In 2009, several additional districts asked to be part of the assessment. The urban assessment is referred to as the Trial Urban District Assessment, or TUDA.

The TUDA provides the opportunity to compare New York City results to those in other large urban districts. Here the results are even more disappointing. While New York City eighth-graders ranked second in reading among the ten urban districts tested in 2002–2003, they had fallen to sixth place by 2006–2007, according to an analysis by the Annenberg Institute for School Reform.[8]

TABLE 2: Change In Percentage of Students Performing at or above Basic Levels from 2002–2003 to 2006–2007; New York State Results Compared with NAEP Results

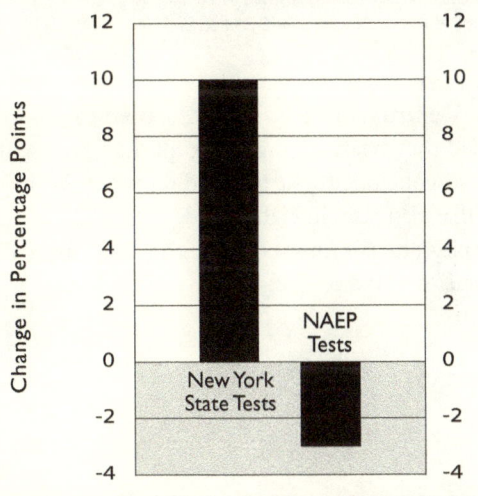

Source: U.S. Department of Education, National Center for Education Statistics, The Nation's Report Card, 2007 Trial Urban District Assessment in Reading; NYCDOE, Annual School Reports, 2002-2003 through 2006-2007; NYC-DOE, results of NYS English Language Arts Test (2003); NYSED, Media File Grades 3–8 English Language Arts (2007)

© 2007 Annenberg Institute for School Reform.

Indeed, New York City was one of only two out of ten cities in which the percentage of students performing at or above Basic in eighth-grade reading actually declined between 2003 and 2007.[9]

Eighth-grade reading levels for Black, Hispanic, and lower income students fell more in New York City than in any other urban district. In fact, New York was the only district in which all of these groups did worse in eighth-grade reading in 2006–2007 than they had in 2002–2003.

TABLE 3:	Change in Percentage of Students Performing at or above Basic on NAEP Eighth-Grade Reading Tests in Major Cities, 2002–2003 to 2006–2007

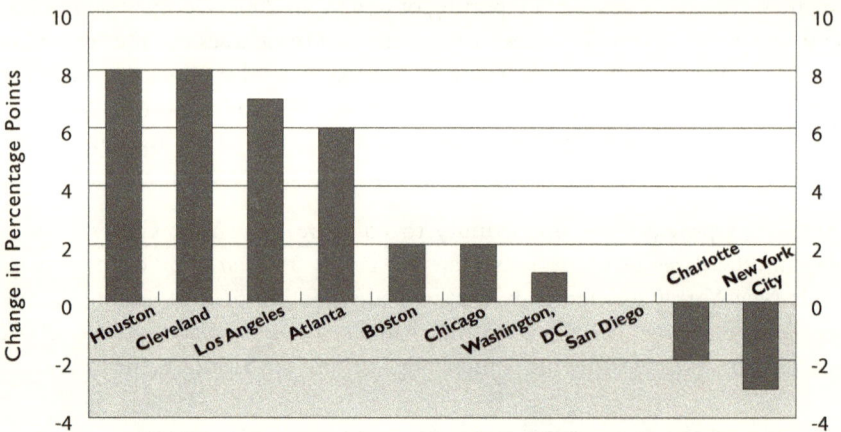

Note: *Where bars are missing for a city, data for the student group were not available. Austin, Texas, is excluded because it did not post 2002–2003 results.*

Source: *U.S. Department of Education, National Center for Education Statistics, The Nation's Report Card 2007, Trial Urban District Assessment in Reading © 2007 Annenberg Institute for School Reform.*

It is unfortunate that officials at the Department of Education choose to ignore and belittle the findings of NAEP. Had they been willing to accept the results and accept accountability, they might have concluded that the reading program they mandated in 2003 was ineffective, or that class sizes in eighth grade were hampering students' opportunity to learn. Our city officials must be willing to learn from all the facts available to them if they hope to make progress in the future.

NOTES

1. See "The Nation's Report Card: The Official Site for Results from the National Assessment of Educaitonal Progress," National Assessment of Educational Progress (NAEP), http://nationsreportcard.gov/.

2. Jennifer Medina, "Little Progress for City Schools on National Test," *New York Times*, November 16, 2007.

3. "City Students Make Gains on National Assessment of Educational Progress (NAEP) Tests," Press release, New York City Department of Education, November 15, 2007, http://schools.nyc.gov/Offices/mediarelations/Newsand Speeches/2007-2008/20071115_naep.htm.

4. Elizabeth Green, "N.Y. Gave the Most Breaks for School Exam," *New York Sun*, November 21, 2007.

5. See Aaron Pallas, "Why NAEP Matters," Gotham Schools, April 17, 2009, http://gothamschools.org/2009/04/17/why-naep-matters.

6. Daniel Koretz, *Measuring Up: What Educational Testing Really Tells Us* (Cambridge: Harvard University Press, 2008).

7. The author served on the National Assessment Governing Board from 1998 to 2004.

8. The following charts and comparative analysis are drawn from "Our Children Can't Wait: A Proposal to Close the Middle Grades Achievement Gap," NYC Coalition for Educational Justice, in collaboration with the Community Involvement Program of the Annenberg Institute for School Reform at Brown University (January 2008), http://www.annenberginstitute.org/pdf/Middle Grades2.pdf.

9. Seven of the ten cities made gains, although the gains were statistically significant only in Houston, Cleveland, Los Angeles, and Atlanta.

The Racial Achievement Gap

- Jennifer L. Jennings and Aaron M. Pallas

On July 17, 2008, New York City Mayor Michael Bloomberg and Schools Chancellor Joel Klein appeared before the US House Committee on Education and Labor and argued that New York City's school reform efforts had substantially closed the racial achievement gap. Klein said:

> Since we started this work in 2002....our African-American and Latino students have gained on their White and Asian peers. In fourth-grade math, for example, the gap separating our African-American and White students has narrowed by more than 16 points. In eighth-grade math, African-American students have closed the gap with White students by almost 5 points. In fourth-grade reading, the gap between African-American and White students has narrowed by more than 6 points. In eighth-grade reading, the gap has closed by about 4 points.[1]

Bloomberg echoed that claim, arguing that "over the past six years, we've done everything possible to narrow the achievement gap—and we have. In some cases, we've reduced it by half."[2]

Over a brief interval of five years, was it possible that New York City schools had made more progress in closing the racial achievement gap than the rest of the country had in the previous thirty? In reality, the average African American and Hispanic student in New York City is as far behind his or her White and Asian peers as in January 2003 when the "Children First" reforms were announced. Only for eighth-grade English Language Arts (ELA) has there been a reduction in the achievement gap–and the size of the reduction is 6 percent rather than the 50 percent reduction Bloomberg claimed. What's worse, the achievement gap in mathematics in both fourth and eighth grades has grown by 12 percent and 22 percent, respectively.

Measuring Achievement Gaps

Government agencies and media observers often use proficiency rates, or the percentage of students passing state tests, to describe the gaps in academic performance between racial and ethnic groups. For example, if 90 percent of White students passed a state test and 65 percent of African-Americans students did, some observers will say that the achievement gap is "25 points." If the gap in proficiency between Black and White students declines from 25 to 22 percentage points, some observers will report that the gap has "closed by 3 points."

Bloomberg and Klein's claim that achievement gaps have closed is based on the difference between the percentages of students that are proficient in each group over time. Proficiency rates can be misleading, though, and educational researchers and testing experts agree that proficiency rates provide an inaccurate measure of achievement gaps.[3] The main problem with this way of assessing the achievement gap is that we cannot differentiate between students who just made it over the proficiency bar and those who scored well above it.

Imagine, for example, two classrooms of students: Classroom A is made up of students who start out as high achievers, and Classroom B of students with middling performance. If every student in both classes answered two more questions correctly than she had in the previous year, it's pretty clear that both classrooms made equal amounts of academic progress. If 95 percent of the students were already proficient when they entered Classroom A, then the additional two questions each child got right is unlikely to have much impact on the passing rate. But in Classroom B, where only 50 percent of the students entered as proficient, the additional two questions answered correctly might boost Classroom B's proficiency rate from 50 percent to 70 percent. Comparing proficiency rates from last year and this year would make Classroom B look more effective than Classroom A, even though the students in both classes actually made the same amount of progress.

Now, imagine that the students in Classroom A are all white or Asian, whereas the students in Classroom B are all African-American or Hispanic. The gap in proficiency rates between the two classrooms at the beginning of the year is 95-50=45 percentage points, and at the end of the year it is 95-70=25 percentage points. It might appear that Classroom B substantially closed the racial/ethnic achievement gap, but that's an illusion: all students made the same academic progress.

In short, proficiency rates can increase substantially by moving a small number of students up a few points—just enough to make the so-called "cut score" for proficiency. In the case of racial achievement gaps, African-American and Hispanic students may still lag far behind their peers even as their proficiency rates increase. Because of this, a more valid way to measure inequality between groups is to compare the average scale scores of White/Asian and Black/Hispanic students.[4] A familiar example of a scale score comes from the SAT, where a student might score a 600 on the verbal section's scale of 0 to 800. Scale scores provide information about how students are progressing both above and below the proficiency bar, and thus are preferable for assessing trends in the racial achievement gap.

Have Racial / Ethnic Achievement Gaps Closed in New York City?

To track achievement gap trends, we analyzed fourth- and eighth-grade test score data from New York State ELA and mathematics tests from 2003 to 2008. We focus on these grade levels because only the fourth- and eighth-grade state tests were consistently administered over this entire time period; until state tests were introduced in 2006, a different set of city tests were administered to New York City students in grades 3, 5, 6, and 7. Moreover, we focus on the years 2003 through 2008 because the "Children First" reforms were announced in January 2003, just as students were taking their state tests that year, and were not introduced into the city's classrooms until September 2003; 2003 thus provides an appropriate baseline for measuring progress in closing the achievement gap under mayoral control.

The data are reported as citywide group average scale scores by grade for Asian, Black, Hispanic and White ethnic groups, along with the citywide average scale scores and standard deviations, for the ELA and mathematics exams. Historically, educational researchers have expressed achievement gaps in standard deviation units as they allow for comparisons across many different tests and time periods.[5] Following this tradition, for each grade and year combination, we calculated the relative position of each ethnic group in relation to the citywide mean. Computationally, this involves subtracting the citywide mean from the ethnic group mean, and dividing by the citywide standard deviation. The resulting value represents the distance of the ethnic group mean from the citywide mean in standard deviation units, which is commonly referred to as a z-score. A standard deviation gap between White and Black students would imply that approximately 84 percent of White students performed above the average Black student.[6]

We start by considering the claim made by Klein above that "our African-American and Latino students have gained on their White and Asian peers." Using the average scale scores of each ethnic group and the number of test takers in each group, we compute a weighted average of White/Asian and Black/Hispanic students' scores for both fourth and eighth grade, and then standardize these scores as described above. (The results of this analysis are displayed in Table 1 on the following page.)

These results show that the achievement gap separating White/Asian from Black/Hispanic students has declined somewhat in eighth-grade ELA (a 6 percent reduction), but is almost the same in fourth-grade ELA as it was in 2003 (a 1 percent reduction). Since many readers will find standard deviation units unfamiliar, we translate these findings to percentile units. The *most promising* achievement gap reduction that we found in New York City between 2003 and 2008—the achievement gap decline from .71 to .66 standard deviations for eighth grade ELA—can be summed up as follows: 76 percent of White and Asian students performed above the average Black and Hispanic student in eighth grade ELA in 2003; in 2008, 75 percent of White/Asian students did. Unfortunately for New York City's Black and Hispanic children, this reduction falls considerably short of the substantial progress claimed by Klein and Bloomberg.

TABLE 1:	New York City 4th- and 8th- Grade Achievement Gaps in State Test Scores, 2003-2008						

ELA

	2003	2004	2005	2006	2007	2008	% Change, 2003 - 2008
4th- GRADE	0.700	0.741	0.706	0.658	0.700	0.691	- 1.3%
8th- GRADE	0.709	0.733	0.738	0.760	0.672	0.664	- 6.3%

MATH

	2003	2004	2005	2006	2007	2008	% Change, 2003 - 2008
4th- GRADE	0.734	0.766	0.741	0.788	0.810	0.820	+ 11.7%
8th- GRADE	0.731	0.721	0.792	0.863	0.889	0.892	+ 22.0%

Note: Gaps in standard deviation units. A larger gap means that White/Asian students are performing better than Black/Hispanic students.

The results are more sobering for fourth- and eighth-grade mathematics, where the gaps separating White/Asian and Black/Hispanic students have grown in both cases. In fourth-grade mathematics, there has been a 12 percent increase in the size of the achievement gap, and in eighth-grade mathematics, there has been a 22 percent increase. Put differently, in 2003, 77 percent of White/Asian students performed above the average Black/Hispanic 8th grader; now 81 percent of White/Asian students do.

In Table 2, we display more detailed achievement comparisons and report Black-White, Black-Asian, Hispanic-White, and Hispanic-Asian achievement gaps. We offer a summary of these trends below:

For fourth-grade New York City students:

- The Black-White achievement gap has increased in both ELA (5 percent) and mathematics (8 percent);

- The Black-Asian achievement gap has decreased slightly in ELA (2 percent) and increased in mathematics (15 percent);

- The Hispanic-White achievement gap has decreased slightly in ELA (2 percent) and increased in mathematics (6 percent);

- The Hispanic-Asian achievement gap has decreased for ELA (7 percent) and increased in mathematics (14 percent).

For eighth-grade New York City students:

- The Black–White achievement gap has decreased in ELA (8 percent) and increased in mathematics (15 percent);

- The Black–Asian achievement gap has decreased in ELA (16 percent) and increased in mathematics (33 percent);

- The Hispanic–White achievement gap has increased slightly in both ELA (1 percent) and mathematics (4 percent);

- The Hispanic–Asian achievement gap has decreased for ELA (7 percent) and increased in mathematics (25 percent).

TABLE 2: New York City Achievement Gaps Between White / Asian Students and Black / Hispanic Students in State Test Scores

4th- Grade ELA

	2003	2004	2005	2006	2007	2008	% Change, 2003 - 2008
ASIAN-BLACK	0.663	0.789	0.750	0.725	0.646	0.653	- 1.5%
ASIAN-HISPANIC	0.741	0.786	0.727	0.696	0.709	0.688	- 7.2%
WHITE-BLACK	0.656	0.705	0.691	0.630	0.683	0.688	+ 4.9%
WHITE-HISPANIC	0.734	0.702	0.668	0.601	0.746	0.723	- 1.5%

4th- Grade MATH

	2003	2004	2005	2006	2007	2008	% Change, 2003 - 2008
ASIAN-BLACK	0.849	0.888	0.870	0.930	0.974	0.980	+ 15.4%
ASIAN-HISPANIC	0.790	0.838	0.826	0.886	0.902	0.901	+ 14.0%
WHITE-BLACK	0.697	0.710	0.669	0.703	0.728	0.753	+ 7.9%
WHITE-HISPANIC	0.638	0.660	0.625	0.659	0.653	0.673	+ 5.5%

8th- Grade ELA

	2003	2004	2005	2006	2007	2008	% Change, 2003 - 2008
ASIAN-BLACK	0.683	0.748	0.736	0.791	0.619	0.572	- 16.2%
ASIAN-HISPANIC	0.732	0.763	0.736	0.754	0.703	0.683	- 6.7%
WHITE-BLACK	0.686	0.708	0.769	0.769	0.635	0.633	- 7.7%
WHITE-HISPANIC	0.735	0.723	0.731	0.731	0.719	0.744	+ 1.2%

8th- Grade MATH

	2003	2004	2005	2006	2007	2008	% Change, 2003 - 2008
ASIAN-BLACK	0.848	0.865	0.992	1.076	1.124	1.129	+ 33.1%
ASIAN-HISPANIC	0.830	0.834	0.932	1.014	1.063	1.041	+ 25.4%
WHITE-BLACK	0.654	0.629	0.675	0.731	0.724	0.751	+ 14.7%
WHITE-HISPANIC	0.637	0.598	0.615	0.669	0.663	0.663	+ 4.2%

Note: Gaps in standard deviation units.

In addition, New York City students' average scale scores from NAEP's Trial Urban District Assessment (TUDA) show no progress in closing racial achievement gaps. In 2003, 2005, and 2007—the time period that can be plausibly attributed to the Bloomberg administration's policies—a sample of fourth-and eighth-grade students in New York City participated in NAEP's urban testing program in both reading and mathematics. The National Center for Educational Statistics' own analyses demonstrated that there were no statistically significant changes in African American-White or Hispanic-White gaps between 2003 and 2007. Based on our own calculations, we find that African American-Asian and Hispanic-Asian gaps in eighth-grade reading, and the Hispanic-Asian gap in mathematics, have grown substantially and these differences are statistically significant.

Finally, in Table 3 we compare change in the White/Asian versus Black/Hispanic achievement gap between 2002 and 2003 and 2003 and 2008.[7] For all tests, we find that the achievement gap closed substantially more between 2002 and 2003 than it did between 2003 and 2008. Specifically, we find:

• In fourth-grade ELA, the gap closed 9 percent between 2002 and 2003, and 1 percent between 2003 and 2008;

• In fourth-grade mathematics, the gap closed 10 percent between 2002-2003, and increased 12 percent between 2003 and 2008;

• In eighth-grade ELA, the gap closed 13 percent between 2002 and 2003, and 6 percent between 2003 and 08;

• In eighth-grade mathematics, the gap closed 18 percent between 2002 and 2003, and increased 22 percent between 2003 and 2008.

TABLE 3: Achievement Gaps Between White / Asian Students and Black / Hispanic Students in New York City: Change Between 2002-2003 and 2003-2008

ELA

	2002	2003	2008	% Change, 2002 - 2003	% Change, 2003 - 2008
4th- GRADE	0.767	0.700	0.691	- 8.7%	- 1.3%
8th- GRADE	0.812	0.709	0.664	- 12.7%	- 6.3%

MATH

	2002	2003	2008	% Change, 2002 - 2003	% Change, 2003 - 2008
4th- GRADE	0.812	0.734	0.820	- 9.6%	+ 11.7%
8th- GRADE	0.888	0.731	0.892	+ 17.7%	+ 22.0%

Note: Gaps in standard deviation units.

Conclusion

In this chapter, we have demonstrated that racial achievement gaps in New York City have remained stubbornly persistent between 2003 and 2008. Contrary to the frequent claims of Mayor Bloomberg and Chancellor Klein that they have substantially reduced the achievement gap, we show that these gaps are largely unchanged or, in many cases, growing.

When confronted with these calculations in summer 2008, Klein "said the achievement gap is 'an issue,' but he said it should not obscure the significant gains Black and Hispanic students have made under his watch."[8] However, most coveted opportunities—jobs, college admission, a good grade in a college course, or a positive evaluation in the workplace—are not divvied up based on students crossing an arbitrary line of proficiency or competence. Educational institutions and workplaces do not have an unlimited number of positions or slots—rather, individuals are competing against one another for access. Everyone who has passed a basic reading test is not assured a job, nor are all students scoring more than a 450 on the verbal SAT assured admission to SUNY-Albany. These decisions are made by comparing the performance of applicants in a pool, and choosing applicants who perform better relative to their peers.

If the goal of the New York City education system is to ensure that every demographic and socioeconomic group is equally prepared to compete in higher education and the workplace, relative achievement measured on a continuous scale is what matters, not proficiency rates. Raising the scores of all groups does not change the representation of minority groups among those who are selected to take advantage of educational and employment opportunities. Only by reducing the real achievement gap can we increase the chances that New York City's Black and Hispanic students have the same opportunities to get ahead as their White and Asian peers. Unfortunately, New York City has made little progress in closing that gap in the last five years.

NOTES

1. Testimony by Joel I. Klein, during U.S. Congress, House Committee on Education and Labor hearings, "Mayor and Superintendant Partnerships in Education: Closing the Achievement Gap," July 17, 2008 (retrieved August 26, 2008), http://edlabor.house.gov/testimony/2008-07-17-JoelKlein.pdf, p. 3.

2. Testimony by Mayor Michael R. Bloomberg, during U.S. Congress, House Committee on Education and Labor hearings, "Mayor and Superintendant Partnerships in Education: Closing the Achievement Gap," July 17, 2008 (retrieved August 26, 2008), http://edlabor.house.gov/testimony/2008-07-17-Michael Bloomberg.pdf, p. 2.

3. Paul E. Barton, "The Right Way to Measure Growth," *Educational Leadership* December/January (2007), pp. 70-73; Andrew D. Ho, "The Problem with 'Proficiency': Limitations of Statistics and Policy Under No Child Left Behind," *Educational Researcher* 37 (2008), pp. 351-360; Daniel Koretz, *Measuring Up: What Education Testing Really Tells Us* (Cambridge: Harvard University Press, 2008); Robert L. Linn, "Validity of Inferences from Test-Based Educational Accountability Systems," *Journal of Personnel Evaluation in Education* 19 (2007), pp 5-15.

4. Ideally, we would be able to compare the test score distributions of the group— that is, compare average scale scores as well as differences between low-scoring White/Asian and Hispanic/Black students (i.e., students scoring at the 10th percentile of their respective groups) and differences between high-scoring students (i.e., students scoring at the 90th percentile of their respective groups). Unfortunately, New York City has not reported these data.

5. See, for example, Christopher Jencks and Meredith Phillips (editors), *The Black-White Test Score Gap* (Washington, DC: Brookings, 1998) and Roland Fryer and Steven Levitt, "The Black-White Test Score Gap Through Third Grade," *American Law and Economics Review* 8: 249-281.

6. This is assuming a normal distribution.

7. Though we would prefer to compare changes in the achievement gap in New York City from 1999-2003 and 2003-2008, the Department of Education has only released scale score data for different racial/ethnic groups from 2002-2008.

8. Elizabeth Green, "'Achievement Gap' in City Schools is Scrutinized: Slight Gains in English are Reported," *New York Sun*, August 5, 2008.

Class Size:

A Promise Broken

- Leonie Haimson

For at least a generation, students in New York City have been disadvantaged by being crammed into far larger classes than students in the rest of the state—with average class sizes as much as 60 percent larger in some grades.[1]

In the early 1990s, class sizes in the city averaged 25 students per class in Kindergarten and 31 students per class in high school, with other grades falling in between, while class sizes averaged between 20 and 22 in all grades elsewhere in the state. Many middle schools in New York City, then as now, have classes of 30 or more, and many high-school classes average 34 students, the maximum allowed under the teachers' union contract.

In 1993, the Campaign for Fiscal Equity (CFE), a group made up of local school board officials, parents, and advocates, filed a constitutional challenge to the state's school aid system, claiming that the state had under-funded New York City's public schools, with the effect of denying students their constitutional right to a sound basic education. In 2003, the Court of Appeals, the state's highest court, ruled in favor of CFE and ordered the state to direct more aid to New York City schools and reform the funding formula.

Class size was a pivotal issue in the case. The court determined, on the basis of expert testimony, that overly large classes had led to tragic outcomes for New York City students:

 • "Plaintiffs presented measurable proof, credited by the trial court, that NYC schools have excessive class sizes, and that class size affects learning";

 • "Plaintiffs' evidence of the advantages of smaller class sizes supports the inference sufficiently to show a meaningful correlation between the large classes in City schools and the outputs . . . of poor academic achievement and high dropout rates";

 • "Tens of thousands of students are placed in overcrowded classrooms . . . The number of children in these straits is large enough to represent a systemic failure." [2]

Even earlier, in 1998, the state legislature had approved targeted funding to reduce class sizes to 20 or less in grades K–3, in the form of grants provided to districts throughout the state to hire extra teachers and form new classes. The federal government also began to provide funding for this purpose. Beginning in the fall of 1999, New York City began to receive about $90 million each in annual state and federal class-size reduction funds.

As a result of this funding, as well as declining enrollment, class sizes in the early grades started to fall in New York City, and the gap in average class size between city schools and those in the rest of the state narrowed. Progress in reducing class size was particularly rapid during the first few years of the program.

In the spring of 2000, I authored a report for the Educational Priorities Panel about the first year of smaller classes in New York City schools.[3] Principals and teachers at the schools where class sizes had been reduced were generally elated, and many proclaimed that this reform had been the best thing that had ever happened at their schools.

Some typical responses were: from a teacher in Queens, "It's ideal"; from a principal in Brooklyn, "It's been incredible. Just phenomenal"; from a teacher in East Harlem, "It's been invaluable." A principal in central Harlem said, "Finally the children in a public school have a fair chance to succeed. The government is investing in our schools the right way, providing the resources the children really need."

Educators interviewed for the report observed that their students appeared to be learning faster; that teachers were able to give individualized attention and small group instruction more effectively; that they could perform more frequent student evaluation and follow-up; that the students participated more in class and were more enthusiastic; and that teacher morale and parent involvement had improved markedly and that disciplinary referrals had declined.

The principal of PS 198 on the edge of Harlem noted that suspensions had dropped 60 percent since class sizes were reduced in her school. She also reported: "For the first time, no new teacher has broken down crying in my office. It's always happened in the past. You could see the lack of morale among the teachers. Now what's being asked of them is realistic."

A second-grade teacher at the same school whose class had been reduced to 19 students from 29 the year before confided that for the first time she knew what it was like to be a teacher rather than an enforcer in the classroom. Educators at all these schools applauded a policy that was *proactive* rather than remedial— ensuring that children succeed to begin with, rather than fall behind and require expensive and often ineffective intervention to catch up. The educators interviewed predicted higher test scores, lower rates of special education referrals, and improved teacher retention as a result.

Their expectations that smaller classes would lead to gains in performance appear to have been confirmed. In the spring of 2003, 322 New York City elementary schools made the state's "most improved" list based on their students' fourth-grade scores.[4] Additionally, of the fifty elementary schools on the state's failing

SURR list in 1998–1999, almost 60 percent had been removed by 2003[5]; that year's fourth-graders were the first to have had the benefit of significantly smaller classes since first grade. In New York City as a whole, the percentages of fourth-graders testing at the lowest levels declined sharply, from 19.4 percent to 8.7 percent in mathematics and from 21.3 percent to 8.8 percent in reading. The percentage of fourth-graders testing at the lowest levels in reading and mathematics was significantly correlated with the decline in average class size, in both reading and mathematics (see Appendix for a statistical analysis). In other words, the districts which reduced class size the most in grades K–3 saw the biggest gains in test scores.

The Chancellor's District, a group of low-performing schools from throughout the city that was placed under then-Chancellor Crew's direct supervision, saw the largest reductions in class size, from 23.2 students per class to 19.4 students per class. In these schools, the percentage of fourth-graders scoring at the lowest level dropped most sharply, with those at Level 1 falling from 35 percent to 9.5 percent in mathematics and from 38 percent to 13.1 percent in reading.

Progress in the Chancellor's District reveals other possible effects of smaller classes. In 1998–1999, before class sizes were reduced, 8.1 percent of students were in full-time special education. By 2001–2002, the number of full-time special education students had fallen to below the citywide average. The percentage of students referred for special education services also declined significantly over the same period.[6]

Teacher retention also rose. In 1998–1999, only 42.2 percent of teachers in the Chancellor's District schools had been in their school for two or more years. By 2002–2003, this figure had risen 12.6 percentage points, to 54.8 percent.

Yet, in 2003, the reduction in class size began to stall, despite a continued fall in enrollment and continued funding. In the spring of 2004, the third-grade teacher at PS 198 reported that her class size had increased from 19 to 23, making it much more difficult for her to give her students the help that they needed.

The Independent Budget Office (IBO) analyzed the city's class size data, and found that in the fall of 2003, average class sizes in grades K–3 had risen in fifteen out of the thirty-four New York City school districts, while in only fourteen districts had class sizes declined.[7] The IBO also discovered that the city had misreported class size data and underestimated the size of classes.[8]

Armed with this information, in January of 2005, City Council Speaker Gifford Miller, Councilmember Robert Jackson, and State Senator Eric Schneiderman requested that the state comptroller perform an audit of the DOE's reporting of class size data and its use of the state early grade class-size reduction funds.[9]

In March of 2006, the state comptroller's office released its audit, showing that the DOE had misused $90 million in annual state class-size reduction funds, and, during in the previous year, had formed only twenty additional classes in grades K–3 over the baseline figure, not the 1,586 classes they had claimed.[10] This meant that only 1.3 percent of the required classes were created, with each one costing the taxpayer over $4 million.[11] Instead, the audit concluded, the DOE had used state funding to supplant their own spending on teaching positions: "We believe that the DOE's calculations are not consistent with the Law, because DOE's method substitutes Program funding for local funding that was used previously for early grade classes (and teachers) that existed prior to the Program's implementation."[12]

The State Comptroller made numerous recommendations on how the city should improve its compliance. In their official response, DOE officials said they would refuse to adopt any of his proposals, and they did not.[13]

In the spring of 2007, as part of the settlement of the Campaign for Fiscal Equity lawsuit, the legislature passed a new law requiring that the city submit a new five-year plan for class-size reduction in all grades in return for receiving hundreds of millions of dollars in additional state aid. After much delay, the city finally submitted its plan, calling for class sizes to be gradually lowered over five years to an average of 20 per class in K–3 and 23 per class in all other grades. In return, in the first year of the program, the city received more than $400 million in additional state aid, of which the city allocated $152.7 million for class-size reduction.

Yet in April 2007, the United Federation of Teachers released a report showing that in the 390 elementary and middle schools that had pledged to spend at least $50,000 on class-size reduction, 48.5 percent did not reduce class sizes at all; and in one-third of these schools, class sizes actually increased. The analysis also found that in 43 percent of all elementary and middle schools citywide, class sizes increased.[14]

In September of 2008, the State Education Department reported that the city had not implemented its class-size reduction plan the previous year. While average class sizes had diminished fractionally, the city had failed to make any of its class-size reduction targets, and class size and/or pupil-to-teacher ratios had increased in more than half of all schools. State officials noted that in seventy schools that received $20 million in class-size reduction funds, both class sizes and student/teacher ratio had increased. These officials concluded that "NYC DOE will be required to improve implementation of the second year of its class size plan."[15]

The following year, the DOE was again provided more than $400 million in additional state aid, of which about $150 million was supposed to be allocated to class-size reduction. That year average class sizes citywide actually rose in all grades except fourth—by the largest amount in over ten years. In grades K–3, the increases were so substantial that they wiped out nearly five years of gradual decline.

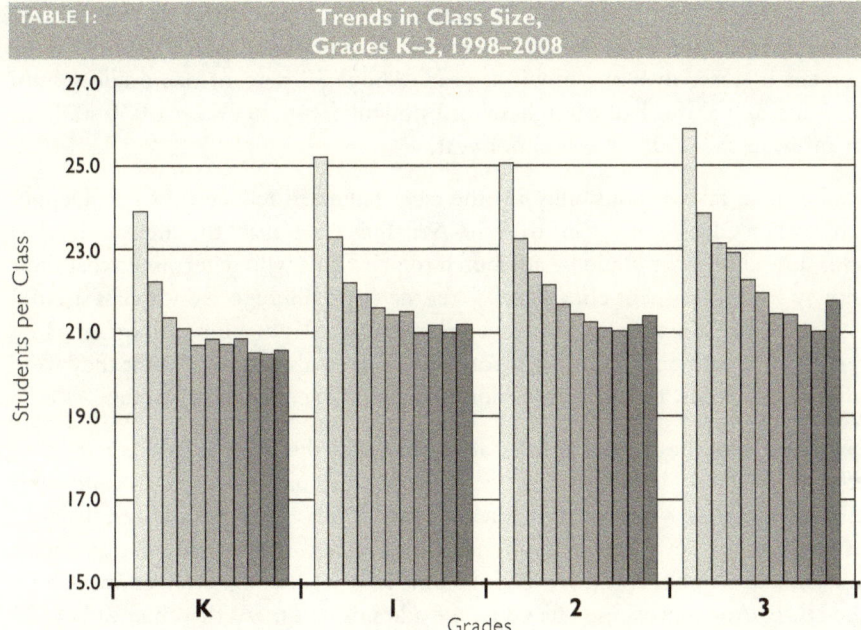

TABLE I: Trends in Class Size, Grades K–3, 1998–2008

In Kindergarten, class sizes jumped to the same average level as in the school year 2002–2003, the first full year of the Bloomberg/Klein administration, despite hundreds of millions of dollars of targeted state funding pumped into the city to lower class size during the intervening years. Class-size reduction in the five years preceding "Children First" actually outpaced the "Children First" years by a factor of thirteen.

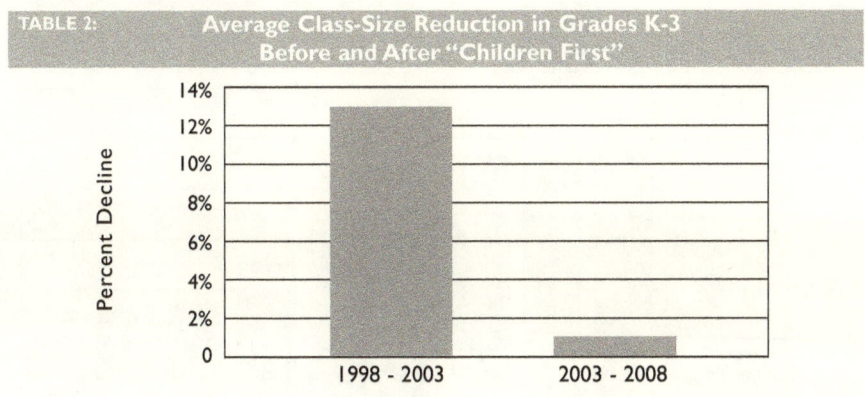

TABLE 2: Average Class-Size Reduction in Grades K-3 Before and After "Children First"

Of course, averages tell only one small part of the story. During the 2008–2009 school year, 25 percent of K–3 students, or 66,895 children, were in classes of 25 or more, compared to 21 percent the year before, amounting to an increase of more than 11,000 children. Seven percent of students in first through third grades, or 13,867 children, were in classes of 28 or more, a 48 percent increase over the previous year. About 38 percent of middle-school students, and about half of high-school students, were in classes of 30 students or more in the 2008–2009 school year.

Rather than take responsibility for the city's failure to reduce class size, Deputy Chancellor Christopher Cerf told the *New York Times* that "the increase in class sizes this school year could be attributed to principals who determined that their money was better spent elsewhere."[16] Yet the city's failure to reduce class size did not occur because principals believed that smaller classes are unimportant. In a recent survey, 86 percent of New York City principals responded that they were unable to provide a quality education because of excessive class sizes.

Garth Harries, the top DOE official in charge of the city's class-size reduction efforts, took the view that class sizes rose because parents "want to send their children to places with successful track records."[18] Yet as of 2008, the vast majority of students in New York City attended their zoned neighborhood elementary and middle schools, and high school admissions were completely controlled by the DOE. Another excuse offered by the administration was that the nearly $150 million allotted for class-size reduction in 2008–2009 was "at best marginal funds." Yet those funds, if used correctly, could have lowered class sizes by more than 1.5 students per class on average in every grade.[19]

Indeed, despite the infusion of nearly a billion dollars of state class-size reduction funds into New York City schools over the last decade, the city has provided fewer K-8 classes and classroom teachers each year of the Bloomberg/Klein administration. Between 2002–2003 and 2008–2009, there was a drop of nearly two thousand classes in these grades. (See Table 3.)

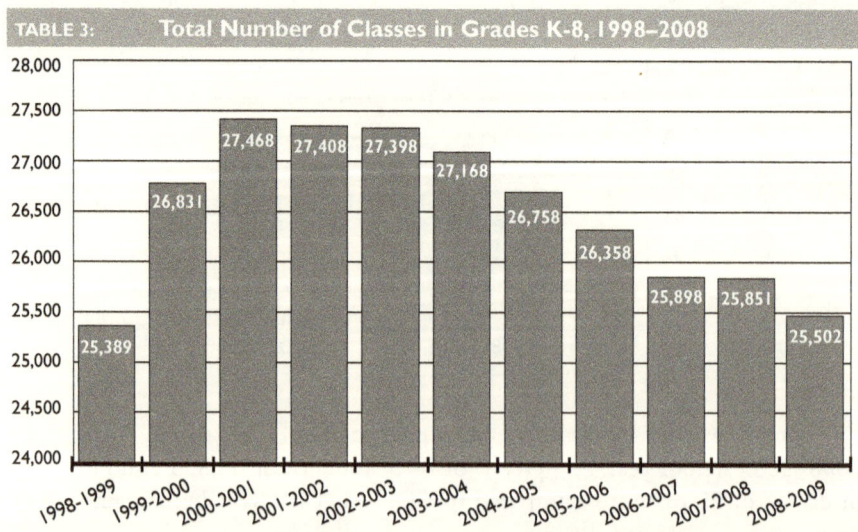

TABLE 3: Total Number of Classes in Grades K-8, 1998–2008

Many New York City parents believe that smaller classes are the reform most needed to improve their children's education. When asked what improvements they would most like to see in the schools, class size reduction remains their top priority.[20] Norma Genao, principal at PS 185 in East Harlem, was one of the educators interviewed for the Educational Priorities Panel report. In 2000, she spoke eloquently about the benefits of smaller classes and how these conditions should be provided to every New York City child:

> Finally the children in a public school ... have a fair chance to succeed. The government is investing in our schools the right way, providing the resources the children really need ... For decades its been the thing we knew would make all the difference for our children, but I never thought I would live to see the day where it would actually happen.
>
> I feel honored that I've seen the day that I could provide these children with the appropriate resources they need to learn. Now it should be expanded to all the schools in the city. All children in this city, this state, this country are entitled to the benefits of smaller classes. Speaking as an educator, it should not be a privilege, it should be a right.

This remains as true today as it was a decade ago.

- APPENDIX -

Statistical analysis by Leonie Haimson and Jacqueline Shannon, showing that decline by district in the percentage of New York City fourth-graders testing at Level 1 from 1999 to 2002 in ELA was significantly correlated with K–3 class-size reduction over the previous four years. In mathematics, there was also a significant correlation between decreased class size and increased number of students testing at or above grade level.

Correlations: Change in fourth-grade mathematics and reading scores 1999–2003, per New York City district, based on average change in class size, K–3, from 1998 to 2002.

			4-year Class Size Change:
MATH: Level 3 & 4	Four Year Change	Pearson Correlation	- .456(**)
		Sig. (1-tailed)	.004
		N	33
MATH: Level 1		Pearson Correlation	.425 (**)
		Sig. (1-tailed)	.007
		N	33

** *Correlation is significant at the 0.01 level (1-tailed).*

			4-year Class Size Change:
ELA: Mean Scale Score	Four Year Change	Pearson Correlation	- .256
		Sig. (1-tailed)	.075
		N	33
ELA: Level 3 & 4		Pearson Correlation	- .152
		Sig. (1-tailed)	.199
		N	33
ELA: Level 1		Pearson Correlation	.322(*)
		Sig. (1-tailed)	.034
		N	33

* *Correlation is significant at the 0.05 level (1-tailed).*

1. The comparative class size data as far back as 1990 are gathered from the New York State Education Department's statistical summaries known as the "Chapter 655 Reports": "A Report to the Governor and the Legislature on the Educational Status of the State's Schools," submitted June 2001.

2. *Campaign for Fiscal Equity, Inc., et al. v. State of New York, et al.*, 100 NY 2d 893, 911-12 (2003).

3. Leonie Haimson, "Smaller is Better: First-Hand Reports of Early Grade Class Size Reduction in New York City Public Schools," Educational Priorities Panel, April 2000, http://www.edpriorities.org/Pubs/Report/Report_Smaller.html.

4. Ellen Yan, "City's Comeback Kids," *Newsday*, February 24, 2004; David M. Herszenhorn, "1,012 Schools Had Big Gains in English and Math Tests Over Five Years, State Says," *New York Times*, Feb. 24, 2004.

5. Deinya Phenix, et.al., "Virtual District, Real Improvement: A Retrospective Evaluation of the Chancellor's District, 1996–2003," Institute for Education and Social Policy, Steinhardt School of Education, New York University, June 2004, p. 21, Table 9.

6. Deinya Phenix, "Virtual District, Real Improvement," p. 18. The citywide average was 5.8 percent. By 2001–2002, the percentage was 4.8.

7. See George Sweeting, Deputy Director, Independent Budget Office, letter to the author, July 19, 2004, http://www.ibo.nyc.ny.us/iboreports/classsizeaug04.pdf and http://www.ibo.nyc.ny.us/iboreports/classsizetablesaug04.pdf. Note in five districts, average class sizes remained unchanged. The IBO reported that in Kindergarten, average class size rose from 20.7 to 20.9 children per class between the 2002–2003 and the 2003–2004 school year. Both these figures differed substantially from the official data reported by the DOE in the Mayor's Management Report.

8. DOE officials later admitted that they had included phantom classes with long-term absent students in their calculations. See letter from Kathleen Grimm, Deputy Chancellor, New York City Department of Education, to State Senator Eric Schneiderman, December 8, 2004, available at http://www. classsizematters.org/Jackson_SCHNEIDERMAN1_EGCSR_1208048.htm.

9. "Department of Education's Admitted Miscalculation of Class Size Numbers Leads to Call for State Audit," Press release, New York City Council, January 30, 2005,http://www.nyccouncil.info/pdf_files/newswire/ 01_30_05_class_size.pdf. See also George Sweeting, Deputy Director, Independent Budget Office, letter to the author, July 19, 2004, available at http://www.ibo.nyc.ny.us/iboreports/classsizeaug04.pdf . The background and full documentation of the audit is posted at http://www.classsizematters.org/timelineclasssizeaudit.html.

10. "New York City Department of Education Administration of the Early Grade Class Size Reduction Program," Report #2005–N–2003, New York State Office of the State Comptroller, March 15, 2006, at http://www.osc.state.ny.us/audits/allaudits/093006/05n3.pdf. See especially Exhibit A, p. 33. See also Erin Einhorn, "City flunks bid to shrink classes, Hevesi says," *Daily News;* David Andreatta, "City Accused of Cheating in Cla$$," *New York Post*; and Elissa Gootman, "Class Sizes Still Too Large in New York, Hevesi Finds," *New York Times*, all dated March 17, 2006.

11. "NYC DOE Administration of the Early Grade Class Size Reduction Program," Exhibit A, p. 33. The audit also found that over the previous four years, the number of early grade classes in New York City schools had declined by 876.

12. "NYC DOE Administration of the Early Grade Class Size Reduction Program," State Comptroller, p.4. If the DOE had actually created the additional classes that city officials had claimed, class sizes in these grades would have averaged 19.1 students, and a majority of students would be in classes of 20 or fewer. Instead, more than 60 percent of New York City students in grades K–3 remained in classes of 21 or larger, with 26 percent in classes of 25 or more.

13. See "NYC Department of Education's Formal Comments on OSC's Draft Audit Report on Early Grade Class Size Reduction," in "NYC DOE Administration of the Early Grade Class Size Reduction Program," State Comptroller, p. 59. These comments were sent to the state comptroller on November 7, 2006–the day of the New York City mayoral election. The authors justify themselves as follows: "instances in which the early grade class size dollars may appear to have been budgeted to classes required under our local commitment represent no deliberate misuse of funds, but rather the difficulty of budgeting across thousands of schools," acknowledging that improper substitution of state dollars for local dollars occurred, yet disclaiming responsibility for the failure to oversee the use of state funds.

14. "Class Size and the Contract for Excellence: Are We Making Progress in NYC's Public Schools?" United Federation of Teachers, April 28, 2008. See also: Carrie Melago, "153M from Albany Can't Uncram Classes," *Daily News*; Yoav Gonen, "Failing to 'Cut' Class: $ize Still Matters," *New York Post*; Elizabeth Green, "Comptroller To Probe City's Class-Size Reduction Effort," *New York Sun*, all from April 29, 2008, and Maisie McAdoo, "Report Shows DOE Refused to Make Headway on Class Size Despite $153M of New Funds," New York Teacher, May 8, 2008, http://www.uft.org/news/teacher/top/doe_refused_headway/.

15. Deputy Commissioner Johanna Duncan-Poitier, "Contracts for Excellence–Monitoring Report, September 8, 2008," New York State Education Department, http://www.regents.nysed.gov/meetings/2008Meetings/September2008/0908 emscd4.htm.

16. Jennifer Medina, "Class Size in New York City Schools Rises, but the Impact Is Debated," *New York Times*, February 21, 2009.

17. Emily Horowitz and Leonie Haimson, "How Crowded Are Our Schools? New Results from a Survey of NYC Public School Principals," Class Size Matters, October 3, 2008, www.classsizematters.org/principal_survey_report_10.08_final .pdf.

18. Medina, "Class Size in New York City Schools Rises."

19. Jennifer Medina, "Class Size Makes Biggest Jump of Bloomberg Tenure," *New York Times*, February 17, 2009. A different DOE official, spokesman Will Haverman, attributed class-size increases to DOE's own budget cuts, which, he argued, resulted in "440 fewer teachers working directly with students" in 2008–2009 than the year before." See Gotham schools Elizabeth Green, "DOE Stands Firm: The Economy Is What Caused Class Sizes to Rise," Gotham Schools, February 17, 2009, http://gothamschools.org/2009/02/17/doe-stands-firm-the-economy-is-what-caused-class-sizes-to-rise. A reduction in the number of teachers violates of the maintenance of effort requirements in the state law. Meanwhile, according to a recent report in the *Daily News*, the headcount at Tweed grew by nearly a hundred. Meredith Kolodner, "Bureaucrats and Class Sizes are Up Sharply," *Daily News*, February 24, 2009.

20. "Learning Environment Survey 2006–2007" and "Learning Environment Survey 2007–2008," New York City Department of Education, http://schools.nyc.gov/ NR/rdonlyres/F3D9A118-C51E-4E23-841C–2003DB5B24C87DC/40757/les 2008citywide.pdf.

Small Schools:
Myth and Reality

- David C. Bloomfield

Since Mayor Michael Bloomberg took control of New York's public schools in 2002, New York City's Department of Education (DOE)[1] reports that it has opened, or plans to open, 333 new schools, serving 5,600 children. Of these, 218 are designated by the DOE as developed with "Gates-funded intermediaries."[2] The Gates Foundation's partnership in this effort is substantial: it has poured over $100 million into the small-school effort, with one of its grantees, New Visions for Public Schools, receiving over $61 million in Gates Foundation grants between 2001 and 2007.[3] These grants have done much to shape the educational landscape of New York City.

Gauging the success of the myriad new programs is an uncertain undertaking. The study sample is by necessity small, since these schools grow annually grade-by-grade. Thus, most of these new schools lack graduating classes, let alone graduation data. Further, thirteen of these schools opened in 2002, prior to Mayor Bloomberg's tenure, although they are generally regarded as within the data set of the small-schools initiative since they served as the model for future new school development. (See Table 1 for a breakdown of new schools by year.)

Small schools have been around for a long time. To some degree, modern urban small high schools are a throwback to the country's pastoral origins[4] and hearken to an era prior to James Conant's postwar call to develop large comprehensive high schools.[5] Whatever data were initially available to Bloomberg, Gates, and their camp followers were based on the small-scale efforts of pioneering, persistent educators serving a select if sometimes academically impoverished student population.[6] There are no studies of systemic implementation of small schools available because no system had ever tried the kind of bold strategy embarked upon by Mayor Bloomberg, underpinned by Gates Foundation funds.

Nonetheless, the mayor chose small schools as his signal high school reform. The notion of personalized, high-quality institutions partnered with community-based organizations for additional support was a compelling model, compelling enough that few asked whether reproducing it throughout a whole system was really feasible. Within a few years hundreds of small schools dotted the cityscape, some inhabiting individual buildings, others sharing space with preexisting schools, other small schools, or both. No doubt was ever expressed by Bloomberg partisans that small high schools would be successful in producing college-ready graduates on on a mass scale. In 2008, approximately 85,000 students were enrolled in high schools with fewer than 600 students, compared to just 29,000 in 2002. (According to DOE enrollment figures, 185,000 students still attend large high schools.)

TABLE 1:	2002-2009 New District Schools								
Grade Level - All New District Schools	2009*	2008	2007	2006	2005	2004	2003	2002	Total
High Schools (9 - 12)	13	26	13	12	25	48	24	12	173
Secondary Schools (6 - 12)	2	5	11	13	11	14	2	1	59
Middle Schools (6 - 8)	14	7	10	10	17	8	-	-	66
Elementary Schools (pre-K - 8)	13	15	4	1	2	-	-	-	35
Total:	**42**	**53**	**38**	**36**	**55**	**70**	**26**	**13**	**333**
Grade Level Gates-Funded Intermediaries	2009*	2008	2007	2006	2005	2004	2003	2002	Total
High Schools (9 - 12)	10	18	10	12	18	48	20	12	148
Secondary Schools (6 - 12)	2	5	8	12	9	14	2	1	53
Middle Schools (6 - 8)	-	2	3	3	1	8	0	0	17
Elementary Schools (Pre-K - 8)	-	-	-	-	-	-	-	-	-
Total:	**12**	**25**	**21**	**27**	**28**	**70**	**22**	**13**	**218**

* As of April 1, 2009, schools planned to open in September 2009.
Source: New York City Department of Education

This frenzy of small school creation was marked by inadequate planning and unprepared leadership. One teacher, who has asked to remain anonymous to avoid retribution to her school, wrote to me when I was serving on the Citywide Council on High Schools:

> As someone who has actually gone through the process of envisioning, applying for, and starting a new small high school in New York City, I have been absolutely shocked by the lack of accountability for the success of this major school reform. The Department of Education, along with the Gates Foundation, New Visions, ISA [Institute for Student Achievement], and other CBOs [community-based organizations], sees small schools as a panacea and do not impose the same level of accountability and scrutiny on the new

schools as they do on the established schools. Especially in this current era of standards and NCLB [the federal No Child Left Behind Act], it is hypocritical, and frankly a disservice to the students in the small schools that there is not more evaluation and accountability.

From my experience, there exists an educational aristocracy of individuals who are personal favorites of Joel Klein or Eric Nadelstern [the director of empowerment schools] and these individuals are given carte-blanche to create their own curricula, hire their own teachers, [create] assessment protocols, etc. I have been witness to highly unethical practices of "creaming students," heavy recruitment of certain students to the small schools, illegal hiring practices, and unreliable and invalid assessment protocols.

There is little rigorous evidence that the small schools work. Why don't the powers that be start on a small-scale, prove the efficacy of their reform, and then scale-up, once small schools are proven a success?

Another teacher, who had just spent the last several months creating and teaching in a small school, wrote to me that "leadership" is the "key to success," but that his school succeeded without effective leadership because their students were all high-performing to start with. "What makes this troubling," he wrote, "is that we receive funds from the Gates Foundation for the explicit purpose of admitting students who are scoring at level 1 and 2 on their 5th grade tests."

Small schools begin with a considerably advantaged position—beyond their substantial foundation support. First is their incubated growth. Bloomberg-era small schools generally start with ninth grades, then when the first class is promoted another grade is added, then another, until the school is fully populated—and enrollment capped—after four years. This policy entails substantial displaced costs onto students attending large high schools. These include severe over-crowding[7] and concentration of the least academically proficient students. This us-against-them bias was even noted by a Gates-funded small schools evaluation team reporting on an initial group of the Gates-funded, Bloomberg-implemented New Century High Schools (NCHS) initiative:

> We have been guilty of pitting NCHS schools against traditional high schools by comparing the two to suggest the superiority of the smaller schools. In the long run what matters, of course, is that drop-out rates decrease and educational achievement increase throughout the system. [8]

The small schools were permitted to ban English language learners (ELLs) and special needs students requiring self-contained classrooms during their first three years of operation (those years from which small school graduation data are derived). As member of the Citywide Council on High Schools I initiated a complaint with the U.S. Office of Civil Rights (OCR) against this practice in

March, 2006.[9] OCR issued a determination based on DOE data that this discriminatory conduct was not illegal since it had not resulted in long-term harm to special needs and ELL students generally. They remarked that for school year 2008–2009, 59 percent of disabled students requiring certain special-education services were matched to the first high school of their choice, while only 50 percent of general education students were matched to their first choice. In addition, 84 percent of these students were matched to one of their first three choices, compared with 76 percent of general education students. As Aaron Pallas has pointed out:

> Rising ninth-graders rank their top 12 choices for high school programs, and a computer algorithm matches students to schools so that students are admitted to their highest-ranked school that also ranked the student as admissible . . . few students, and their parents, would be willing to "burn" a top high school choice on a school that they felt would be unlikely to admit them. If the message is clear that a particular high school doesn't welcome disabled or LEP (limited English proficiency) students—and the low numbers of such students in the school is a pretty clear message—why would a student list that school as a top choice in the admissions process?[10]

In my view the decision was faulty and the city's small-school policies remain descriminatory.

Indeed, writing in 2008, based on a study of small schools established between 1993 and 2003, the research team of Iatarola, Schwartz, Stiefel, and Chellman concluded that small schools had negative impacts on desegregation, equitable resource allocation, and achievement:

> Segregation worsened for poor students, recent immigrants, and Asians, who were increasingly isolated from other groups of students; improved for White (because of increased exposure to Asian students) and Black students, who were less isolated from other groups of students; and held steady for LEP and Hispanic students. The dispersion of resources grew over time, and noninstructional spending continued to be more disparate than total spending and instructional spending.[11]

Simply put, no fair comparisons are possible between small and large New York City public high schools since at every turn the small schools were advantaged by central policies and their outside benefactors. They were better funded, were permitted capped enrollments, avoided upper grade transfers, and were not expected to educate those with the greatest instructional challenges. Additionally, small schools were accorded a designated development/advocacy office at DOE headquarters directly reporting to the chancellor, special staff recruitment, dedicated high school fairs, and a politically motivated public-relations effort.

Nevertheless, small schools have pitfalls of which their proponents failed to take adequate account and which have ultimately been borne out by disappointing results. What happens when their short-term advantages of special incubation and attention are past and they need to cope with the normal issues of leadership and staff succession, student mobility, overcapacity, and decreased outside funding? Because of their size, small schools usually lack diverse curricula; depth in specialized faculty, particularly in math and sciences; professional guidance and college counseling; and other strengths of comprehensive schools. Many of them share space with other schools within the same building. According to the DOE, more than eight hundred of 1,626 school programs shared facilities as of February 2009.[12] These conditions create strains on shared spaces, loss of space to duplicated administration, and, often, overcrowding in the host school. Many predate the mayor's new schools initiative but this oft-difficult coexistence has clearly been exacerbated by large-scale insertion of small schools into existing schools. Neither traditional large comprehensive high schools nor their pendulum-swing reaction, small schools, automatically provide the necessities of a twenty-first-century education to twenty-first-century urban adolescents.

And indeed so far the achievement in the small schools does not seem to be keeping pace with comprehensive high schools in teaching higher-level subject matter. One small-school teacher told me:

> I also don't think that anyone was monitoring graduation rate for a school like that—TC [Teachers College] connected, etc. Here's a telling example: There were four English teachers. Two teachers taught 9th grade. I taught 10th grade with pretty large classes: 28, etc. and one person taught both 11th and 12th grades. Hmm...what does that [say] about #s by the time they got to 11th and 12th grades??

According to the U.S. Department of Education's What Works Clearinghouse ("WWC") evaluation of the New Century High Schools, the claim that Bloomberg's small schools are effective in dropout prevention cannot be substantiated.[13]

Graduation with marketable skills for post-secondary opportunities is also falling short. Small school achievement of the New York State Regents diplomas, a minimum standard demonstrating mastery of state curriculum requirements, is not encouraging. Even passing scores of 65 on the Regents exams do not meet State or City University of New York requirements to avoid remedial classes and yet, according to Policy Studies Associates, New Century High Schools fell short of a control group attending large high schools even of this measure:

> Examination of the Class of 2006 graduates in the two groups of schools indicates that graduates of comparison-group schools were more likely to earn a Regents diploma or Advanced Regents diploma, however, than were NCHS graduates (67 percent versus 46 percent). When the unit of comparison is students rather than graduates,

however, the difference is less stark, with 41 percent of comparison-group students and 36 percent of NCHS students earning a Regents or Advanced Regents diploma.[14]

Like their large-school colleagues, most New York City small school graduates earned so called "local diplomas," rather than Regents diplomas; these are so deficient that New York State is eliminating them because they fail to meet accepted standards of college readiness. It appears that, counter to their stated mission, the small schools are putting graduation over education without the academic rigor that advocates claim.

Emphasizing the local diploma option places graduation more easily within reach for small-school graduates; small schools have also tended toward defining success as "credit accumulation" rather than subject mastery, allowing even greater ease on meeting graduation requirements. This practice permits the use of "credit recovery" toward graduation, a method of giving students course credits for classes they would otherwise have failed by giving special assignments when regular homework, test scores, and other standard measures of achievement have not been met.[15]

One small school teacher described for me how her school avoided the stigma of low graduation rates: the principal refused to have a self-contained class for special education students, so that he would not attract special ed students to his school. Hence students with Individualized Instructional Programs (IEPs) calling for such classrooms were thrown in with the regular population. He told a reporter with a child with special needs that there was no room in the school. He worked to get kids with behavioral problems kicked out. There was, she said,

> no plan or idea about working with difficult kids . . . Rather than challenging the kids intellectually . . . the idea was to pass the kids on, in order to graduate them. I (and another teacher who was rigorous) were questioned about our failure rates. Why did we fail so many kids? . . .

> The seniors were given 3 classes and then were free for the day, rather than giving them the preparation they needed for college. The point was graduation rate rather than real preparation for what lay ahead. A couple of students transferred because they didn't feel they were getting real preparation.

What, then, continues to attract the administration to this approach to high schools that does not work for its own population and harms the population it excludes? In the end, it is not small schools' quality, but the assembly-line approach of interchangeable educational modules that can be slid in or out of larger institutions that appears to have grabbed the mayor, allowing him to stay one step ahead of federal and state timelines for failing school closure. Rather than doing the hard work of instructional improvement—an area in which the mayor and chancellor seem disinterested and clearly inexpert—schools that receive embarrassingly low marks can be quickly terminated, replaced by untested programs from a veritable warehouse of pre-approved "schools" developed from within the bureaucracy. Thus the mayor's own failures become a kind of success: "Look what we've done! Replaced a failing school with a new one!" without admitting that the initial failure took place on the mayor's watch, that real students have been the victims of the original school's supposed free fall, and that the new school's prospects are really no better than the first's unless the academic profile of incoming students is improved, a DOE contrivance well documented by Jennifer Jennings and Aaron Pallas.[16]

In the end, small schools as a group have proven to provide no assurance of academic success. Their reckless, politics-driven creation has resulted in untold numbers of large-school students displaced and given insufficient instructional attention so that the Bloomberg administration could claim a political victory. Small school students, too, have suffered from their schools' focus on reaching the administration's self-defined benchmarks rather than providing a substantive, well rounded education preparatory to post-secondary opportunities. The Gates Foundation has explicitly moved on and no longer supports a small schools program.[17] Even the Bloomberg administration has tried to divert attention from its failures by now promoting a "portfolio" of small schools, large schools, and "small learning communities" integrated within a single school.

But the legacy of the failed small school experiment lives on in limited curricular opportunities; low standards; displaced students; excluded special needs and ELL students who might truly have benefited by a more personalized environment; an assembly-line approach to school creation and destruction, with inadequate appreciation of the human costs to affected students; and a newly entrenched political constituency of not-for-profit small school managers and "support organizations" enriched by DOE and outside contracts— all measured not by human observers but by privatized data gathering and evaluation systems operating outside public scrutiny.

NOTES

1. While the statutory name for New York City's public schools continues to be the "Board of Education," or the "City School District of the City of New York," the mayor has denominated it the "Department of Education," so that term is used here.

2. "2002–2009 New District Schools," New York City Department of Education, 2009. The Gates-funded new school intermediary partners in New York City are the Asia Society, CUNY, the Coalition of Essential Schools, The College Board, Diploma Plus, Good Shepherd Services, Internationals Network for Public Schools, the Institute for Student Achievement, National Academy Foundation, the National Council of La Raza, NYC Outward Bound, New Visions for Public Schools, Replications, Inc., The Urban Assembly, and Young Women's Leadership Foundation.

3. See www.gatesfoundation.com/grants.

4. Judith Kafka, "Thinking Big about Getting Small: An Ideological History of Small School Reform," Teachers College Record, 110:9 (September 2008), pp. 1802-1836.

5. See, e.g., James B. Conant, *The American High School Today: A Report to Interested Citizens* (New York: McGraw-Hill, 1959) and *The Comprehensive High School: A Second Report to Interested Citizens* (New York: McGraw-Hill, 1967).

6. Seymour Fliegel and James McGuire, *Miracle in East Harlem* (New York: Times Books, 1993).

7. See, David C. Bloomfield, "High School Reform: The Downside of Scaling Up," Politics of Education Association Bulletin 30:1 (Fall, 2005) and "Come Clean on Small Schools," *Education Week*, January 25, 2006.

8. Eileen M. Foley, et al., "Evaluation Of New Century High Schools: Report on the Third Year" (Washington, D.C., Policy Studies Associates, June, 2006), p. 65.

9. Citywide Council on High Schools, Complaint to the U.S. Department of Education, Office of Civil Rights, March 2006, reprinted in David C. Bloomfield, *American Public Education Law* (New York: Peter Lang, 2007).

10. Aaron Pallas, "Questioning the Office of Civil Rights Decision about Small High Schools," Gotham Schools, January 20, 2009, http://gothamschools.org/2009/02/20/questioning-the-office-of-civil-rights-decision-about-small-high-schools/.

11. Patrice Iatarola, Amy Ellen Schwartz, Leanna Stiefel, and Colin C. Chellman, "Small Schools, Large Districts: Small-School Reform and New York City's Students," Teachers College Record, Volume 110, Number 9 (September 2008), pp. 1837–1878.

12. See http://schools.nyc.gov/Facilities/CampusManagement/default.htm.

13. "The New Century High Schools Initiative," U.S. Department of Education, Institute of Education Sciences, What Works Clearinghouse (August 2008).

14. Eileen M. Foley, et al., "Evaluation Of New Century High Schools: Profile of an Initiative to Create and Sustain Small, Successful High Schools," Final Report, (Washington, D.C., Policy Studies Associates, 2007, Revised 2008), p. i.

15. See, Elissa Gootman and Sharona Coutts, "Lacking Credits, Some Students Learn a Shortcut," *New York Times,* April 11, 2008.

16. See Jennifer Jennings writing as Eduwonkette, "Why Has the Education Press Missed the Boat? The Case of Small Schools," *Education Week,* vol. 27, no. 39, June 4, 2008 and Jennifer L. Jennings and Aaron Pallas, "Who Attends Small Schools?," presented at the American Educational Research Association annual conference, San Diego, CA, April 13-17, 2009.

17. See, William Gates, "2009 Annual Letter from Bill Gates: U.S. Education" at http://www.gatesfoundation.org/annual-letter/Pages/2009-united-states-education.aspx.

School Overcrowding in NYC:

What Principals Say

- *Emily Horowitz*

Overcrowding in New York City schools remains a systemic problem throughout the city, despite claims otherwise by the Department of Education (DOE).[1] The Bloomberg/Klein administration has failed to build sufficient new schools, and some of its major initiatives have served to worsen rather than alleviate overcrowding. Moreover, the "Blue Book," the official DOE document that lists the enrollment and school capacity for each school and calculates utilization based on these figures,[2] is severely flawed and does not adequately reflect the seriousness of overcrowding on the ground. Parents, educators, and advocates have protested that schools listed as underutilized in the Blue Book are actually overcrowded, but historically these critics have only had access to anecdotal data as evidence.

New York City has a legal responsibility to relieve overcrowding. In 2003, the New York State Court of Appeals (the state's highest court) ruled in favor of the plaintiffs in the Campaign for Fiscal Equity (CFE) lawsuit. The plaintiffs maintained that the New York state finance system underfunded New York City public schools and thereby denied its students their constitutional right to a sound basic education. The court ruled that the state must undertake sweeping reforms. Overcrowding and excessive class sizes in New York City public schools were major elements of the case. The court found that over-crowding had a deleterious impact on the quality of education that the city could provide. Here is an excerpt from the Court of Appeals' decision:

> Some facts that the trial court classified as purely "physical" facilities inputs are inseparable from overcrowding and excessive class size—conditions whose measurable effect on students plaintiffs have shown. One symptom of an overcrowded school system is the encroachment of ordinary classroom activities into what would otherwise be specialized spaces: libraries, laboratories, auditoriums and the like. There was considerable evidence of a shortage of such spaces.[3]

As a result of this decision, the state legislature provided an additional $8.3 billion in financing to New York City for school construction in the spring of 2006. The reimbursement rate for new school construction in the city was also raised to 50 percent, meaning that the city now receives back from the state half of every dollar spent to build new schools.

Unfortunately, the DOE did not respond to this new infusion of funds by expanding its capital plan, but instead cut back on the number of new seats by 3,000, to 63,000. Then, in the fall of 2008, the DOE introduced a new five-year capital plan that even more sharply curtailed new school construction.

In 2007, City Councilmember Robert Jackson, one of the key litigants in the CFE lawsuit, funded a survey of New York City public school principals in order to learn more about the discrepancy between claims by advocates and the DOE data. This principal survey represents the first effort to quantify the true extent of overcrowding in New York City public schools, by asking principals throughout the city about their schools' actual capacity and needs.[4]

Official Estimates

The Blue Book assigns each school a figure in percentage form to represent school utilization, based on the official capacity of each school—the estimate of how many students the school should be able to hold and adequately educate. If the utilization figure is above 100 percent, this means that the school has more students than capacity, and if it is under 100 percent, this means that there is extra space in the school.

According to the Blue Book from the 2006–2007 school year, 38 percent of New York City public school students attended schools in buildings that were above 100 percent utilization. 47 percent of elementary school students were in school buildings that were overutilized, 19 percent of middle school students, and 51 percent of high school students.[5]

While the DOE's official figures for the number of students in overcrowded school buildings are discouraging enough, the results of the principal survey reveal that these figures significantly understate the actual level of overcrowding in the New York City school system, for reasons explained below.

Survey Results

The survey received responses from 550 principals, more than one-third of the city's total.[6] The distribution by borough was very close to that of the city as a whole. The average length of time our respondents had been principals was five and half years. Sixty-one percent of them prepared their school's "turn-around" document on which the Blue Book utilization rates are based. Their schools had significantly lower official utilization rates than schools in New York City as a whole. Twenty-eight percent of respondents were at schools that the Blue Book reported as 100 percent or above, compared to 38 percent of schools overall. The Appendix includes details about responses and respondents.

Nearly half (49 percent) of our respondents believed that the official utilization rate for their own school as reported in the Blue Book was inaccurate. For principals of schools whose official utilization rates were reported as under 100 percent, slightly more than half (51 percent) said that the DOE utilization rate was incorrect and understated the actual level of overcrowding at their school. Fifty-one percent of all principals said that the enrollment at their school was not capped at a level to prevent overcrowding.

The capacity formula in the Blue Book relies upon "target" class sizes that are substantially larger than class sizes average currently and much larger than the goals in the city's five-year class size reduction plan.[7] For example, the Blue Book formula assumes class sizes of twenty-eight students per class in fourth through eighth grades, and thirty-four students in high school. Compare that to the class sizes of twenty-three to twenty-seven in these grades that are the current average and to the target of twenty-three students per class in the city's Class Size Reduction Plan.[8] If the Class Size Reduction Plan targets were used to calculate utilization, many more of the city's schools would register as overcrowded, and by much higher margins.

Not surprisingly, in our survey, 86 percent of principals responded that they were unable to provide a quality education because of excessive class sizes. The primary impediments to achieving smaller classes, they reported, were lack of space and lack of control over enrollment, with insufficient funding coming in third.

Unsafe Conditions and Curtailed Programs

Slightly more than half of principals surveyed (51 percent) said that overcrowding sometimes leads to unsafe conditions for students or staff; 43 percent said that overcrowding makes it difficult for students and/or staff to get to class on time. Forty-three percent of all principals said that their schools were too crowded to be able to provide important afterschool programs or services, such as tutoring, sports, clubs, and the like. More than one-fourth (26 percent) of all middle and high school principals said that overcrowding sometimes made it difficult for their students to receive the credits and/or courses they need to graduate on time.

Lost Cluster Rooms and Access to School Facilities

The DOE capacity formula does not reflect the fact that many schools over time have lost cluster rooms (dedicated to art, music, science, etc.) to regular academic classrooms, and that this process is ongoing. One quarter of principals surveyed (25 percent) reported losing their art, music, or dance rooms to academic classroom space; 20 percent said they had lost their computer rooms; 18 percent had lost their science rooms; 14 percent had lost their reading enrichment rooms; and 10 percent had lost their library space. As one principal noted, "Over the years we have eliminated our art room & science room, and at-risk/intervention rooms. We are now going to request that our computer lab be converted to classrooms because we need another room for a class."

The official capacity estimates do not consider whether the level of overcrowding prevents students from having regular access to the cafeteria, the auditorium, the library, and/or the gymnasium. At 17 percent of schools, students have no regular access to the school's library, and at 29 percent of schools, lunch starts at 10:30 a.m. or earlier. Almost half of all schools (47 percent) have less than one hour of gym per week.[9] In 11 percent of schools, students have no access to an auditorium at all. Many schools have no science labs. One principal observed: "We have over 1000 students in this building, the overwhelming majority of whom are in high school, with only a partial science lab that seats 12."

In addition, many principals reported using inadequate space for remediation or special education services. For example: "We are using closet space for speech, SETTS, and SPINS."[10] Another: "The classroom that we presently have our 12:1 is too small.[11] It was the Dean's office space that was for our SAVE Room detainees (total 8.) The students are sitting on top of each other. Our SAVE Room is desperately needed. Disruptive students are placed in another classroom or sit with the A.P. [Assistant Principal] or Principal."[12] And yet another: "We lost our Science Lab and Art Studio. Most if not all of our AIS [Academic Intervention Services] Instruction is in our hallways and inappropriate offices in the Gym."

Substandard Rooms and Temporary Spaces

Many schools are obliged to use non-standard space for classrooms, preventing their true capacity from being properly assessed under the DOE formula. For example, some principals said their schools had especially small rooms that cannot hold more than twenty-five students; others described classrooms with columns that obstruct the students' view of the teacher or blackboard. In addition, 20 percent of principals reported that their schools have classrooms with no windows. One example: "Our art lab and music room is in the basement. It was never suitable for classrooms."

In our survey, 17 percent of principals said that their schools had one or more temporary spaces (trailers or Temporary Classroom Units). Several principals said their schools are reported as underutilized even though they need annexes and/or transportables to accommodate all their students. As one principal observed: "My school occupies two buildings due to overcrowding in the main building. We have an annex which is one mile away from the main building and students are bussed there by yellow shuttle buses. There are 4 portable classrooms in the schoolyard, however due to the way that the DOE calculates space utilization, it does not deem my building as overcrowded."

Expanding Capacity Ratings and Enrollment

Seventeen percent of respondents said that their school's official capacity had been increased by DOE in recent years—that is, the number of students that the DOE claims the school can safely hold and educate. In many cases, this increase in the school's capacity occurred without any significant renovations or classroom additions, leading many principals to distrust the results. As one principal observed, "The blue book estimates change annually based on the needs of our school system. Really has no bearing on reality."

Several principals reported ongoing battles with the Department of School Facilities over their capacity ratings. Asked whether they had had their ratings raised in recent years, one principal replied, "I have fought this off. We successfully had the capacity lowered from 1000 to 900 but only with 5 meetings that were very contentious. I believe NYC is the only city who expects students to do more with less—in this case less space and area for movement."

Many principals also argue that DOE's Office of Student Enrollment, Planning, and Operations (OSEPO) assigns more students to their schools than they can hold. Principals are reluctant to use state money to reduce class size, fearing OSEPO will send more students, although DOE has insisted in hearings that this is not their policy. A typical comment: "Once OSEPO sees on ATS that a class has fallen below 30 they send another student."[13] Another: "There is a problem when a school chooses to use their own money to lower class size (instead of an extra pullout or support position). Then DOE determines that you have space in the classroom and sends you extra students. You get punished for trying to lower class size." Also, several principals reported that overcrowding had worsened when the DOE changed the grade configurations of their schools.

External Encroachments on Space

The Bloomberg/Klein administration has made a priority of the rapid formation of new small schools and charter schools, with more than three hundred created during this administration. Very few of these new schools have come with their own buildings. The vast majority of these schools have been put in buildings that already housed schools. Indeed, 42 percent of the 1,577 traditional public and charter schools in New York City share their building with at least one other school.[14] Not surprisingly, the rapid explosion of new schools has led to even more overcrowding, as each new school requires its own administrative, specialty, and cluster spaces.[15] In the survey, 27 percent of principals responded that overcrowding in their schools had worsened as a result of new schools or programs moved into their buildings in recent years.

In sum, our principals report a situation in which overcrowding severely compromises the learning environment. The formula used by the DOE to determine the actual level of school overcrowding should be significantly revised to more accurately take into account these conditions and to ensure student and staff safety, reduce class size, provide necessary special education and intervention services, and improve access of students to gymnasiums, libraries, cafeterias, and auditoriums.

The formula should also be adjusted to reflect the ongoing loss of cluster space, including art, music, and science rooms, and the existence of substandard and temporary spaces such as annexes, trailers, and temporary units at many schools.

School Capacity

The city has had a disappointing record in recent years in investing in new capacity. The administration claims that the current school capital plan is the most ambitious in the city's history; the reality is otherwise. Data drawn directly from Mayor's Management Reports since FY 1997 show that fewer seats were created during the first six years of the Bloomberg administration than during the last six years of the previous administration, that of Rudy Giuliani.[16]

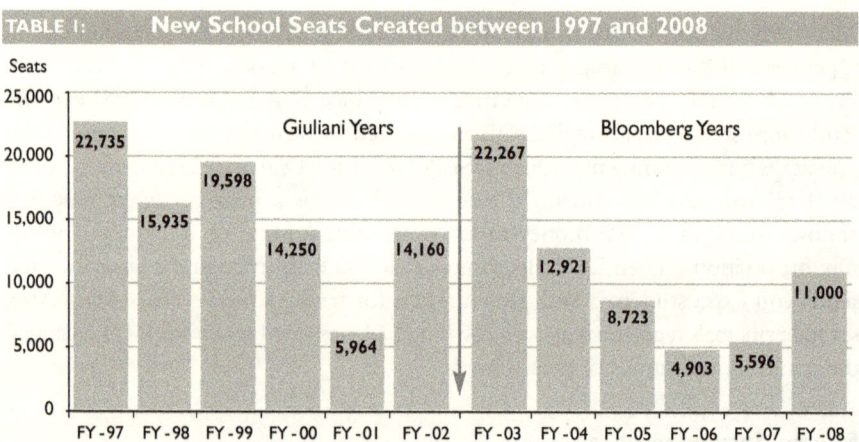

TABLE 1:   New School Seats Created between 1997 and 2008

Seats

- FY-97: 22,735
- FY-98: 15,935
- FY-99: 19,598
- FY-00: 14,250
- FY-01: 5,964
- FY-02: 14,160
- FY-03: 22,267
- FY-04: 12,921
- FY-05: 8,723
- FY-06: 4,903
- FY-07: 5,596
- FY-08: 11,000

Giuliani Years — Bloomberg Years

Source: Mayor's Management Reports, FY 2000, FY 2004, and FY 2007

The Giuliani administration built on average 15,440 seats per year during its last six years, compared to 10,895 per year for the first six years of the Bloomberg administration.

In 2003, the Bloomberg administration created 22,267 seats, the high point in recent years. Even then, most of the new seats were the result not of school construction, but of "classroom conversions"—conversions that, in many cases, cost schools their art rooms, computer rooms, and other specialty spaces (e.g. . science labs, music rooms, parent association spaces). (See Table 2.)

The DOE and School Construction Authority (SCA) have also been slow to deliver promised seats. Of the 63,000 seats in the current capital plan, only about one-third—21,000—will be completed by June 2009. Another 34,000 seats are due to be finished by 2012, and 8,000 seats will never be built.

This decline in the provision of new capacity comes in the face of many indications of increasing need. Both the Manhattan Borough President and the New York

City Comptroller released reports in 2008 critiquing the DOE's mechanisms for identifying and responding to enrollment trends. Both reports identified

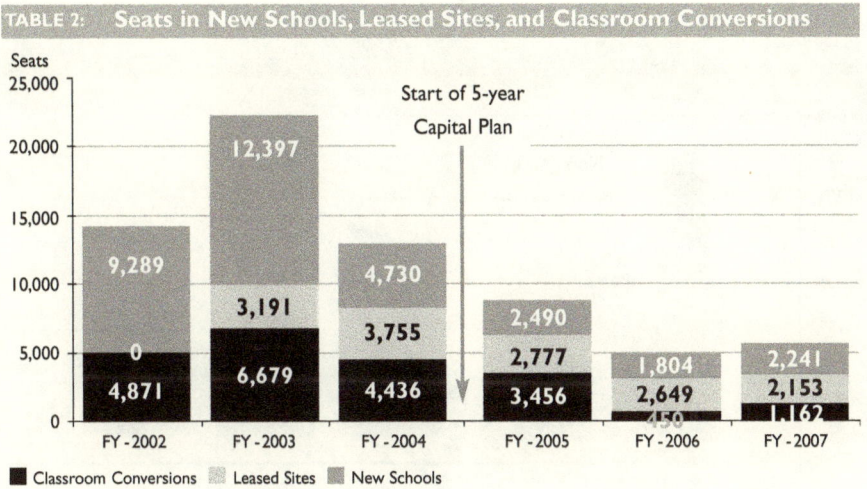

TABLE 2: Seats in New Schools, Leased Sites, and Classroom Conversions

Source: Mayor's Management Reports, FY 2006 and FY 2007

neighborhoods where extensive residential development had failed to trigger an increase in school seats and predicted, correctly, that a number of zoned schools would soon be unable to accommodate local children. PLANYC, a sustainability task force founded by the mayor to provide a comprehensive plan for new infrastructure and municipal services for the estimated one million new city residents predicted by 2030, neglected to mention any need for new school space in its report.[17]

In October 2008, a coalition of more than seventy advocacy groups and elected officials on the local, state, and federal levels signed a letter urging the city to adopt a better capital plan.[18] They urged the city to address existing school overcrowding and provide sufficient space for smaller classes; to be ready for enrollment growth, and to plan at the neighborhood level; and to correct the faulty capacity estimates which have the effect of depriving schools of the space necessary for art, science, special services, and other programs necessary for a well-rounded education. The Manhattan Borough President's Task Force on Overcrowding has estimated that the proposed capital plan will provide only approximately one-third the need for new capacity citywide, based on the data in the Blue Book, which, as we have seen, underestimates the level of overcrowding in our schools.[19]

Yet instead of expanding and improving the current plan, in November the administration released a new proposed five-year capital plan that was dramatically smaller—and contained only 25,000 new seats. If the eight thousand seats "rolled over" from the current plan are excluded, this plan will provide only one-fifth of number of new seats promised by the current plan.

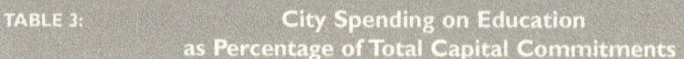

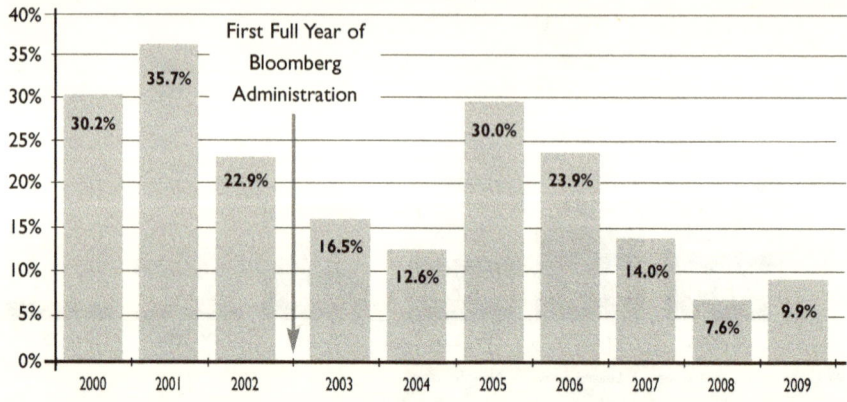

Source: Independent Budget Office, Analysis of the Mayor's preliminary budget for 2009 (March 2008)

This proposed plan continues the overall decline in the number of new seats created by the Bloomberg administration; it also continues the overall declining share of city dollars invested in schools. The percent of city capital spending devoted to schools under this administration has fallen from 30 percent in 2005 to 7.6 percent in 2008.

The thrust of the Department of Education's current management philosophy assumes that the educators at each school are primarily responsible for the success or failure of their students. Accordingly, the administration has devolved more responsibility and autonomy to principals to improve academic results, with the presumption that they have at their disposal most of the tools they need to succeed. Yet principals say that they have no control over some of the most important factors determining the quality of their schools: the allocation of space and the number of students assigned to them. These remain entirely within the control of the DOE.

In the view of an overwhelming majority of principals, the resulting overcrowding prevents them from reducing class size to appropriate levels and being able to provide space for critical programs, such as art, science, and special services, necessary for a quality education. The data from the survey of principals adds to a growing body of incontrovertible evidence that this administration has not been honest with the public about the need for more schools.

- APPENDIX -

Survey Background

BOROUGH	OUR RESPONDENTS	ALL NYC PUBLIC SCHOOLS
Manhattan	20%	17%
Bronx	22%	23%
Brooklyn	31%	30%
Queens	21%	22%
Staten Island	5%	4%
SCHOOL LEVEL		
PS	47%	64%
IS	28%	17%
HS	23%	19%

Survey Details

	OUR RESPONDENTS
Principals represented out of all NYC principals:	38%
Students represented out of all NYC public school students	41%
Principals in our survey at schools the Blue Book says are OVER 100%:	32%
Schools in all of NYC the Blue Book says are OVER 100%:	39%
Principals with 5 years or more experience:	47%
Principals who believe official utilization rate is inaccurate:	49%
Principals at schools under 100% who believe official utilization rate is inaccurate:	51%
Principals who feel that enrollment is NOT capped at an appropriate level to prevent overcrowding:	51%
Principals who say overcrowding always OR sometimes creates	
- unsafe conditions for students/staff:	51%
- difficulty for students/staff to get to class on time:	43%
- difficulty providing adequate afterschool programs (e.g. tutoring, sports, clubs):	43%
- difficulty for students to receive enough credits or courses needed to graduate:	26%
Principals who say their class sizes are small enough for a quality education:	14%
Reasons why principals have difficulty achieving classes of quality size	
- lack of control over total enrollment:	44%
- lack of space:	44%
- lack of funding:	35%
Cluster rooms converted to general education / academic classrooms	
- computer/tech lab:	20%
- reading enrichment:	14%
- art, music, dance, drama, or foreign language:	25%
- science:	18%
- library:	10%

Schools where students have NO regular weekly library access:	17%
Schools that start lunch at 10:30 or earlier:	29%
Schools with LESS than 60 minutes of gym per week:	47%

Average minutes per week in gym class

- elementary:	60
- middle school:	60
- high school:	120

Principals who say that their official capacity rating has been raised in recent years:	17%
Principals who say that they have had space taken away in recent years:	18%
Schools with no auditorium or no access to an auditorium:	11%
Schools that can't fit ALL students into the auditorium at one time:	76%
Schools with one or more academic classrooms with no windows:	20%
Principals who say that overcrowding has increased because of new schools or programs being added to their building:	27%
Schools without sufficient electrical power:	59%
Schools with one or more temporary spaces: (e.g. trailers, TCU's, annexes)	17%

What SHOULD class sizes be to provide a quality education?	**K - 3**	**4 - 5**	**6 - 8**	**9 - 12**
Mean:	20	23	24	24
Median:	20	22	25	25
Mode:	20	20	25	25

NOTES

1. For example, in their most recent proposed capital plan: "In most cases, over-crowding and larger class sizes are very local phenomena, reflecting school admissions zones that are poorly designed for the building, and/or reflecting deeply popular schools into which the press of parents creates larger class size. Local neighborhood planning will help identify and solve these issues..." NYC Department of Education, "Building on Success: Proposed 2010-2014 Five-Year Capital Plan," February 2009 Revision, http://source.nycsca.org/pdf/capital plan/11-08_2010-14_CapitalPlan.pdf.

2. NYC Department of Education and School Construction Authority, "Enrollment, Capacity and Utilization Report, Classic Edition, Building and School Enrollment and Utilization Data for School Year 2007–2008" (November, 2008), http://schools.nyc.gov/Offices/SCA/Reports/CapPlan/ECUReport07-08Classic.htm.

3. Campaign for Fiscal Equity, Inc., et al. v. State of New York, et al., 100 NY 2d 893, 911-12 (2003).

4. For the full text of the report see Emily Horowitz and Leonie Haimson, "How Crowded Are Our Schools? New Results from a Survey of NYC Public School Principals," Class Size Matters, October 3, 2008, http://www.classsizematters.org/principal_survey_report_10.08_final.pdf.

5. We are using target utilization rates, as reported in an Excel version (2006–2007) of the Blue Book provided by the DOE. The DOE reports lower overall figures for overcrowding, calculating how many students attend overcrowded schools rather than attend schools in overcrowded buildings.

6. In 2007–2008, 550 principals represented more than one third of New York City public school principals, and their schools contained about 397,000 students, 42 percent of the total public-school population.

7. In 2007, pursuant to the Contract for Excellence requirements in the state budget passed as a result of the Campaign for Fiscal Equity lawsuit, the DOE submitted, and the New York State Education Department ultimately approved, a class size reduction plan committing the city to reduce class size in all grades over five years as a condition for receiving state aid. (See the approved NYCDOE 5-Year Class Size Reducation Plan [November 8, 2007]). This plan calls for class sizes of twenty for K-3 and twenty-three in all other grades.

8. See the discussion of this issue in "A Better Capital Plan," a report from the Manhattan Task Force on School Overcrowding, Class Size Matters, the United Federation of Teachers, and The Center for Arts Education (October, 2008), http://www.classsizematters.org/abettercapitalplan.html.

9. The New York State Department of Education Commissioner's regulations require that all children in kindergarten through third grade participate in physical education classes every day and that children in fourth through sixth grade participate in physical education classes a minimum of three times per week for a total of at least 120 minutes.

10. SETTS is an acronym for Special Education Teacher Support Service—mandated special education services. SPINS is unknown to the authors of the report.

11. A 12:1 classroom is for students with learning disabilities whose state-mandated Individualized Education Program calls for one special education teacher to twelve students.

12. SAVE is the room reserved for students being disciplined—after the Schools Against Violence in Education Act.

13. ATS stands for Automate the Schools, the school-based system which automates the collection and reporting of data for all New York City public schools.

14. Elissa Gootman, "In Cramped Spaces, Small School Benefits," *New York Times,* December 20, 2008.

15. See "Capital promises: why NYC children don't have the school buildings they need," Educational Priorities Panel, April 2007. For example, "…a middle school in the Bronx…was restructured to host other smaller schools. Students of the host school no longer had any access to the science lab, which was used exclusively by a small middle school with higher-performing students. All students in the school lost the use of the library, which was transformed into a space for special education conferences and for various staff meetings" (p. 40).

16. The city's fiscal year runs July 1 to June 30.

17. "Crowded Out: School Construction Fails to Keep Up with Manhattan Building Boom," Office of Manhattan Borough President Scott Stringer, April 2008, and "Growing Pains: Reforming Department of Education Capital Planning to Keep Pace with New York City's Residential Construction," Policy Report of the New York City Office of the Comptroller, Office of Policy Management, May 2008, and see Mayor Michael R. Bloomberg, "PLANYC: A Greener, Greater New York," The City of New York, Office of the Mayor, April 22, 2007, http://www.nyc.gov/html/planyc2030/downloads/pdf/full_report.pdf.

18. See http://abccampaign.wordpress.com/our-letter-to-the-mayor-and-chancellor/.

19. "A Better Capital Plan," Manhattan Task Force on School Overcrowding, et al.

Inside the Panel for Educational Policy

- Patrick J. Sullivan

The New York State Education Law lays it out clearly: "The board of education of the city school district of the city of New York is hereby continued. Such board of education shall consist of thirteen members: one member to be appointed by each borough president of the city of New York; seven members to be appointed by the mayor of the city of New York; and the chancellor."[1] But Mayor Michael Bloomberg sought a clean break with the past. He renamed his school board the "Panel for Educational Policy." Intended to provide oversight and serve as a check on the extraordinary authority granted to the mayor by the state legislature in 2002, the Panel had been significantly weakened long before I was appointed by Manhattan Borough President Scott M. Stringer as a public school parent member in June of 2007. Early in its existence, the mayor had enforced his will over the Panel by summarily dismissing two of his appointees who threatened to vote contrary to his desire.

A month before my first meeting as a member, I sat in the audience to watch the Panel transact its business. What I saw was distressing. The Panel passed a $17 billion operating budget, approved a major labor contract, reviewed a student achievement database costing $80 million, and heard a ten-minute presentation by parents seeking to move their school out of trailers. All this in under fifty minutes. Only two questions were asked by the Panel members, and just a handful of spectators were on hand to witness the heavily scripted proceedings. The Panel for Educational Policy seemed more a misplaced relic of the Brezhnev-era Soviet Union than a functioning board of directors overseeing the education of 1.1 million children.

As a Panel member, I quickly learned how it had been engineered to deliver on the administration's agenda. By dispensing with the rules of order customary for deliberative body and frequently flouting its few bylaws, Chancellor Joel Klein has run the school system as his personal fiefdom, with minimal regard for transparency and accountability.

For example:

- Meeting agendas are typically distributed only a few days in advance;

- Presentation materials are rarely made available to members before the meeting; when they are provided it is typically within twenty-four hours of the meeting;

- Under its bylaws the Panel is supposed to meet in executive session once a year to discuss how to improve its processes, but this meeting has never been held, at least since I joined almost two years ago;

- Members may request roll-call votes under the bylaws but my attempts to do so have been refused; in any event, votes are taken before public comment, rather than afterwards;

- There are no transcripts; meeting minutes have not been distributed since early 2007;

- There is no audit committee, as required by state law;

- Investigative reports of the Special Commissioner for Investigation are not provided to the board as required by the mayor's executive order.

These poor practices serve to obscure the workings of the board and inhibit communication between the Panel members and the public school families they are supposed to represent. Unfortunately, there is little appetite among members to challenge the chancellor's rules of order, as the mayor's eight appointees vote in lockstep to support every one of his positions. The fact that the mayor's appointees rarely ever ask questions or comment on the board's business suggests they have little interest in functioning as a truly deliberative body in any event. I am certain that at least two and possibly more of the members of the Panel have never actually spoken during a public session.

Budget Decisions

The Panel is required by law to approve both the capital budget and operating budget of the school system. A separate vote is held to approve the mechanism for allocating operating funds to individual schools. I have the good fortune to be appointed and supported by Borough President Stringer, who has insisted that we always represent the best interest of children even if it means drawing the ire of the mayor and chancellor. As a result I have frequently dissented from the mayor's position. I am often the only member to do so.

Fair Student Funding

My first Panel vote was a swift introduction to the heavily top-down approach employed by the Bloomberg Administration. Robert Gordon, a prominent policy analyst now serving in the Obama administration, was responsible for the development of "Fair Student Funding" formulae for allocating funds to schools. His approach tied all school funding, including that for teacher salaries, to the number and type of children in the school; kids were to be allocated more per capita when they have special needs, such as English-language instruction and special education. When the individual school budgets were provided before the vote to approve Gordon's scheme, I was surprised to see the formulae would lead to substantial budget cuts to two-thirds of schools in District 4 (East Harlem) and District 5 (Central Harlem)—the poorest areas in the borough—including six of the seven schools considered failing by the state in District 4. While the formulae were not fully implemented due to widespread protests and an eleventh-hour agreement with the teachers union, these schools were effectively blocked from receiving more state aid. It didn't make sense to me. New state funding was supposed to be directed to higher poverty areas. And Mayor Bloomberg had publicly argued that Fair Student Funding would provide more equity by ensuring that wealthier, more politically connected communities could not garner more than their share of school funds.

The chancellor asked me to sit down with Robert Gordon so he could explain the results. But when I did, Gordon could not explain why he had slated these schools for cuts. Moreover, he felt no obligation to investigate the consequences of such shift in funds, let alone brief the district superintendents or meet with the principals of the affected schools. I realized that to him, the process of allocating funds to schools was an abstract technocratic exercise that might be pitched as "fair" but was not connected to potential effects on actual schools—or their students. The self-declared experts at Tweed and my colleagues on the Panel felt no need to question or even examine closely the real-world effects of this change in policy.

Operating Budget

When in the spring of 2008, the chancellor presented a budget for the 2008-2009 school year that would result in steep cuts in operating funds for many schools, I objected. I explained that by state law we are charged with proposing a budget sufficient to fund school operations, and we should not approve a budget that clearly did not do so. We had, furthermore, been provided insufficient documentation to understand the precise allocations of the budget we were expected to approve—a major budget funding school operations for thousands of schools. The 2008-2009 budget was approved with eight votes in favor and my sole vote against. Nevertheless, the City Council determined that the budget was insufficient to fund the schools and subsequently restored enough funds to prevent cuts to instruction or services to children. (Ironically, when class sizes increased substantially in the fall of 2008–by the largest amount in ten years— the Department of Education (DOE) attributed these increases to the very budget cuts they had previously promised would not affect schools.) Rather than put forward a transparent budget with the "total sum of money deemed necessary" for school operations as state law requires, the chancellor and a Panel beholden to the mayor approved a budget drafted to the mayor's specifications and defining "school needs" from there.

Capital Budget

The Panel's vote on the 2009 capital budget again demonstrated a quiescence that shortchanges the city's children. Approving the capital budget is one of the Panel's legislated responsibilities: the schools' capital budget is approved every five years with annual amendments. In presenting the proposed 2009 amendment both DOE and the School Construction Authority asserted that the current plan, now in its final year, would improbably accomplish all its goals: the reduction of class sizes to twenty in every kindergarten through third-grade classroom, the elimination of portables units to provide emergency seats, and an end to split sessions (overcrowded schools teaching two full school days in sequence in one day). The proposed amendment offered no comment on how how spending would achieve the city's class size reduction goals required by state statutes and regulations, which are considerably more ambitious.

The Panel declined to enter into a serious discussion of school overcrowding and the capital plan's ability to address it. When I asked Chancellor Klein why PS 290 was the most overcrowded elementary school in Manhattan, he told me "because too many parents want to send their children there." The mayor and his chancellor control school siting, construction, zoning, and placement and even receive matching funds from the State for school construction, yet somehow they cannot be held accountable for the fact that on their watch a neighborhood zoned school has swelled to 155 percent of capacity. Instead, they blame parents.

Despite the demonstrable inadequacy of the plan, it was passed again with only my dissenting vote.

The administration has now put forward a proposed five-year capital plan for 2009-2014. The Panel must vote on the plan in the Spring of 2009, yet no needs analysis or demographic assessment of the enrollment expectations underlying the plan has been provided to its members. (A report by the Manhattan Borough President's Task Force on Overcrowding, which I co-chair, has estimated that the plan provides only about one third of the seats currently necessary to eliminate overcrowding and reduce class size to state-mandated levels—even ignoring the well documented enrollment growth in many city neighborhoods).[2] The Panel is simply expected to believe that whatever the mayor is willing to spend is exactly what the city's children need.

Special Education System Contract

When I read in the press that the DOE was about to sign a $55 million contract for a new special-education computer system, I asked the DOE general counsel if the Panel would vote to approve the contract. I pointed to state law requiring approval of any contract which would "significantly impact the provision of educational services or programming." He explained that the new system "is not changing either the nature of the services we deliver or the manner in which we deliver them" and therefore no vote is required. When at the January Panel meeting, I objected on the record, Chancellor Klein questioned what the purpose of such a vote would be. I explained that before voting, I would make sure that all the Community District Education Councils (the elected parent bodies that replaced our local school boards) and especially the Citywide Council on Special Education (CCSE), which represents parents of special needs children, had the chance to review the system requirements and provide input.

But the chancellor did not see the need for, or benefit of, such collaboration. The CCSE was never asked their opinion. Instead, John Englert, the president of CCSE read about this new system in the press. The chancellor explained that the Panel had been functioning this way for seven years. He didn't see any need for it to change. But someone should be reviewing these massive expenditures. The intent of the state education law was for the board to provide oversight of significant contracts. The Bloomberg administration routinely cites the weakest of pretexts to ignore any possibility of public review or independent evaluation of costly contracts. To this date, I have not seen the Panel vote on a single procurement contract.

Gifted and Talented Admissions

The new Gifted and Talented admissions policy has been a comprehensive failure of educational policy. Ostensibly seeking to improve equity for "underserved" communities, the chancellor swept away the various admissions criteria employed by the schools and districts and replaced them with absolute benchmarks on two standardized tests. Like many, I warned Marcia Lyles, Deputy chancellor for Teaching and Learning, that the new exams, focusing more on preparedness than giftedness, would have a racially disparate effect and would significantly reduce the number G&T seats in low-income neighborhoods. Even one of the mayor's appointees told me I was "100 percent correct on this issue." Now the damage has been done, with fewer programs overall and many programs closed in predominantly minority and low-income neighborhoods. This policy change was approved, again, with only my vote cast in opposition. The lack of independence of the Panel's members and their indifferent attitudes directly resulted in the adoption of this poorly considered policy.

Grade Retention

The original Panel was opposed to the mayor's proposed program to hold back third-graders who did not pass the two standardized tests given by the state. Members were aware of research that indicated that such policies were not effective. For example, Advocates for Children argued at the time in a letter to the mayor and chancellor that leading academic organizations including the American Educational Research Association, the National Academy of Science, and even the two largest test publishers, Harcourt and McGraw Hill, all strongly discouraged use of single test to determine grade advancement.[3] A single test, in their view, is too prone to error to compel such a disruption in a student's career. Separately, studies of existing grade retention programs showed they were not effective in improving achievement. The seminal study of a Chicago grade-retention program conducted by the Research Consortium for the Chicago Public Schools found retained students had higher drop-out rates despite the (enormously costly) additional year of school.[4]

To secure the Panel's approval of the program, Bloomberg terminated two of his appointees and the Staten Island Borough President, a political ally of the mayor's, replaced his in the hours before they were to vote. The mayor appointed in their place the head of the New York City Hospital Corporation and the head of the City Housing Authority. City employees are barred by law from serving as mayoral appointees on the Panel, but the mayor eluded this provision by appointing the directors of public authorities, who though not officially city employees nevertheless owe their jobs to the mayor. Never again did any of the mayoral appointees to the Panel challenge his position on an issue. This incident is remembered as "The Monday Night Massacre," and it heralded the mayor's conclusive suppression of the Panel's legislative powers.

By the time I was appointed to the Panel, the policy of holding back students had been extended to fifth and seventh grades, and, in March of 2008, we were asked to approve a similar policy for eighth graders. Students would have to pass all five core courses as well as the two state standardized tests before entering high school. At a public hearing, a number of advocates and academics opposed the proposal, based once again on the extensive body of research showing that such policies didn't work. Speakers urged the administration to focus instead on creating programs to improve achievement in the city's underperforming middle schools. As the March 17 vote on the policy neared, I repeatedly asked the chancellor and his senior staff to make available to the Panel research on grade retention that had been commissioned as part of a compromise vote on fifth-grade retention: now two years after the RAND Corporation had been commissioned by the DOE to study this policy, no findings had been released. I was finally provided with 479 pages of reports on a Saturday, two days before the Monday night vote. The rest of the Panel was granted access only at 8 p.m. on Sunday night.

What I found in the reports was disturbing and suggested we were on course to repeat the failures of the past. While a thorough analysis of student performance had not yet been completed, the reports contained the results of extensive surveys with elementary school principals, summer school administrators, and Academic Intervention Services (AIS) specialists. Summer school leaders were coping with the latest DOE reorganization and complained they could not get any specific information on the students assigned to their programs. AIS leaders found that small class sizes were the most effective tool to help struggling students but less than a third of at-risk children had access to smaller classes. Principals felt the retention policy relied too much on standardized tests and was damaging to student self-esteem. Most troubling of all: none of these findings had been made public.

RAND had provided the DOE with reports annually since 2006. To this day, the administration refuses to release any of these findings, despite the fact that much of the information would be highly valuable in the effort to improve our middle schools. The lack of transparency is inexcusable. This information, paid for by taxpayer funds, should be available to the public, in order to inform the discussion and understanding of this important educational policy.

My experience as a member of what the State still calls "the New York City Board of Education" has taught me that the Bloomberg administration has little interest in accountability, transparency, or a meaningful consultation with parents, teachers, education experts, and other interested citizens on school governance. In its current form the Panel does not make policy or even meaningfully advise the chancellor. These roles are reserved for a closed circle of management consultants and foundations operated by wealthy men: the Broad Foundation, the Gates Foundation, the Dell Foundation. This is not the model of school governance envisioned by the New York State legislators or desired by parents or community members.

Real insight into the challenges of urban education lies in communities, School Leadership Teams, PTAs, and Community Education Councils. Mayor Bloomberg and Chancellor Klein have chosen to turn their backs on this insight and to eviscerate the institutions that might foster it. We will never have real improvement in our schools until we listen to those who live with our schools and whose lives are changed by them every day.

NOTES

1. New York Education Law Section 2590-b, http://law.onecle.com/new-york/education/EDN02590-B_2590-B.html.

2. "A Better Capital Plan," a report of The Campaign for a Better Capital Plan, The Manhattan Task Force on School Overcrowding, Class Size Matters, The United Federation of Teachers, and The Center for Arts Education (October, 2008).

3. Letter available at http://www.classsizematters.org/retentionletter.html; full report available at: http://www.advocatesforchildren.org/pubs/2005/retention.pdf.

4. Elaine Allensworth, "Ending Social Promotion, Dropout Rates in Chicago After Implementing the 8th Grade Promotion Gate," Consortium on Chicago Schools Research (March 2004), http://ccsr.uchicago.edu/publications/p69.pdf.

Discharge and Graduation Rates

- Jennifer L. Jennings and Leonie Haimson

In 2002, Advocates for Children (AFC) and the Public Advocate of New York City published a landmark report revealing the large number of New York City high school students who are "discharged" from the school system without graduating.[1] Discharged students are removed from the city's enrollment rolls entirely; they are not counted as dropouts, nor are they counted in the denominator when graduation rates are calculated. As the number of discharges rises, so too does the graduation rate. Based on evidence that high schools had illegally ejected students entitled to continue attending public schools, Advocates for Children described these students as "push-outs" and subsequently filed three class action complaints against the city.[2]

In the summer of 2003, Chancellor Joel Klein condemned the practice. "The problem of what's happening to the students is a tragedy," Klein said. "It's not just a few instances, it's a real issue."[3] In a message to principals, Klein made it "unequivocally clear" that he did not support this practice and would take steps to end it: "It is a disservice to our students and ourselves to rely on shortcuts or play numbers games in order to make things look better than they really are."[4] Following the AFC lawsuits, the New York City Department of Education (DOE) revised its policy on transfers and discharges in January 2004 to bar schools from discharging students without their consent and required schools to conduct planning interviews before discharging students to programs that do not grant high school diplomas.[5] In addition, the DOE created an "Office of Multiple Pathways" in order to better serve overage students who had earned few high school credits.

Since the 2002 report, there has been no comprehensive update on high school discharges in New York City. This chapter summarizes the findings of a report analyzing trends in the discharge rate using data from the classes of 2000 to 2007 disaggregated by race, gender, English language proficiency, and special education status; school-level discharge data; GED data provided by the New York State Education Department; and data from the United States Census American Community Survey.[6] Taken together, our analysis suggests that the high school discharge system continues to provide a loosely regulated loophole that can be used to inflate graduation rates by pushing at-risk students out of school.

There are Nine Key Findings:

1. High school discharge rates have not declined since the 2002 AFC/Public Advocate report was published. In fact, the percentage of all students discharged has *increased* from 17.5 percent for the Class of 2000 to 21.1 percent for the Class of 2007.[7] Between the graduating high school classes of 2000 and 2007,[8] a total of 142,262 New York City students were discharged. None of these students was counted as a dropout, and all were excluded from the denominator —that is, the total cohort—used for graduation rate calculations. Because discharges are reported as only one category and schools' discharge records are not independently audited, it is currently impossible to distinguish legitimate discharges from those students who would be better understood as dropouts.

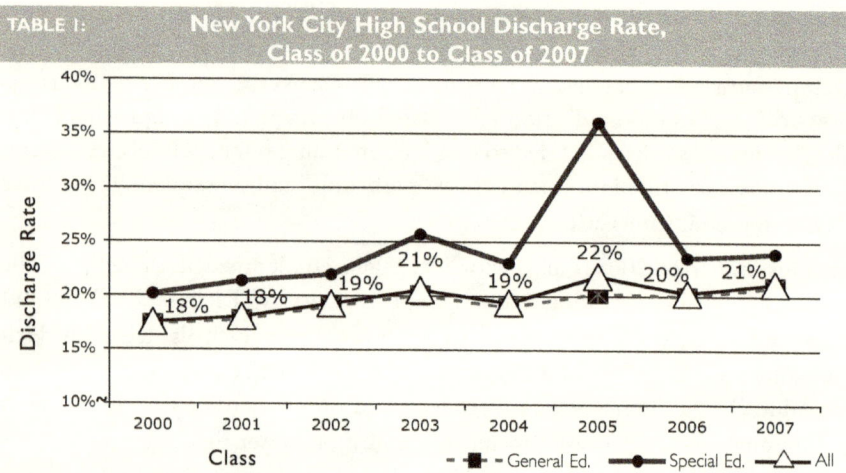

TABLE 1: New York City High School Discharge Rate, Class of 2000 to Class of 2007

2. The increase in the overall discharge rate has been primarily driven by a *doubling in the discharge rate for students in the first year of high school*. This finding is of serious concern as a central goal of the public school system is to provide all students with the support needed to graduate successfully from high school. It also raises questions as to whether schools are responding to accountability incentives to discharge students earlier in their high school careers.[9] For the general education Class of 2000, the discharge rate for first-year high school students was 3.8 percent; by the Class of 2007, that rate was 7.5 percent. For the special education cohort, which includes only self-contained students and students in District 75, the discharge rate for first-year students was 2.9 percent for the Class of 2000 and 5.8 percent for the Class of 2007. The explanation for the increase in the first-year discharge rate is not clear, as students cannot be discharged from New York City public schools except in limited circumstances before completing the school year in which they turn seventeen.

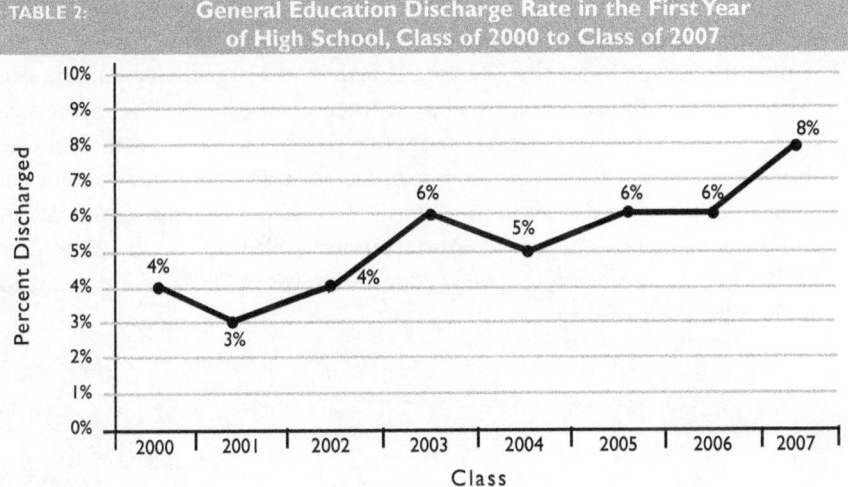

TABLE 2: General Education Discharge Rate in the First Year of High School, Class of 2000 to Class of 2007

3. The special education discharge rate is especially high, and has increased over time for students in self-contained classes. Twenty-three percent of self-contained special education students in the Class of 2007 were discharged; for students in District 75, that rate was 28 percent. The entire increase in the special education discharge rate has been driven by a rising discharge rate for students in self-contained classes. Between the Classes of 2000 and 2007, this rate increased from 17 percent to 23 percent, including a spike to a startling 39 percent for the Class of 2005.

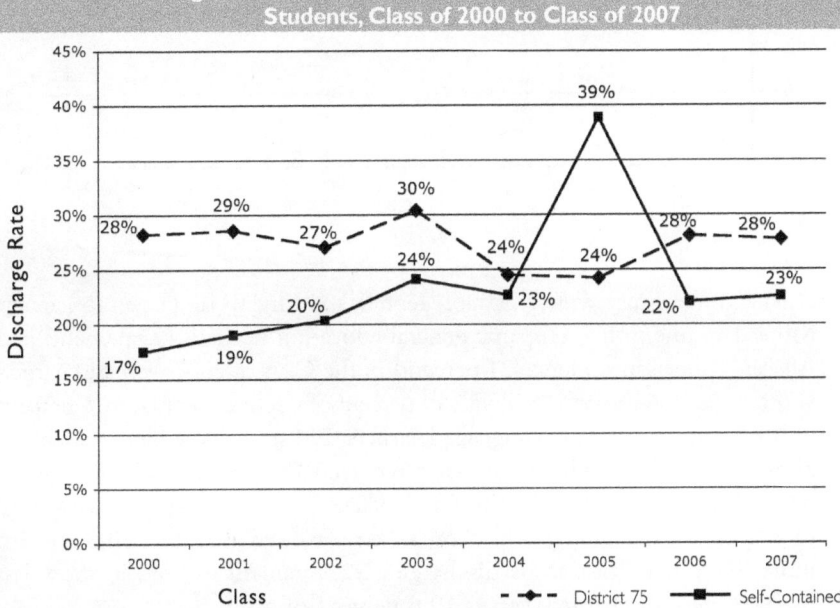

TABLE 3: Discharge Rates for District 75 and Self-Contained Special Education Students, Class of 2000 to Class of 2007

4. A close review of the DOE's longitudinal graduation reports suggests that there are dramatic shifts in reported populations that require further explanation. For example, for the Class of 2005, there is a large increase in the size of the special education cohort, and a contemporaneous decline in the size of the general education cohort. It appears that in that class, more than one thousand students may have been transferred from the general education cohort to the special education cohort[10] and then been discharged at an extremely high rate—39 percent. Also requiring explanation is why 21 percent of the students in the entire special education Class of 2005 were discharged in their first year of high school.

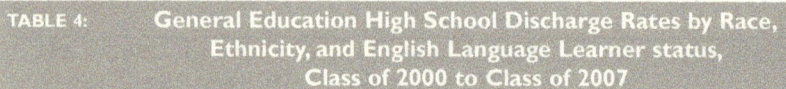

TABLE 4: General Education High School Discharge Rates by Race, Ethnicity, and English Language Learner status, Class of 2000 to Class of 2007

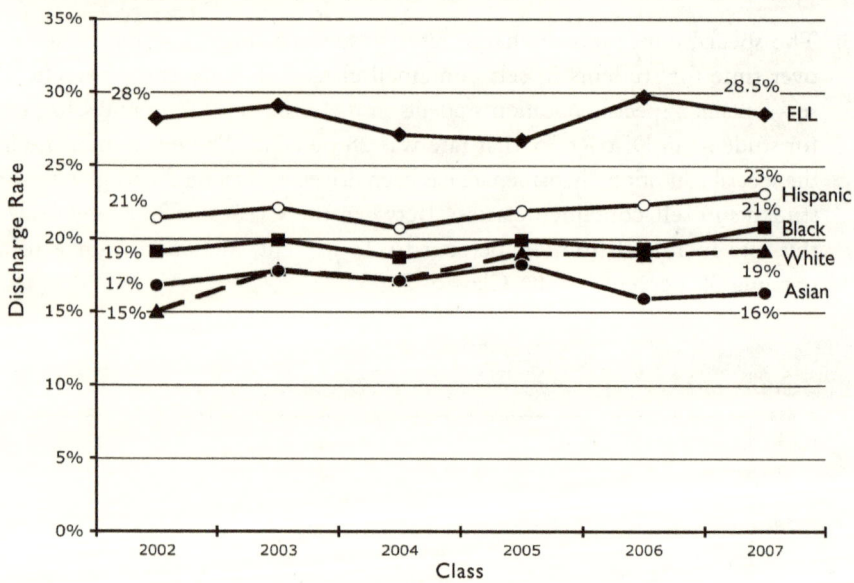

5. Discharge rates vary widely by race, gender, and English language proficiency. More than one in five Hispanic general education students (23 percent) and African-American students (21 percent) in the Class of 2007 were discharged without graduating, compared with 19 percent of white students and 16 percent of Asian students. English Language Learners (ELLs) also have higher discharge rates than students who have never received ELL services. Twenty-nine percent of ELL students in the Class of 2007 were discharged, compared to 22 percent of students who were never classified as ELLs. Boys are also more likely than girls to be discharged: 22.1 percent of boys in the Class of 2007 were discharged, versus 19.6 percent of girls.

6. Graduation rates in New York City would be substantially lower if discharges were included in the calculation. We caution that these discharge-adjusted figures surely represent an underestimate of the graduation rate. Nonetheless, they point to the substantial impact that discharges can have on the graduation rate and thus demonstrate the importance of carefully accounting for discharged students. While the city's reported four-year general education graduation rate was 62 percent for the Class of 2007, the graduation rate would have been 57.6 percent if students in the special education cohort were also included, 45.5 percent if all discharges were counted as dropouts, and 43.6 percent if students earning GEDs rather than high school diplomas were excluded. If discharges were counted as dropouts and GEDs were not counted as graduates, the African-American general education graduation rate for the Class of 2007 would fall to 44 percent, the Hispanic graduation rate to 39 percent, the male graduation rate to 42 percent, the ELL graduation rate to 21 percent, and the special education graduation rate to 6 percent.

TABLE 5: **Official and Discharge-Adjusted Graduation Rates, All Students: Class of 2000 to Class of 2007**

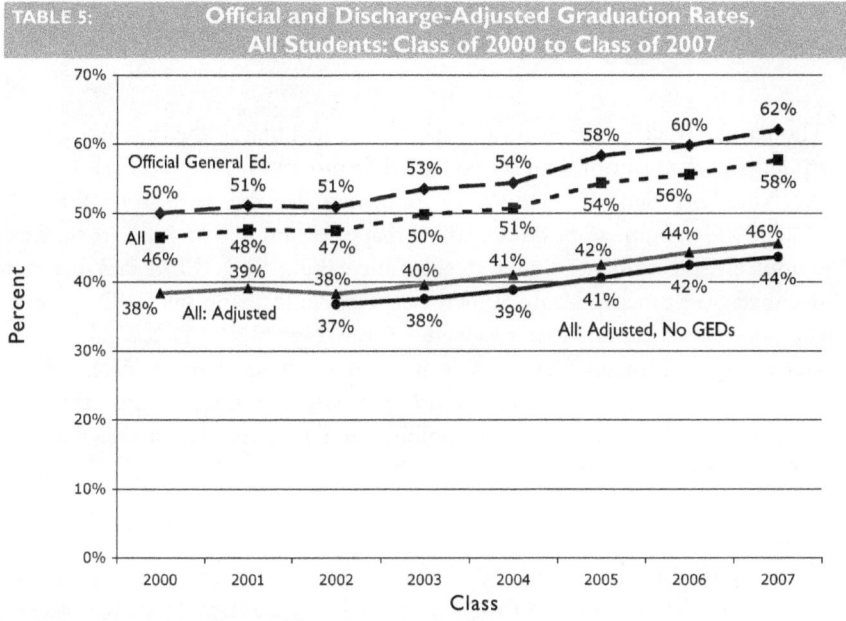

7. Schools vary considerably in their discharge rates. For approximately one in three New York City high schools[12] —eighty-seven high schools—Class of 2007 graduation rates would drop by 15 percentage points or more if discharges were counted as dropouts in the graduation calculation. Almost three in four of these schools (72 percent) received A's or B's on their 2007 school Progress Report.[13] Large comprehensive high schools that are phasing out have much higher discharge rates for their final graduating classes. For example, the last graduating class of Morris High School had a discharge rate of 55 percent, compared to 33 percent the year before.

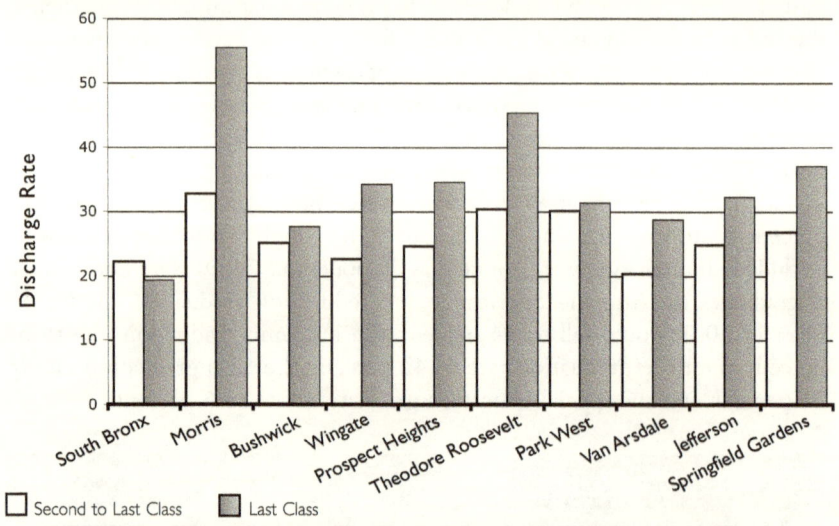

TABLE 6: Discharge Rates of Closing Comprehensive High Schools, Final Two Graduating Classes

☐ Second to Last Class   ■ Last Class

8. Though the AFC/Public Advocate report drew attention to the large number of students pushed out of high school to GED programs, GED data released by the New York State Department of Education for the 2002–2003 through 2007–2008 school years demonstrate that the number of New York City school-eligible students under twenty-one taking the GED exam has not declined over time, and only 59 percent of students taking the GED exam in the 2007–2008 school year received a GED. Notably, GED test-taking has increased for Hispanics even as it has remained unchanged, declined, or increased by smaller increments for other racial and ethnic groups. Yet only 39 percent of Hispanic school-eligible test takers received a GED in the 2007–2008 school year.

9. A survey of data from the U.S. Census American Community Survey and enrollment data from New York City parochial schools suggests that recent increases in the discharge rate do not appear to be explained by increased student migration out of the city, increased international out-migration, or increasing parochial school enrollments.

To be sure, many of these discharged students represent legitimate transfers to parochial or private schools or diploma-granting schools outside of the city. But it is impossible to evaluate the legitimacy of these discharges until the Department of Education publicly reports data by the category of discharge, commits to independent audits of schools' discharge records, and makes these audits publicly available.

Based on our findings, we recommend that the DOE publicly release comprehensive discharge code data for both the general education and special education cohorts from 2000–2007 and annually in the future as part of the "Four Year Longitudinal Graduation Report." These data should be disaggregated by discharge code and by race, gender, English language proficiency, socioeconomic status, special education status, and age. In addition to disaggregating graduation rates for the general and special education cohorts, the Four Year Longitudinal Graduation Reports should report an overall graduation rate that includes all high school students served in New York City, including special education students served in self-contained and District 75 classes.

The New York State Comptroller and/or the New York City Comptroller should also audit the discharge and graduation rate data for New York City high schools. A recent audit by the State Comptroller found significant reporting errors in schools' graduation and dropout data elsewhere in the state, but no comparable audit has performed for New York City high schools in many years. An independent party should produce a report analyzing the discharge data since the AFC/Public Advocate report to make clear who the discharged students are, why they were discharged, why the discharge rate has increased over time, and why the discharge rate of first-year students in particular has doubled.[14]

The city's Progress Report school grading system and the state accountability system should be evaluated to determine whether high schools face perverse incentives to discharge students earlier in their high school careers. The DOE should further explore incorporating certain categories of discharges into its Progress Reports to ensure that schools have an incentive to retain at-risk students and provide them with the supports necessary to ensure that they graduate with high school diplomas.

Finally, the discharge codes should be carefully examined to see if they conform to national standards. Some of the students who are currently defined as "discharges" in New York City should not be excluded from the cohort for the purpose of calculating graduation rates and should more accurately be redefined as "dropouts."[15]

In the July 2003 *New York Times* article, Chancellor Klein argued for more transparency regarding high school discharges, saying, "The information should be out there, and it should be clear. You're never going to change the system unless you're brutally candid."[16]

More than five years later, much of the information needed to evaluate the validity of New York City's high school discharges remains hidden. The public still does not have access to full information about who discharged students are, why they were discharged, why the discharge rate has increased over time, and why the discharge rate for students in their first year of high school in particular has doubled. Furthermore, in the absence of a regular and independent auditing mechanism, the public cannot have confidence that students who are discharged to educational settings outside of the New York City public schools are actually enrolling at these schools. As state and city accountability systems continue to raise the stakes for schools to improve graduation rates, an independent auditing mechanism is more necessary than ever before.

NOTES

1. "Pushing Out At-Risk Students: An Analysis of High School Discharge Figures," Advocates for Children and the Public Advocate for the City of New York, November 21, 2002, http://www.advocatesforchildren.org/pubs/2005 discharge. pdf.

2. *R. V. v. New York City Dept. of Educ.*, 321 F. Supp. 2d 538 (E.D.N.Y. 2004). These suits were ultimately settled to allow students at the three cited campuses the right to reenroll at their campuses or other schools, as well as priority for summer and night school.

3. Tamar Lewin and Jennifer Medina, "To Cut Failure, Schools Shed Students," *New York Times,* July 31, 2003.

4. Jennifer Medina and Tamar Lewin, "High School Under Scrutiny for Giving Up on Its Students," *New York Times,* August 1, 2003.

5. Elisa Hyman, "School Push-Outs: An Urban Case Study," *Clearinghouse Review Journal of Poverty Law and Policy,* January/February 2005, pp. 684-689.

6. Jennifer L. Jennings and Leonie Haimson, "High School Discharges Revisited: Trends in New York City's Discharge Rates 2000–2007," Public Advocate of the City of New York (May, 2009), http://pubadvocate.nyc.gov/new_news/documents /DischargesRevisited.pdf.

7. These figures include both what we refer to in this report as the "general education cohort"—students in general education classes as well as special education students in less restrictive settings—and the special education cohort—students in self-contained classes and District 75 classes.

8. The DOE calls the Class of 2007 the group of students that entered high school four years earlier and thus should have graduated in 2007.

9. For example, one of the specific measurements used in the DOE's school Progress Reports is the percentage of students at a school who accumulated ten or more academic credits in their first year of high school. If there are students who appear unlikely to accumulate these credits in the ninth grade, the accountability system as structured may encourage schools to discharge them as quickly as possible. In addition, the New York state system for tracking graduation rates under the No Child Left Behind Act excludes from the school's graduation rate any student who attended a given school for less than five months. As a result, schools may have an incentive to discharge students before this point so that they do not count towards their graduation rate. Though the data we report are not sufficient to establish a causal link between these accountability measures and the rising ninth-grade discharge rate, we believe this issue warrants further investigation.

10. Almost all of the increases in the special education cohort for the Class of 2005 were in the self-contained population, not the District 75 population; 39 percent of self-contained students in the Class of 2005 were discharged.

11. These figures are all for general education students; we did not have access to special education discharges disaggregated by race, ethnicity, and English language proficiency.

12. There are 292 high schools with graduation data reported for the Class of 2007.

13. Seventy-nine of these eighty-seven schools received a Progress Report grade for 2007. We make use of the Progress Report grades for 2007 because they are based on graduation data from the Class of 2007, the most recent class for which graduation data are available.

14. While the "Multiple Pathways Research and Development: Summary Findings and Strategic Solutions for Overage, Under-Credited Youth" report by the Office of Multiple Pathways provided a profile of overage, under-credited students, it did not provide a profile of discharges ("Multiple Pathways Research and Development: Summary Findings and Strategic Solutions for Overage, Under-Credited Youth," Office of Multiple Pathways, New York City Department of Education, undated, http://schools.nyc.gov/NR/rdonlyres/B5EC6D1C-F88A-4610-8F0F-A14D63420115/0/FindingsofOMPG.pdf).

15. For example, students who leave school after their twenty-first birthday, voluntarily withdraw because of pregnancy, enroll in a full-time GED program outside the New York City public school system, or are expelled are all considered dropouts by federal standards but discharges by the DOE. Students who transfer to a full-time GED program inside the New York City public school system and pass the GED exam are considered graduates by the DOE, though are not recognized as graduates under the guidelines of the national No Child Left Behind Act.

16. Lewin and Medina, "To Cut Failure, Schools Shed Students."

Test Score Inflation:
Campbell's Law at Work

- *Steve Koss*

...we're creating an illusion of success that is really nice
for everybody in the system except the kids.
- Daniel Koretz, Harvard School of Education[1]

Not everything that can be counted counts,
and not everything that counts can be counted.
- Albert Einstein

Performance measurement has always been an important element of modern education. For much of the last century, those measurements consisted of how individual teachers rated their students' mastery of their course work as exhibited by their performance on unit exams, classroom performance, and homework. Report cards served as communication to parents of their children's progress as well as motivators to the students themselves. Teaching and learning took precedence; measurement was necessary but not the primary objective.

In the six years since Chancellor Joel Klein took the reins of the New York City Department of Education (DOE), the performance measurement concept has been turned on its head, converted from student motivator to Damoclean sword. The federal No Child Left Behind Act (NCLB), which mandated that states set and reach performance benchmarks on standardized tests, placed these exams in the center of the curriculum, where they have taken the place of student report cards as the primary focus of administrators and teachers. These high-stakes exams have proliferated, and the DOE has institutionalized their widespread use as the basis for decision-making regarding school closure, personnel retention and compensation, and student promotion and graduation. This one-dimensional focus on measurability, soft-pedaled by the mayor and chancellor as "accountability," has affected people at every level of the public education system, from students to administrators.

For elementary and middle school students, their promotion to the next grade is now predicated on standardized test results. As more of the city's high schools become "screened" schools, students' seventh grade mathematics and ELA results are used in admissions decisions. In an effort to focus students' attention even further on test results, the DOE has adopted experimental programs to pay students for taking and scoring well on standardized exams.[2]

For parents and the community at large, schoolwide performance on standardized tests from third to eighth grades constitutes 85 percent of the raw score in the school's Progress Report, which assigns an overall letter grade from A to F to each school. These letter grades affect prospective parents' perceptions of a school, particularly in light of the DOE's repeated practice of shuttering schools that receive a D or F rather than dedicating increased resources and coaching assistance to improve them.

For school principals, year-to-year progress on standardized test results has become the major component of their annual performance assessment. Not only can firing decisions be based on these results, but cash performance bonuses of as much as $25,000 (on typical base salaries of $125,000 or more) are at stake.[3] Similarly, under a program first piloted at 205 schools in 2007, a school's entire staff can receive bonuses of up to $3,000 per full-time teacher based on their schools' combined, measured progress on the annual mathematics and English Language Arts exams.[4]

Measures of success are different for the city's public high schools, but the guiding philosophy is the same. Principals, teachers, and students are rewarded for the school's results on New York State Regents exams, most notably on five baseline subject-area exams: Global History and Geography, American History and Government, Comprehensive English, first-level Math (now called Integrated Algebra I), and Science (typically Living Environment or Earth Science). In addition to pass rates on these Regents exams, high schools' Progress Reports include measures of credit accumulation and graduation rates.

Campbell's Law: The Fallout from High-Stakes Measurement Systems

Educators and education researchers have long been wary of high-stakes tests, since they inherently create conflicts of interest and are fraught with unintended consequences. The higher the stakes, the more likely behavior contrary to the original intent of the measurement system will result. In 1976, sociologist Donald T. Campbell described this tendency toward subversion in what became known as Campbell's Law:

> The more any quantitative social indicator is used for social decision making, the more subject it will be to corruption pressures and the more apt it will be to distort and corrupt the social processes it is intended to monitor.[5]

The accountability pressures levied by NCLB and State Education Departments inevitably lead to their own manifestations of Campbell's Law: dumbing down exams, falsifying reported results, excluding low-scoring groups from taking the exams, and various forms of teacher- or administrator-abetted cheating. Such outcomes have already been documented in several major cities, including Dallas[6], Houston[7], Chicago[8], Oakland (CA)[9], and Charleston (SC).[10] Many of these corrupting behaviors can be grouped together under what is commonly referred to as "test score inflation,"[11] artificially boosting results on high-stakes standardized exams. Some examples of score inflation include:

- Designing tests so they are easier to pass (that is, to reach the minimum level deemed proficient);

- Lowering the minimum passing score, commonly called the "cut score";

- Teaching to the test, focusing on the content and question formats most likely to appear on the exams;

- Systematically excluding students likely to score poorly from taking the test (by retaining them in lower grades, suspending them, and/or encouraging them to be absent or away on a class trip on the day of the test);

- Increasing classroom time spent on tested subjects (mathematics, English) to the detriment of social studies, science, art, music, physical education, and other untested subjects;

- Systematic cheating by teachers or principals during the test (coaching, extended time, leaving helpful materials on display in the classroom) or afterwards (changing students' incorrect answers, improperly inflating the point value of students' answers on essays and open-ended questions);

- Focusing undue teacher attention and additional resources on so-called "bubble children" (students viewed as being just below or near enough to the proficiency level) to the detriment of other students. Pushing a small number of bubble children's scores over the proficiency cut score can have a sizable impact on a school's reported progress.

Other measures that influence Progress Report ratings, such as high-school credits awarded, graduation rates, and school safety, can each be manipulated in their own individual ways to yield favorable results, whether privately by individual school administrators or systematically through methods encouraged by high-level officials. Events over the past six years suggest strongly that the deleterious effects of Campbell's Law has been at work in New York State, and its effects have been amplified in New York City by the policies of Mayor Bloomberg and Chancellor Klein.

Impact of Campbell's Law in New York State

New York State has employed Regents (high school) exams for well over a century. Through the 1980s and early 1990s, Regents exams served primarily as diploma differentiators, signifying a higher level of subject-area proficiency than "local" diplomas. Beginning with ninth graders entering high school in 1996, students were required to pass a minimum of five Regents exams to receive a high school diploma. Initially, passing meant scoring at least a 55 percent on each exam, but over the years, the passing level has been increased to 65 percent and the number of exams that have to be passed has gradually been raised as well. Students entering ninth grade in Fall 2008 will be the first cohort required to pass all five required Regents exams with scores of at least 65 percent.

With this increased demand for proficiency has come a dramatic easing in scoring. For example, in June 1998, New York City high school students needed to earn 65 of the 100 available points to achieve a passing grade of 65 on the ninth-grade Regents exam in mathematics, then known as Sequential I. That test contained twenty-two multiple-choice questions (44 percent of the maximum score), thirteen short-answer questions, and seven moderately complex, multi-part questions from which students had to answer four.

Ten years later, in June 2008, students only needed to garner 34 percent of the available points (30 out of 87) to be awarded a scaled passing grade of 65 in the equivalent-level Integrated Algebra I exam. Furthermore, the 2008 test was far less challenging, with thirty multiple-choice questions (69 percent of the maximum score), lower demands for algebra skills, and a helpful formula sheet. Test questions included finding the volume of a cube and the surface area of a rectangular box, calculating miles per gallon, and figuring out what percentage discount results when a store marks down an item from $18.00 to $15.00–questions most educators would regard as middle-school level.

The pattern on the U.S. History Regents exam was similar. In 1998, students who achieved a passing grade of 65 had to earn at least 53 percent of the 93 available points. In June 2008, students could pass with a grade of 65 by scoring only 40 percent, and multiple-choice questions comprised two-thirds of the exam, compared to 55 percent in 1998. In 1998, students had to retrieve content knowledge from memory; in 2008, half the essay section, a significant portion of the multiple-choice questions, and all the short-answer questions could be completed from material provided in the test document itself. One question, for example, contained a photograph captioned, "…federal troops escort the Little Rock Nine to their classes at Central High School" and then asked, "Based on the photograph, what was the job of the United States Army troops in Little Rock, Arkansas?"

Even a cursory review of current Regents exams against those of 1998 makes it clear that today's pass rates would fall dramatically if the earlier standards and content were still in place. To make the tests easier and passing scores lower, and then claim higher success rates, misleads the public and undermines the credibility of those who claim progress in our schools.

Tests have also been dumbed down in elementary and middle schools. In 2007, the New York *Daily News* reviewed the fourth-grade mathematics tests for the preceding six years and discovered that "in every year when scores went up, test makers identified the questions as easier during pretest trials."[12] Another study, this one conducted by the New York City teachers' union in 2006, demonstrated that a state reading exam dropped as many as six grade levels in difficulty, from ninth grade to third or fourth grade, between 2004 and 2005.[13]

Impact of Campbell's Law in New York City

New York City's Department of Education cannot directly alter the content or cut scores of state exams. However, since the appointment of Chancellor Klein, the DOE has implemented numerous programs and initiatives that magnify and exacerbate the Campbell's Law effects of high-stakes testing.

For elementary- and middle-school students, the DOE reports proficiency levels and rates (how many students passed a bar, called the "cut score," labeled proficient) rather than average scale scores across the spectrum. A school (or a system) can appear to show improvement by pushing relatively small numbers of "bubble students" across the cut-score boundary for proficiency, while performance by students on either side of the boundary can go in any direction. Indeed, disturbing evidence exists that the number of students scoring at the highest performance levels is in fact falling, presumably due to increased tailoring of classroom time and activities toward children at the proficiency margin, a perverse form of educational triage.[14]

Progress Report grades impose enormous pressure on teachers and principals. The pressure to show annual improvement in test scores has resulted in increased emphasis on test preparation and "teaching to the test" while shrinking the time spent in other curricular areas and activities including history, science, music, and art. Chancellor Klein's implementation of teacher bonus pay adds financial incentives for teachers to focus their attention on standardized test results. Another DOE program, designed to measure individual teachers' value-added performance based on their students' test scores, adds more "corruption pressures" (as Campbell termed such behavior modifiers) to teach to the test or falsify results.

At the high-school level, anecdotal reports abound of score padding for marginal students and other forms of cheating. The temptation to do so is exacerbated by the fact that teachers score the Regents exams of students at their own schools. Strong motivations exist for administrators not to report school safety incidents or to classify them as lesser infractions, and reports of principals instructing teachers to (in so many words) "dumb down" their classes (enabling more students to achieve at least ten credits for the year) elicit little public outcry.[15] The pressure to improve graduation rates may well be linked to an increase in high school credit recovery programs.[16] For students who fail a class due to poor performance, principals may pressure teachers to assign projects or make-up exams whose successful completion enables the student to receive ex post course credit. Credit recovery thereby improves the school's Progress Report metrics twice over—once by increasing the percentage of students achieving ten credits for the year, and a second time by increasing a now-debased graduation rate.

Not surprisingly, incidents of administrator and teacher cheating in standardized exam scoring have proliferated as Chancellor Klein has steadily raised the stakes. Incidents have been reported throughout the city, some of them at schools lauded just months earlier by the mayor or chancellor for their extraordinary achievement. Cheating scandals have occurred in recent years at Susan Wagner High School (Staten Island),[17] the High School for Contemporary Arts (Bronx),[18] P.S. 33 (Bronx),[19] P.S. 48 (Bronx),[20] the High School for Youth and Community Development (Brooklyn),[21] John F. Kennedy High School (Bronx),[22] and the Cobble Hill School of American Studies (Brooklyn),[23] to name only a few that have been publicly reported. Many others go unreported or operate on a smaller, less egregious scale.

Even parents are affected by the increased pressure of Progress Reports. Not wanting to see their children's school receive a lower report card grade or risk being closed, they may feel compelled (or even be encouraged by school staff or well-intentioned parent leaders) to inflate their positive responses. Sadly, parent insights and criticisms are effectively stifled when the price for honesty may result in lower grades for their children's school.

Conclusion

Thoughtful independent observers might well ask for whose benefit all this measurement and incentivizing has been implemented. Despite the DOE's heavily publicized claims of test score improvements, it is fair to ask if higher test scores translate as improved education. With such intense focus on standardized exam scores, it is increasingly difficult for public school teachers in New York City to keep in view the larger goals of developing their students' critical and creative thinking skills. Rather, the system operates on a politicized platform that serves the interests of adults, from the mayor and chancellor to principals and teachers.

For New York City public school students, education has lost much of the excitement of exploration or discovery. The very concept of education is perverted, and the negative effects of Campbell's Law prevail.

It is worth noting that in the same 1976 paper in which he introduced his theory, Donald Campbell wrote: "achievement tests may well be valuable indicators of general school achievement under conditions of normal teaching aimed at general competence. But when test scores become the goal of the teaching process, they both lose their value as indicators of educational status and distort the educational process in undesirable ways."[24] But Tom Chapin's song, "Not on the Test," offers perhaps the best summary of what New York City's public school system has become under Mayor Bloomberg and Chancellor Klein:

Go on to sleep now, third grader of mine.
The test is tomorrow but you'll do just fine.
It's reading and math, forget all the rest.
You don't need to know what is not on the test.

Each box that you mark on each test that you take,
Remember your teachers, their jobs are at stake.
Your score is their score, but don't get all stressed.
They'd never teach anything not on the test...

Thinking's important. It's good to know how.
And someday you'll learn to but someday's not now.
Go on to sleep, now. You need your rest.
Don't think about thinking. It's not on the test. [25]

NOTES

1. Quoted in Bob Herbert, "High Stakes Flimflam," *New York Times,* October 9, 2007.

2. Jennifer Medina, "Schools Plan to Pay Cash for Marks," *New York Times,* June 19, 2007.

3. Principals' salary schedule from 2003–2010 Salary Schedule, downloaded as an Excel file from Council of School Supervisors and Administrators, http://www.csa-New YorkCity.org/ps/pscontract.php. Performance bonus information from David Herszenhorn, and Julie Bosman, "Under Pact, Principals Get Bonus to Lead Tough Schools," *New York Times,* April 24, 2007.

4. New York City Department of Education, "98% of Eligible Schools Opt to Participate in Second Year of School-Wide Performance Bonus Program," press release, November 20, 2008, http://schools.NewYorkCity.gov/Offices/mediarelations/NewsandSpeeches/2008-2009/20081120_schoolwide_bonus.htm.

5. Donald T. Campbell, "Assessing the Impact of Planned Social Change," The Public Affairs Center, Dartmouth College, Hanover, NH (December 1976), p. 49, www.wmich.edu/evalctr/pubs/ops/ops08.pdf.

6.   Joshua Benton and Holly K. Hacker, "Analysis Shows TAKS Cheating Rampant," *Dallas Morning News*, June 3, 2007, http://www.dallasnews.com/sharedcontent /dws/dn/latestnews/stories/060307dnmetcheating.433e87c.html).

7.   Benton and Hacker, "Analysis Shows TAKS Cheating Rampant." *Dallas Morning News,* June 3, 2007,

8.   Kris Axtman, "When Tests' Cheaters Are the Teachers," *Christian Science Monitor,* January 11, 2005, http://www.csmonitor.com/2005/0111/p01s03-ussc.html.

9.   Ed Attanasio, "Cheating Allegations Hit Oakland High School Hard," *BrooWaha San Francisco,* July 8, 2007, http://www.broowaha.com/article.php?id=1951.

10. Diette Courrégé, "School Under Scrutiny," *Post and Courier,* September 10, 2008, http://www.charleston.net/news/2008/sep/10/school_under_scrutiny53611/; and "High-Stakes Testing Puts Pressure on Educators," *Post and Courier*, September 14, 2008, ttp://www.charleston.net/news/2008/sep/14/high_stakes_ testing_puts_pressure_on_edu54514/; and Adam Nossiter, "School's Success Gives Way to Doubt," *New York Times,* October 31, 2008.

11. The methods described here are summarized from Kevin Carey, "The Pangloss Index: How States Game the No Child Left Behind Act," *Education Sector,* November 2007, pp. 6-11, http://www.educationsector.org/research/research_ show.htm?doc_id=582446.

12. Erin Einhorn, "Daily News Exam Finds Math Scores Up When Difficulty Rating Went Down," *Daily News,* September 4, 2007.

13. Elizabeth Green, "State Guts Its Test of Reading," *New York Sun*, September 7, 2007.

14. Andrew Wolf, "Middle Management," *New York Sun,* June 27, 2008.

15. Ethan Rouen, and Erin Einhorn, "Dumb Down Class, Asks Principal Memo," *Daily News,* December 13, 2007.

16. Elissa Gootman and Sharona Coutts, "Lacking Credits, Some Students Learn a Shortcut," *New York Times,* April 11, 2008.

17. Jim Callaghan, "Wagner HS Teachers Vindicated After Release of Cheating Scandal Report," *New York Teacher,* January 17, 2008, http://www.uft.org/news/teacher/ top/vindicated.

18. Elissa Gootman, "School Official to Be Fired After Cheating Is Found," *New York Times,* December 4, 2008.

19. Andrew Wolf, "Resorting to Cheating," *New York Sun,* January 4, 2008.

20. Elizabeth Green, "High Test Scores, and Criticism, Follow a South Bronx Principal," *New York Sun,* June 30, 2008.

21. Richard Steier, "Fault Principal for Cheating on Regents," *The Chief,* December 29, 2006, http://www.thechief-leader.com/news/2006/1229/news/014.html.

22. "Cheating Reports Continue to Erupt," FairTest, May 2006, http://www.fairtest.org/cheating-reports-continue-erupt.

23. David Herszenhorn, "Principal Hid Fraud on Tests in Brooklyn," *New York Times,* July 1, 2005.

24. Campbell, "Assessing the Impact of Planned Social Change."

25. See http://www.notonthetest.com.

Has the Bloomberg/Klein Agenda Served the Cause of Equity?

- Hazel N. Dukes

The policies and programs implemented in New York City public schools will determine the quality, character, and readiness of the students who will become our future leaders. For the past six years, the members of our NAACP branches and other advocates have been receiving complaints from parents and other community members who believe they have a right to be included in decision-making when it comes to the policies implemented in our public schools. Too often, the New York City Department of Education's policies have been top-down, with insufficient inclusion of stakeholder groups—and as a result, the decisions made have often had damaging effects, particularly on children of color.

To begin with, there's the issue of class size. New York City students continue to be forced to endure the largest class sizes in the state—even though class size reduction is one of only two systemic education reforms that have been shown to narrow the achievement gap—along with increased access to pre-Kindergarten programs.[1] And yet this administration has done everything it can to block smaller classes from becoming a priority for our schools.

The NAACP is a core member of New Yorkers for Smaller Classes, a coalition of many advocacy groups and unions working to promote smaller classes in New York City public schools. A few years ago, we helped collect over 100,000 signatures to put a proposition on the ballot that would require smaller classes in our schools by amending the City Charter. The Mayor successfully blocked this proposition from appearing on the ballot.

Subsequently, we helped push for a measure passed by the state legislature in 2007. In return for receiving hundreds of millions of dollars in new state aid, the state required the New York City Department of Education to submit a plan to use a portion of these funds to reduce class size in all grades. After much resistance, Chancellor Klein finally did submit such a plan, but he has consistently refused to implement it.

The result has been that in 2007–2008, the first year of the program, class sizes, as well as the student-teacher ratio, actually increased in half of all New York City schools.[2] And though, overall, average class sizes declined fractionally citywide, primarily due to enrollment decline, the state criticized the city for failing to make any of its class-size targets.[3]

This year, the administration's record was even worse. The data shows that this fall class sizes increased in all grades but fourth—by the largest amount in ten years.[4] Class-size increases were especially sharp in the early grades—which are widely believed to be the most critical years for narrowing the achievement gap and ensuring that children in our high-needs communities have the best possible start.

Many of the other policies pursued by this administration have also served to put low-income and minority students at a disadvantage. In October 2007, Chancellor Klein announced that he would impose uniform cut-offs on high stakes tests for admissions to gifted and talented programs. Previously, admissions to these classes were controlled by district administrators who used different selection processes, adjusted to the needs of their communities, to make these decisions. Though the chancellor claimed that his intention was to expand access to gifted and talented programs in underserved areas, experts warned that if admissions to these programs were based solely on the results of high-stakes exams, especially ones designed to test for school preparedness rather than innate ability, this would cause a significant drop in the numbers of Black and Hispanic students admitted. Educators warned that the DOE was "using two instruments [that] we know for a fact, provide racially biased results."[5]

Yet the experts were ignored and the chancellor went ahead anyway. What they warned indeed occurred. There was a sharp decline in the number of Black and Hispanic students admitted to gifted and talented programs this fall, and a drop in the number of gifted classes in districts with high poverty rates. The percentage of Black students entering gifted programs declined precipitously, falling from 31 percent to 13 percent.[6] Seven predominantly minority districts of thirty-two citywide lack gifted programs this year, compared to only two last year. How does this serve the cause of equity?

Another issue that concerns us greatly is that the declining share of African-American teachers hired to teach in New York City public schools. The percentage has dropped by more than half over the course of this administration, falling from 27 percent in 2001–2002 to 13 percent last year. This is tragic, especially given the fact that our schools are increasingly made up of non-white students.[7]

Finally, the proportion and number of minority students enrolled in our selective, specialized high schools such as Stuyvesant and Bronx Science has also declined under this administration. Fewer Black and Hispanic students now take the admissions exam to these elite schools and even lower percentages pass, compared to years past. Among the 21,490 public school students who last year took the exam for our specialized high schools, only 6 percent of Blacks and 7 percent of Hispanics were admitted, compared with 35 percent of Asians and 31 percent of white students. This compares to an overall city school population that is 40 percent Hispanic, 32 percent Black, 14 percent Asian, and 14 percent White. Meanwhile, the special program designed to help high-needs students gain entrance to these schools by means of afterschool and Saturday sessions has been sharply curtailed—enrolling only 2,800 students this year compared to 3,800 students in 2006.[8]

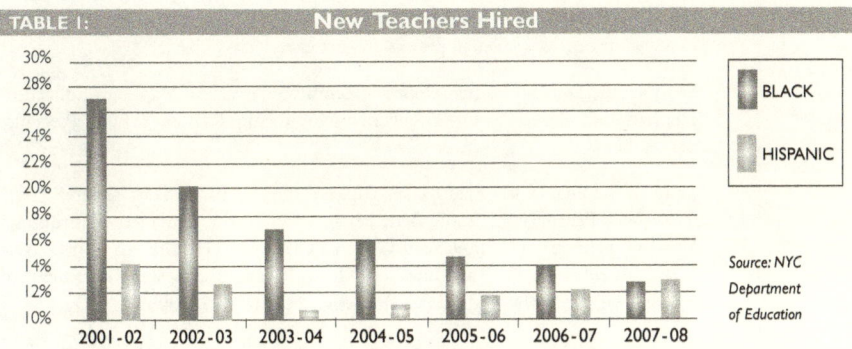

TABLE 1: New Teachers Hired

Source: NYC Department of Education

Joshua Feinman, an economist, has concluded that the admissions exam used for our selective high schools is highly unreliable, and has not been analyzed for racial bias.[9] While state law mandates that a high-stakes exam be the sole criterion of entrance to three New York City high schools, namely Stuyvesant, Bronx Science, and Brooklyn Tech, there is nothing that mandates that any test be used that has never been analyzed for racial bias. Moreover, Chancellor Klein has unilaterally imposed the use of this high-stakes exam on schools that once had a more holistic admissions process, such as Staten Island Technical High School, as well as several newly created high schools, including the High School for Mathematics, Science and Engineering at City College, the High School of American Studies at Lehman College, the Queens High School for the Sciences at York College, and Brooklyn Latin.

According to Feinman, as well as other experts, "Overwhelmingly, studies have found that multiple criteria, used in tandem, provide a better guide to future student performance than a single one."[10] The fact that DOE has undertaken no validity studies on the admissions test for our elite high schools, nor any analysis to assess whether it may be racially biased, and instead has broadened the application of these tests to more and more schools, is unacceptable. These policies have had unfortunate effect of excluding minority students from our top public schools, from which many of our future leaders will be drawn.

1. See, for example, David W. Grissmer, et al., *Improving Student Achievement: What State NAEP Scores Tell Us,* RAND: Santa Monica, CA, 2000.

2. Carrie Melago, "153M from Albany can't uncram classes," *Daily News,* April 29, 2008; Yoav Gonen, "Failing to 'Cut' Class: $ize Still Matters," *New York Post,* April 29, 2008; Elizabeth Green, "Comptroller To Probe City's Class-Size Reduction Effort," *New York Sun,* April 29, 2008; United Federation of Teachers, "DOE flouts state class-size reduction mandates," Press release, April 28, 2008, http://www.uft.org/news/issues/press/state-mandated_class_size/.

3. See Johanna Duncan Poitier, Deputy Commissioner of the NY State Education Department, Contracts for Excellence-Monitoring Report to the Regents, September 8, 2008.

4. Jennifer Medina, "Class Size Makes Biggest Jump of Bloomberg Tenure," *New York Times,* February 17, 2009; Beth Fertig, "New York's Crowded Classrooms," WNYC, February 17, 2009; Yoav Gonen, "Class Size Has Growth Spurt," *New York Post,* February 17, 2009; Elizabeth Green, "Updated data show class sizes are up, especially in early grades," *New York Sun,* February 17, 2009.

5. See, for example, Deborah Meier, "Deborah Meier on the Chancellor's inequitable G and T proposal," NYC Public School Parents blog, November 2, 2007, http://nycpublicschoolparents.blogspot.com/2007/11/deborah-meier-on-chancellors.html.

6. Elissa Gootman, "Fewer Children Entering Gifted Programs," *New York Times,* October 29, 2008.

7. These data are from a file provided by DOE. See also Elizabeth Green, "Fewer Blacks, More Whites Are Hired as City Teachers," *New York Sun,* September 25, 2008.

8. Javier C. Hernandez, "Racial Imbalance Persists at Elite Public Schools," *New York Times,* November 7, 2008.

9. Joshua Feinman, Ph.D., "High Stakes, but Low Validity? A Case Study of Standardized Tests and Admissions into New York City Specialized High Schools," Education Policy Research Unit, Arizona State University, October 2008.

10. Josh Feinman, "All is not well with the admissions practices of the specialized high schools," NYC Public School Parents blog, November 28, 2008 at: http://nycpublicschoolparents.blogspot.com/2008/11/all-is-not-well-with-admissions.html.

"Progress" Reports

- Aaron M. Pallas and Jennifer L. Jennings

Schools give report cards that evaluate how students are performing in different areas, examining whether their performance is up to the school's standards and seeking to motivate students to work harder. Is giving report cards to schools a good idea? In this essay, we describe the New York City School Progress Reports and their strengths and weaknesses. Evaluating how schools are performing might be useful, but not, we suggest, if it is done poorly. In our analysis, the Progress Reports produce results that are unreliable, confusing, and create unintended negative consequences.

A key component of the "Children First" initiative developed by Chancellor Joel Klein is the accountability system, whose most visible elements are school-level Progress Reports and Quality Reviews. The Progress Reports and Quality Reviews are tools to hold schools, and the leaders and teachers within them, accountable for school performance. The principals and teachers at schools that perform well on these indicators are eligible for cash awards, whereas schools that perform poorly can be threatened with restructuring or closure. Principals in schools that receive low ratings are at risk of being fired. Teachers who work at schools that are "restructured" or closed must look for new jobs or enter the absent teacher reserve, where they can be assigned to classes that they are not qualified to teach or be obliged to become substitute teachers.

The Progress Reports were piloted in 2006–2007, with schools receiving their first official reports in October 2007; the second round of reports was released in the fall of 2008. The reports assess a school's performance in three domains: school environment, student performance, and student progress. Scores in these three domains are combined, along with extra credit for raising achievement for particular student subgroups, to derive an overall score, and schools are assigned a letter grade ranging from A to F based on this overall score.

In the 2008 Progress Reports, the school environment contributed 15 percent to the overall score, with student performance representing 25 percent and student progress 60 percent. At the elementary school level, the "school environment" is measured by student attendance and teachers' and parents' responses to a survey made available to teachers and parents in the spring of the year. Student performance is indicated by the percentage of students who meet the cutoff for proficiency on state tests in grades three through eight in mathematics and

English Language Arts (ELA), as well as the median student proficiency, which is based loosely on students' scaled scores on those tests. Student progress is based on the percentage of students who make a year's worth of progress on the mathematics and ELA exams from the previous year to this year, and the average change in proficiency ratings from the previous year to this year, considering lower- and higher-achieving students separately. A total of thirty-four components go into the elementary/middle school Progress Report score, and additional extra credit components may also come into play. There is a different mix of components at the high school level, including students' responses to the learning environment survey.

By design, each elementary/middle school and each high school is compared both with a peer group of forty schools with similar demographic characteristics and with all schools across the city at that grade level. Three-quarters of a school's score in a given area is based on a school's position relative to other peer schools, whereas one-quarter of a school's score is based on how well a school does relative to other schools across New York City. A school could perform well in relation to its peer group, but poorly in relation to schools citywide, as might be expected if we examined the mathematics and ELA proficiency rates in schools serving high concentrations of poor children and/or English language learners.

In 2007, 61 percent of elementary and middle schools received letter grades of A or B, with 9 percent receiving D's and 4 percent receiving F's. The overall distribution of grades shifted upward from 2007 to 2008, as 79 percent of elementary and middle schools received A's or B's, with only 5 percent receiving D's and 2 percent receiving F's. This shift corresponded to the statewide increase in performance on the state mathematics and ELA assessments.

Of the 35 elementary and middle schools receiving an F in 2007, not one received an F in 2008, and only one received a D. Seventy-seven percent of the schools receiving an F in 2007 vaulted to an A or B in 2008. The most favorable interpretation of this pattern is that the schools receiving an F dramatically over-hauled instruction, which resulted in sharp upticks in student performance and the school's learning environment. A more plausible explanation might be that the letter grades are based heavily on an unreliable measure of student progress. It is just not credible that all 35 failing elementary and middle schools turned themselves around in the space of one year.

There are two key strengths to the Progress Reports. The first is that they are designed so that schools are judged primarily in relation to schools serving similar populations—comparing apples to apples rather than to oranges. The use of peer groups as a basis for three-quarters of the overall Progress Report grade is an effort to take account of the fact that different kinds of students enroll in different schools, and that a school serving students with high learning needs faces greater challenges than a school serving students already achieving at high levels. It makes little sense, for example, to compare the performance of students in a highly selective high school like Stuyvesant with the performance of students in a zoned comprehensive high school. The peer group approach, although not perfect, is an effort to introduce an adjustment for relevant differences in the student population of each school.

The second strength of the Progress Reports is that they seek to rate a school on a diverse set of attributes. To be sure, most of a school's score is based on test scores, but the results of surveys are also taken into account, including subjective measures of academic expectation, communication, engagement, safety, and respect, as well as student attendance. At the high-school level, measures include four- and six-year graduation rates, percentage of students earning ten or more credits in a given year, and their pass rates on Regents examinations.

The limitations of the Progress Reports, however, greatly outnumber their strengths. We note the following four deficiencies, each of which we discuss in detail below. First, the Progress Reports introduce confusion and complexity into the ways in which schools are held accountable for their performance. Second, the Progress Reports for elementary and middle schools are based primarily on an unreliable measure of students' progress from one year to the next. Third, the Progress Reports create a false sense of precision about the relative performance of schools, suggesting that schools can easily be distinguished from one another, when in fact only a small number doing very well or poorly can really be identified as different from the vast majority in the middle. And finally, the measures on the School Progress Reports are vulnerable to manipulation that can distort true progress in schools.

Confusion and Complexity

The federal No Child Left Behind Act, which predates the Progress Reports by more than five years, had already introduced a high-stakes accountability system in which schools are judged on whether they are making Adequate Yearly Progress (AYP) towards universal proficiency in reading and mathematics. Schools that fail to make AYP for two or more years are judged Schools in Need of Improvement (SINI) and subject to a progressive system of supports and sanctions, including eventual closure. The criteria for AYP, however, differ substantially from the measurements in the Progress Reports, creating the possibility that a school may fare well under one accountability system but poorly under the other. Moreover, the state Board of Regents administers a Registration Review Process that represents New York State's efforts to identify schools that are not meeting state performance benchmarks and in need of improvement. The list of Schools Under Registration Review (SURR) is yet another accountability metric that may be at odds with the criteria on which the Progress Reports are based. This is confusing to educators in the school and to the public, who might struggle to make sense of these discrepant evaluations.

We found that, in 2008, 74 percent of the elementary and middle schools that received A's on their Progress Reports were in good standing with NCLB; but 89 percent of the schools that received F's were also in good standing. The fact that a higher percentage of F schools were in good standing with the federal NCLB requirements than schools that received A's is indicative of the potential for confusion.

The other central component of the city's accountability system is the Quality Review. To prepare a school's Quality Review, outside educators visit a school for one or two days and examine how well it generates and uses available information to monitor student performance and progress, as well as its planning and goal-setting for promoting student achievement. Schools are rated Well-Developed, Proficient, Underdeveloped with Proficient Features, or Underdeveloped. The Quality Reviews introduce yet another variant measure of accountability. In 2008, 44 percent of the elementary schools receiving an F on the Progress Report received a Well-Developed in their Quality Review, the highest possible rating, and 94 percent of F schools received a rating of Well-Developed or Proficient—the same as the percentage of C schools receiving these ratings. It is extremely confusing for parents and others to be able to judge which of these ratings to trust. The Klein Administration has endeavored to introduce "choice" and market strategies into schools, but how is the public to weigh these mutually contradictory measures of schools' success?

Unreliable Measures of Student Progress

Most of an elementary or middle school's letter grade is based on the progress that students made on the state mathematics and ELA exam from one year to the next. If some schools really are better than others at promoting growth, then we would expect that the schools producing high growth in achievement in one year will show growth again in the next, even allowing for the possibility that some schools will move up or down a bit. Similarly, schools not as successful in promoting growth should prove consistently low in this measure from one year to the next. If schools that are rated as high-growth in one year turn out to be low-growth the next, and low-growth schools one year are found to be high-growth the following year, then we have to wonder if the school progress measures are really telling us anything meaningful about which schools are good and which ones are not.

Our analysis of the student progress component on last year's and this year's Progress Reports suggests that it is unreliable. We compared the scores of elementary, K–8, and middle schools on the school progress measure in on both last year's and this year's reports. The schools that the progress reports identified as high growth last year were just as likely to be named low growth this year. You could actually do better randomly picking schools out of a hat to identify those that would receive high scores for student progress, than by relying on last year's reports as a predictor.[1]

The reason is that much of the changes in student performance within a particular school on a test from one year to the next is due to random error, or "statistical noise," rather than genuine change. It takes a lot more information—either from a larger number of students or across more years—to sort real gains from illusions. The Progress Reports, by looking at short-term changes from one year to the next, rather than performance over a several-year period, cannot be counted on to provide a solid measure of the school's contribution to student progress over time.

A False Sense of Precision

Each of the components of the Progress Reports—Learning Environment Surveys, student test scores, pass rates for Regents exams, and so on—is based on a sample of parents, teachers, or students in a school. In some cases, these samples are small, as when the school itself is small, or if only 10 percent of the parents at a particular school respond to the survey. Just as in a political poll, which is reported with a margin of error, the components that go into the Progress Reports are simply estimates of what is going on. The general rule of thumb is, the more information available in a sample, the less uncertainty in the estimate. This is as true for estimates of the relative performance of schools and teachers as it is for political polls. One would not want to place too much faith in a particular estimate if one knew that another sample of the same size might yield a quite different value.

The calculations that go into the Progress Reports do not acknowledge that the components are imprecise and that most schools are statistically indistinguishable from one another. For example, an elementary school that has 58 percent of its students making a year's progress in English could just as easily have had 51 percent or 65 percent doing so. Yet even when these statistical differences are not significant, the Progress Reports pretend that they are real. Some schools may be doing substantially better than others; the problem is that the School Progress Reports fail to provide enough information to judge which ones.

Vulnerability to Manipulation

All accountability systems are vulnerable to manipulation, but there are two features of the Progress Reports that are particularly so. The first is the Learning Environment Survey, which makes up 10 percent of a school's letter grade. At the elementary- school level, these surveys are completed by parents and teachers, whereas at the middle- and high-school level, students are surveyed along with parents and teachers. Knowing that a poor grade on the Progress Report may lead to closure, on the one hand, or to financial rewards for staff on the other, provides a powerful incentive to parents and teachers to report a rosy picture— regardless of what the reality might be. And this will be especially true for schools that received a D or an F on their Progress Report the previous year.

Reports from students are apparently harder to affect in this way.

Our analyses show that parents and teachers in D and F schools reported much sharper improvements in areas such as safety and engagement than did the students in these schools.[2] On the other hand, the improvements reported by parents and teachers in A and B schools were about the same as those reported by their students. This suggests that the pressure on parents and teachers may be leading them to inflate responses on the surveys to avoid the negative consequences of a poor rating. The *New York Post* reported in December, 2008 that some principals were encouraged to keep the survey away from "toxic" parents, teachers, and students, and numerous teachers have reported efforts to influence their responses.[3]

A second factor that is vulnerable to manipulation is credit accumulation. High-school Progress Reports measure the fraction of students who earn ten or more credits in their first year. This measure creates incentives for schools to create non-traditional ways for students to "recover" credits when they have failed to pass a course. These practices may help students in the short-run, but if they enable students to move ahead when they have not mastered the underlying material, it will ultimately shortchange them. We cannot know for sure how measuring credit accumulation for the Progress Reports is affecting the standards for completing a course successfully, but steep increases in the percentage of first year students accumulating ten or more credits in some high schools raise troubling questions. For example, only 6 percent of the first-year students at the Secondary School for Journalism earned 10 or more credits in 2007, but 60 percent of the first-year students earned 10 or more credits in 2008. Substantial gains from 2007 to 2008 were also observed at the Rachel Carson High School for Coastal Studies, Canarsie High School, the Law, Government and Community Service High School, and the Cobble Hill School of American Studies. Since so much of the student progress score for high schools is based on credit accumulation, the School Progress Reports may be contributing to this unfortunate practice.

In short, rather than holding schools accountable for performance, the Progress Reports provide unreliable ratings, are confusing, and create perverse incentives that may in the long run actually harm rather than help New York City students.

NOTES

1. See Skoolboy, "Could a Monkey Do a Better Job of Predicting Which Schools Show Student Progress on English Skills than the New York City Department of Education?," Eduwonkette, September 24, 2008, http://blogs.edweek.org/ed week/2008/09/could_a_monkey _do_a_better_job.

2. Eduwonkette, "Irreconcilable Differences: Why NYC's Surveys Provide a Misleading Portrait of School Quality," September 16, 2008, http://blogs.edweek. org/edweek/eduwonkette/2008/09/irreconcilable_differences_ why.html.

3. Yoav Gonen, "Schools Fixed Grade Survey," *New York Post,* December 1, 2008.

New York City Public School Student Improvement Before & After Mayoral Control

- The Honorable James F. Brennan[1]

This essay examines changes in the test scores, spending, and programming before and after mayoral control, to understand the impact of the mayor's reforms compared to the impact of earlier reforms. In the 1998-1999 school year, New York State began its new testing program for fourth- and eighth-grade students. These tests have been administered continuously since, providing a useful baseline for comparing student performance before and after mayoral control.[2] New York City public school spending virtually doubled from 1998–1999 to 2007–2008. Over this same period fourth-grade ELA and mathematics scores increased by about 30 percentage points. Eighth-grade mathematics scores increased by nearly 37 points and eighth-grade ELA scores increased by 8 points. An examination of New York State test results from 1998–1999 to 2007–2008 reveals that the groundwork for student improvement had largely been laid prior to the mayor's reforms.

Historical Background

In 1995, the New York State Board of Regents developed a three-tiered plan for raising standards for all students that included: setting higher learning standards and revising the assessment system; building the capacity of schools to support student learning; and developing an institutional accountability system with public reporting. In 1996 the Regents adopted a set of twenty-eight learning standards for seven subject areas and issued a series of core curricula related to the standards. The New York State Education Department and school districts began the testing program during the 1998–1999 school year in fourth and eighth grades. In addition, new federal and state efforts were introduced in 1998 to reduce early-grade class sizes. Further, in 1997, the New York State legislature and the governor agreed to a new plan for universal pre-Kindergarten, placing New York at the forefront of the universal pre-Kindergarten movement. In June 2002, the New York State legislature approved mayoral control of the New York City public schools. The momentum created by these reform efforts from 1998–1999 to 2007–2008 was complemented by increased spending on education in New York City. These policy changes are examined further below.

New York City School Spending

Over these past ten school years, from 1998–1999 to 2007–2008, the city's education budget has nearly doubled, from $9.79 billion to $18.34 billion. Spending rose from 1998–1999 to 2002–2003, growing from $9.79 billion to $12.71 billion, or by 30 percent. From 2002–2003 to 2005–2006 the budget continued to increase from $12.71 billion to $15.99, billion or by 26 percent. Spending after the 2005–2006 school year continued to increase to $17.26 billion in 2006–2007, to $18.34 billion in 2008–2009. This represents a 44 percent increase from 2002–2003 to 2007–2008. It should be noted that the figures from 1998–1999 to 2005–2006 are based on New York City Department of Education School Based Expenditure Reports, whereas the 2006–2007 and 2007–2008 figures come from Financial Status Reports. The two reports are calculated somewhat differently, but they are comparable. All of the above figures include all categories of spending with the exception of "pass-throughs" (funds diverted to non-public schools, largely special-education preschools).

During this same period, New York City public school enrollment declined slightly. In 1998–1999 the total student enrollment in New York City schools was 1,088,079. Enrollment increased slightly for the next two years and then decreased every year after 2000–2001. By 2006–2007 enrollment had fallen to 1,042,100 students, 45,879 fewer students than were enrolled in 1998–1999.

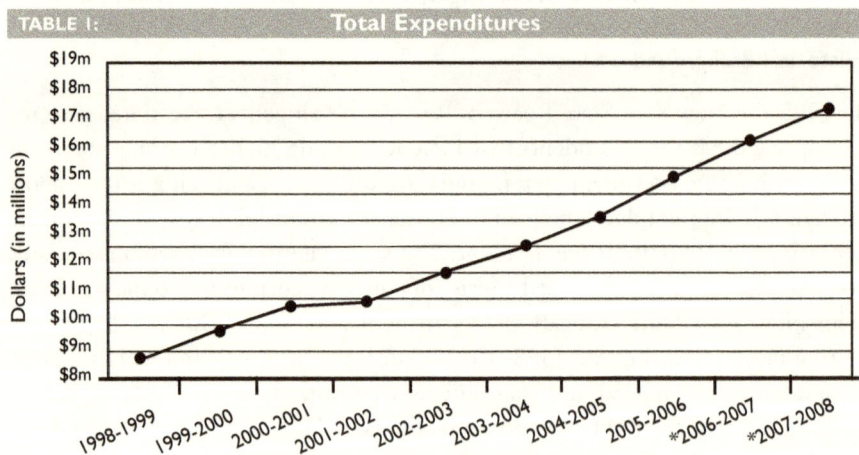

TABLE 1: Total Expenditures

* 2006-2007 and 2007-2008 do not exclude pass-throughs

TABLE 2: Total Enrollment (DOE)

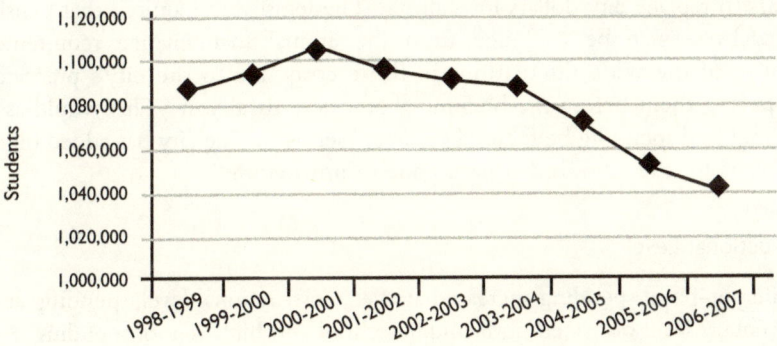

Declining enrollment, combined with the rise in spending, increased the per-pupil expenditures significantly. From 1998–1999 to 2002–2003 per-pupil spending rose from $8,957 to $11,640 or a $2,683 overall per-pupil increase, which represents an increase of $671 per student per year. Thus, from 1998–1999 to 2002–2003 the average per-pupil expenditure rose by 29 percent. From 2002–2003 to 2006–2007, per-pupil spending rose from $11,640 to $16,566 or a $4,926 increase, which represents an average annual per-pupil increase of $1,232. This is a per-pupil expenditure increase of 42 percent from 2002–2003 to 2006–2007. Overall, from 1998–1999 to 2006–2007, the average per-pupil expenditure rose by 85 percent, from $8,957 to $16,566. When controlling for inflation, per-pupil spending from 1998–1999 to 2006–2007 rose by 49 percent.

TABLE 3: Per Pupil Expenditures

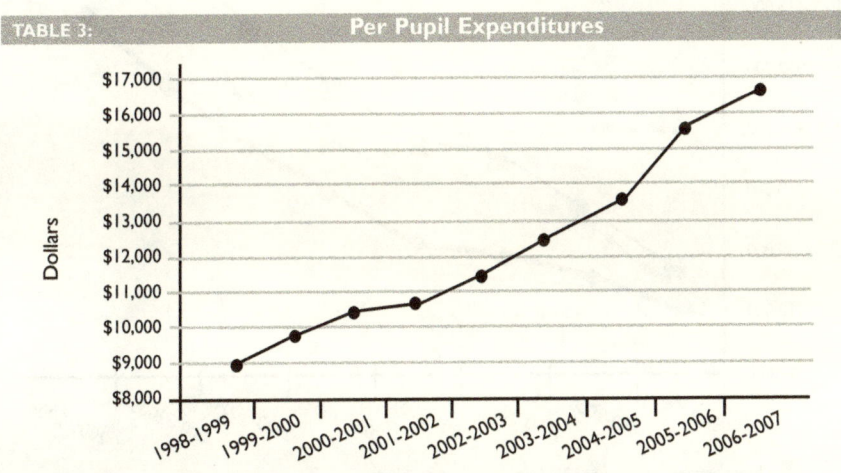

In 2002, the state passed the maintenance of effort law requiring the city to maintain its own level of school funding and preventing it from using state dollars to replace city dollars for schools. The legislature required that pensions and debt service be excluded from the annual maintenance requirements because of the wide fluctuations in those costs due to the city's practice of pre-paying them before the beginning of a new fiscal year. This would assure that required spending be focused on actual services. The city has added billions of dollars for the schools that have gone to instruction.

Instructional Level

While per-pupil spending increased at every instructional level, spending at the elementary level outpaced both middle-school and high-school spending. From 1998–1999 to 2002–2003 the per-pupil expenditure for elementary school increased by 37 percent. For middle school the per-pupil expenditure increased by 26 percent, and for high school it increase by 24 percent. From 2002–2003 to 2005-06 the increases for elementary, middle, and high school were 31 percent, 34 percent, and 31 percent, respectively. Per-pupil spending for elementary school students increased by 79 percent from 1998–1999 to 2005–2006. For middle school and high school the increase for the same time period was 69 percent and 62 percent respectively.

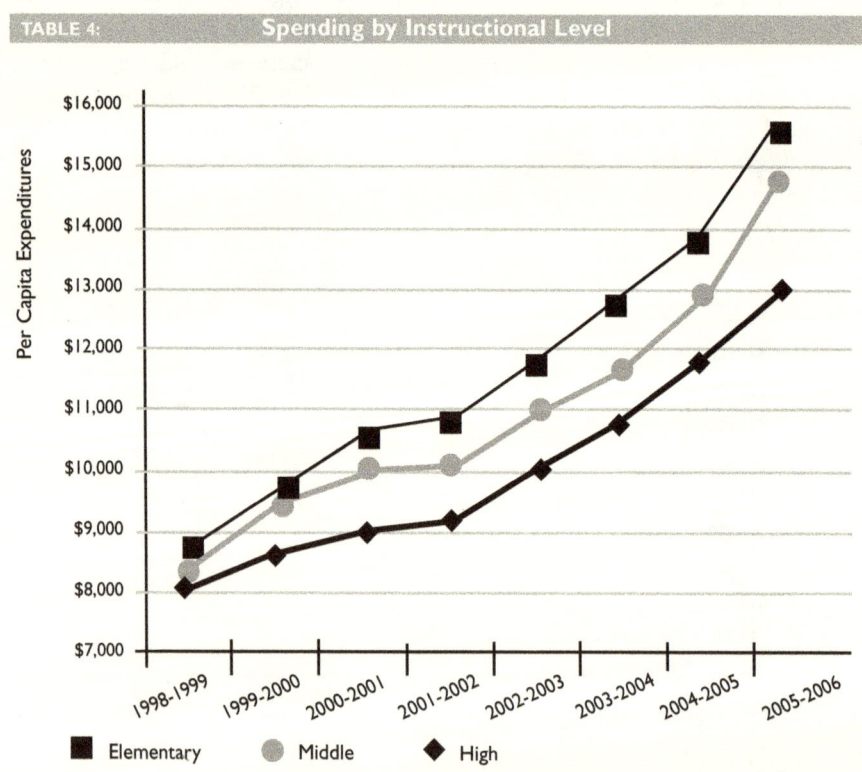

TABLE 4: Spending by Instructional Level

Revenue Sources

All sources of funds—city, state, and federal—rose significantly during the 1998–1999 to 2007–2008 period. City funds rose from $4.9 billion in 1998–1999 to $5.7 billion in 2002–2003, then to $9.97 billion in 2007–2008. State funds rose from $4.4 billion in 1998–1999 to $5.38 billion in 2002–2003, to $7.88 billion in 2007–2008. Federal funds rose from $1.07 billion in 1998–1999 to $1.58 billion in 2002–2003 and up to $1.89 billion in 2007–2008.

Test Results

From 1998–1999 to 2007–2008 the percentages of students scoring at levels 3 and 4 in the fourth and eighth grades in both English Language Arts (ELA) and mathematics increased. In 1998–1999, 32.7 percent of students in the fourth grade scored at levels 3 and 4 in ELA. In 2002–2003, 52.4 percent of students in the fourth grade scored at levels 3 and 4 in ELA. Thus, from 1998–1999 to 2002–2003, the period prior to mayoral reforms, the percentage of fourth-graders that scored at levels 3 and 4 increased by 19.7 percentage points. In 2007–2008, the percentage of fourth-grade students who scored at levels 3 and 4 continued to increase to 61.3 percent. This represents an 8.9 percentage-point gain from the five-year period from 2002–2003 to 2007–2008, the period after the implementation of mayoral reforms. The largest single-year gain made on the fourth-grade ELA occurred in 2004–2005, which saw a 9.9 point gain over the previous year's scores. The greatest decrease occurred in 2006–2007, when the percentage of students scoring at levels 3 and 4 declined by 2.9 points from the previous year. Overall, from 1998–1999 to 2007–2008, fourth-grade students scoring at levels 3 and 4 on the ELA exam increased by 28.6 percentage points.

Similar gains were made by fourth-graders in mathematics. From 1998–1999 to 2002–2003, prior to mayoral reforms, the percentage of fourth-graders at levels 3 and 4 went from 49.6 percent to 66.7 percent or a gain of 17.1 percentage points. Following mayoral reforms from 2002–2003 to 2007–2008, the percentage of fourth-graders at levels 3 and 4 in mathematics increased by 13 points from 66.7 percent to 79.7 percent. The greatest single-year increase was 14.7 percentage points and occurred in 2002–2003. The biggest one-year decrease in fourth-grade mathematics was 6.5 percentage points in 2005–2006. Overall, from 1998–1999 to 2007–2008, fourth-grade students scoring at levels 3 and 4 on the mathematics exam increased by 30.1 percentage points.

Prior to mayoral reforms, the percentage of eighth-grade students scoring at levels 3 and 4 on the ELA decreased by 2.7 percentage points from 1998–1999 to 2002–2003 (a drop from 35.2 percent to 32.5 percent). From 2002–2003 to 2007–2008 the percentage of eighth-grade students scoring at levels 3 and 4 increased from 32.5 percent to 43 percent, or an increase of 10.5 percentage points. The largest one-year gain occurred in 2005–2006, a 5.2 percentage-point increase. The greatest loss occurred in 2001–2002, which was a loss of 3.5

percentage points. From 1998–1999 to 2007–2008, eighth-grade students scoring at levels 3 and 4 on the ELA increased by 7.8 percentage points.

In 1998–1999, 22.8 percent of eighth-grade students scored at levels 3 and 4 in mathematics. In 2002–2003, 34.4 percent did so, which represents 11.6 percentage-point increase that occurred prior to mayoral reforms. From 2002–2003 to 2007–2008, the percentage of eighth-grade students scoring at levels 3 and 4 on the mathematics exam increased from 34.4 percent to 59.6 percent, a 25.2 percentage-point gain, occurring after mayoral reforms. The greatest single-year increase in eighth grade mathematics scores was 14 percentage points and occurred in 2007–2008. The biggest one-year decrease in eighth-grade mathematics was 1.9 percentage points in 2005–2006. Overall, from 1998–1999 to 2007–2008, eighth-grade students scoring at levels 3 and 4 on the mathematics exam increased by 36.8 percentage points.

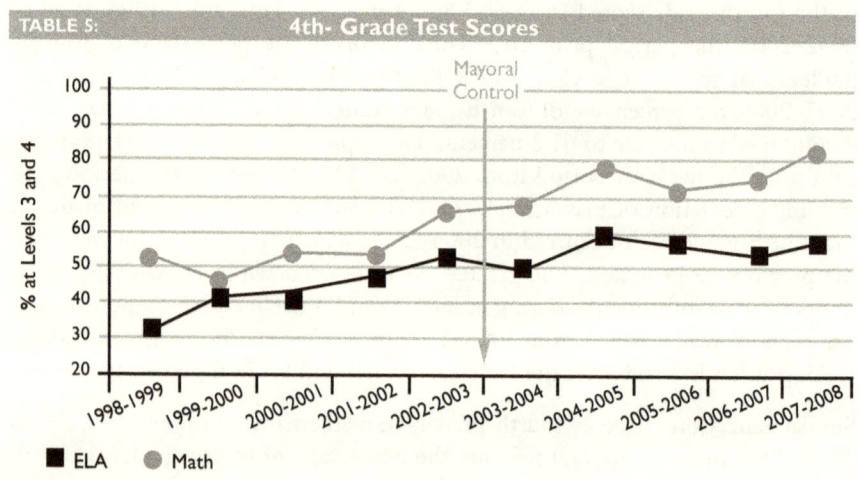

TABLE 5: 4th- Grade Test Scores

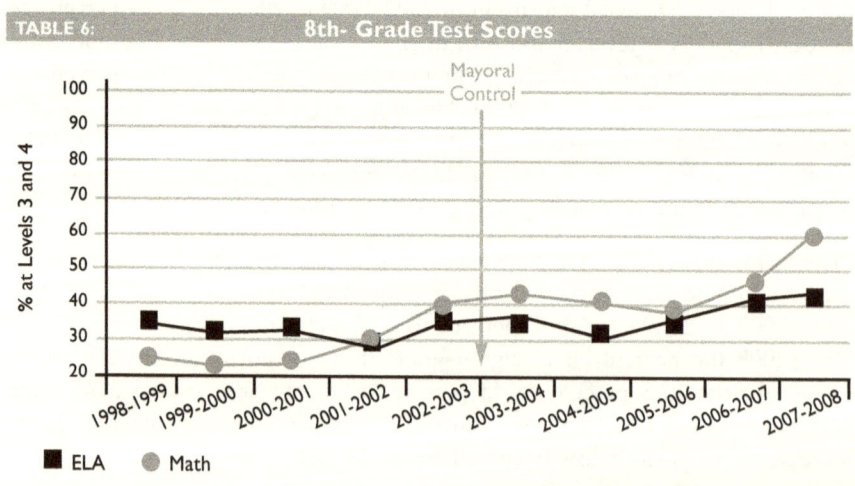

TABLE 6: 8th- Grade Test Scores

Proper Benchmarking of Test Results

In the years since mayoral control, Mayor Bloomberg and Chancellor Klein have claimed credit for improved student achievement based on rising test scores for New York City fourth- and eighth-graders compared with 2002 test results. However, the New York State legislature did not approve mayoral control of the schools until June 2002. Mayor Bloomberg announced his overhaul of the school system on January 15, 2003, at a New York Urban League Dr. Martin Luther King, Jr. symposium. This was one day after the eighth-grade ELA testing had begun and only three weeks before the fourth-grade tests. Following the announcement of the mayor's curriculum and administrative overhauls, the legal basis for some of the changes were challenged in a lawsuit. On June 13, 2003, after the administration of the fourth- and eighth-grade ELA and mathematics exams, an agreement to resolve the legal challenges was announced. Thus, substantive curricular, administrative, and instructional approaches to education were implemented by the Bloomberg administration in September 2003.

To be clear, since the school year begins in September but statewide tests are all administered in and after January, a test given in 2002 pertains to the 2001–2002 school year. Thus, in order to analyze student achievement under mayoral control of the schools, the 2003 scores from the 2002–2003 school year should be the reference point.

In 2003, 52.4 percent of New York City's fourth-grade students performed on the ELA at or above grade level. In September 2006, the DOE announced that the percentage of fourth-graders reading at or above grade level increased to 58.9 percent, marking a 6.5 percentage-point increase above the 2003 results. However the DOE claimed the 2002 to 2006 increases of 12.4 percentage points (from 46.5 percent to 58.9 percent), which is not the correct benchmark in relation to mayoral control. The 6.5 percent improvement still compares favorably with gains made statewide; however the margin reported by the Department of Education was overstated. New York City students outpaced the improvement rate of the New York statewide average by 2.2 percentage points, rather than the 7.1 percentage points noted in the DOE's September 21, 2006, press release. New York City schools did not double the rate of improvement vis à vis New York State as a whole, as they claimed.

Similarly, in 2003, 32.5 percent of New York City's eighth-grade students met or exceeded standards on the state ELA. The Department of Education claimed that the eighth-grade students at or exceeding standards increased by 7.1 percentage points when comparing 2006 to 2002 test scores. However, when correctly applying the 2003 scores as a baseline, the eighth-grade students increased their scores by a more modest 4.1 percentage points.

Conclusion

Educational achievement as measured by the state test scores of New York City public school students has improved significantly. To understand how new initiatives have contributed to these improvements, they must be examined in light of the impact they have had on cohorts of students over time. When viewed in this manner, many major school initiatives predate or are roughly contemporaneous with the onset of mayoral reforms.

About two-thirds of the improvements in fourth-grade test results predate the implementation of mayoral control. In 1998–1999, 32.7 percent of students scored at levels 3 and 4 on the ELA test; in 2002–2003 52.4 percent reach those levels. By 2007–2008, 61.5 percent have reached levels 3 and 4. In 1998–1999 49.6 percent of students score 3 and 4 in mathematics; by 2002–2003, 66.7 percent reach those levels. By 2007–2008, 79.7 percent score at levels 3 and 4. Furthermore, the National Assessment of Educational Progress (NAEP) results confirm the 1998–2003 gains in New York, but not those of 2003–2008.

Contemporaneously, pre-Kindergarten enrollments were rising rapidly as the state universal pre-Kindergarten program was implemented, and early grade class sizes were reduced from about twenty-five to nearly twenty-one before the mayor's program began. Pre-Kindergarten enrollment rose from 14,000 in 1997 to 24,000 in 1998; 34,000 in 1999 and 41,000 in 2000; to 42,000 in 2002. A comprehensive summer school program for students needing help was developed in the years immediately preceding mayoral control and already incorporated into the system. New reading, mathematics, and academic intervention services were introduced and expanded as a result of state initiatives, and professional development expenditures increased by 179 percent and teacher compensation increased by 40 percent. The cohorts of students affected by these policies, as they reach the fourth and eighth grades in later years, perform substantially better than earlier groups of students.[3] From a spending perspective, Mayor Bloomberg's main contribution was substantially increased teacher compensation.

Mayor Bloomberg and Chancellor Klein regionalized the former school districts in 2003–2004, and directed regional superintendents, local instructional superintendents, and curriculum coaches to form a new supervisory system to oversee teaching and learning. The mayor and chancellor introduced new accountability initiatives and empowerment schools in the 2006–2007 school year, but generally speaking the overwhelming proportion of student improvements in the past ten years had already occurred by 2006–2007, and new reforms had little relevance to improved student achievement. Far more relevant is the doubling of spending, with teacher compensation, early childhood initiatives, and elementary school investments paving the way for a strengthened foundation for learning.

1. This chapter was written with Shawn Campbell, Legislative Aide. It is a condensation of Assemblymember Brennan's report "New York City Public School Achievement Before and After Mayoral Control," January 28, 2009, www.assembly.state.ny.us/member_files/044/20090128.

2. Fourth- and eighth-grade tests are notable benchmarks. The fourth grade test scores demonstrate the extent to which children have gained the skills that will prepare them for higher learning. Eighth-grade results demonstrate high-school readiness. In 2005–2006, the New York State Education Department expanded English Language Arts (ELA) and mathematics testing to grades three through eight; these tests were previously administered only by the city.

3. Our full report details increased investments in pre-Kindergarten, early grade class size reduction, curriculum programs, summer school, professional development and teacher compensation, and demonstrates the relationship between these investments and student achievement.

Institutional Cheating

- Sol Stern and Andrew Wolf

Recently, the New Jersey town of Fort Lee was in the news. It seems that students there have been getting unusually high grades, and as a result more and more of them are being admitted to the most prestigious colleges.

Are students in Fort Lee really getting smarter? Unfortunately not. It turns out they got a bit of an assist from a benevolent guidance counselor with a big eraser, changing grades on student transcripts to give them a leg up in the college admissions process.[1]

Cheating is as old as testing. As long as standardized tests have been used to measure academic achievement and the tests have had consequences, students have had an incentive to copy answers from their neighbors, smuggle in crib sheets, and even steal advance copies of exams. But increasingly it is not the students alone who benefit from improving test outcomes. Under the Bloomberg/Klein administration student test scores and graduation rates have been tied to teacher and principal salaries and promotions as well as school closures. This creates clear potential for conflicts of interest among teachers and administrators that requires extra monitoring. The problem is that in New York City under mayoral control there is *less* monitoring to detect cheating than there was before.

Regrettably, New York State has repeatedly been cited for a widening gap between results on the standardized tests that the State Education Department administers in grades three through eight and the NAEP (National Assessment of Educational Progress) also known as the "nation's report card." Moreover, even as student scores on the state tests continue to climb, the improvements are not mirrored in better outcomes on key standardized measures such as the SAT. These results can have several causes, such as easier state tests and more forgiving means of calculating the results, but they might also be evidence of cheating.

Furthermore, although the change to mayoral control was supposed to bring greater accountability to New York City's education system, one unintended consequence was tying the mayor's own political fortunes to rising test scores. Both the mayor and the principals that he is now supposed to supervise have a mutual interest in driving test scores up—sometimes by any means necessary.

Without any independent oversight, this lethal combination could undermine the integrity of the testing system. This hypothetical danger was realized during Mayor Bloomberg's first reelection campaign.

One morning in May 2005, the mayor's office bused the City Hall press corps to PS 33, an elementary school in one of the Bronx's poorest neighborhoods. In the school's auditorium, overflowing with happy children and teachers, the mayor proclaimed a miracle. With a student enrollment that was 95 percent Hispanic and Black, and with 100 percent of the students poor enough to qualify for free lunch, PS 33 had hit the jackpot on the state's fourth-grade reading test. Over 83 percent of the school's 140 fourth-graders scored at or above proficiency (or grade level), the mayor explained, compared with only 35.8 percent in 2004—an unheard-of one-year gain of close to 50 percentage points. The school's spectacular test-score results were just four percentage points below the average for the richest suburban districts in the state. In one giant leap the kids of the South Bronx had achieved Scarsdale academic outcomes.

The PS 33 success story was the cherry topping a very sweet election-year gift for Mayor Bloomberg. At the press conference, he was also able to report "historic" and "record-breaking" gains in reading all across the city—59.5 percent of all Gotham fourth-graders had achieved proficiency on the state test, a gain of nearly 10 percentage points from the year before. The test results proved, the mayor contended, that his education reforms "really are paying off for those who were previously left behind."

Media coverage the next day echoed the mayor's claims. It was clear that mayoral candidate Bloomberg had hit a home run right on the home field of his likeliest Democratic challenger, Bronx Borough President Fernando Ferrer. Bloomberg eventually went on to trounce Ferrer in the general election just five months later. It is important to note that once this dramatic press event was held at PS 33, the education issue was effectively removed from campaign discussion and debate from that day forward, as the mayor's opponents were unable to argue with such impressive indicators of "success."

When the 2006 reading scores on the state tests came out one year later, Mayor Bloomberg was in California, burnishing his national political image and spreading the gospel about the benefits of mayoral control of urban school districts. It was up to Chancellor Joel Klein to discuss the 2006 results at a reporters' "roundtable" at his Tweed Courthouse headquarters (no gala press conference that year, no miracle schools to visit). Klein acknowledged that fourth-grade reading was down slightly overall but noted that Gotham remained ahead of most of the state's urban districts. And though eighth-grade reading was still dreadfully low—only 36.6 percent of city students had attained proficiency—it was up three points over 2005.

The city's education reporters seemed rather incurious about what happened to the PS 33 fourth-graders whom they celebrated as heroes a year earlier. That's too bad, because it would have been easy to find out. The reporters certainly knew that the federal No Child Left Behind law now required state education authorities to test students in grades three through eight and make the scores public. Thus, for the first time it was possible to track a student cohort's test scores on the same battery of state tests as they moved from grade to grade.

It was now clear that the miraculous achievement of PS 33's fourth-graders in 2005 almost completely evaporated in 2006, with the pass rate of those same students plummeting back to 41.1 percent in the fifth grade. The 2006 fourth-graders at the school achieved proficiency at only a 47.5 percent rate. The miracle of 2005 was not a miracle at all, just an election-year opportunity to make political hay.

Put aside the raw numbers and consider the human consequences of this discrepancy. One year the Mayor publicly honored 120 poor Hispanic and Black children for beating the odds and acing the reading test. A year later, half of those kids discovered that they were failures after all. In 2005 they shone as stars of a mayoral campaign. In 2006 they were truly "left behind."

No one from City Hall or the DOE came to the school to explain how so many kids could be high achievers one year and failures the next. Nor was the school's miracle principal, Elba Lopez, around to explain the shocking setback to the parents. After the mayor's triumphant press conference in May 2005 she retired, collecting a $15,000 bonus for her school's spectacular test score performance, thus boosting her pension by an estimated $12,000 a year for life.

With no plausible explanation for the sudden jump in scores and then the melt-down, it is hard to avoid the conclusion that it happened as the result of some adult manipulation. In fact, the school's wildly fluctuating test numbers were so unbelievable that this story should have immediately attracted the attention of state education authorities.

Indeed, if Mayor Bloomberg had really introduced accountability into the city's education system, the implausible PS 33 scores would have immediately raised red flags at the DOE and perhaps even prompted a fraud referral to the city's Special Commissioner of Investigation for the New York City School District. But in 2005, as the man in charge of both the schools and the appointing officer for the Special Investigator, the mayor—candidate for reelection—had no interest in challenging these apparent gains.

Before mayoral control, under the old "unaccountable" Board of Education, the then-Special Commissioner of Investigation, the late Edward Stancik, would have likely investigated such an improbable fluctuation in test scores. In fact, in 1999, in a widely reported incident, a number of principals and teachers were accused of cheating on behalf of their students based on test gains less than half of those achieved by the PS 33 fourth-graders. Commissioner Stancik personally took an interest in the case, the charges were thoroughly investigated, and the perpetrators of the cheating scam were suspended from their positions.

After both of us published articles in 2006 about the suspicious test scores at PS 33, the DOE was finally forced to take a second look. Chancellor Klein concluded in December 2006 that enough evidence of possible fraud existed to ask DOE counsel Michael Best to make a referral to the Special Commissioner of Investigations.

Yet the DOE counsel subsequently claimed that he somehow "forgot" to make the referral. "I just goofed," said Mr. Best in acknowledging the delay to Sol Stern in June 2007. The referral was finally made, but only after another inquiry by Andrew Wolf. The Commissioner immediately, and in our opinion wrongly, then sent the referral back to DOE without any action.

According to the DOE, after the allegations of cheating at PS 33 were referred back by the Special Commissioner, it began its own investigation. A Utah-based company called Caveon Test Security has developed a "data forensics computer analysis" of test scores, and has won contracts in eleven states. Unfortunately, because of the department's practice of destroying test documents within a year of the date of the test, it was not possible to conduct a forensic examination of the PS 33 test papers to detect cheating. That left DOE investigators with only the word of the very interested parties at PS 33.

As of this writing, almost three years after the 2006 test scores were released, the DOE claims it has interviewed many PS 33 students, parents, and teachers, as well as principal Lopez, but no report on the case has been issued. With the mayor now in an election campaign for a third term, it's unlikely that his administration will be looking to shine a light on how the PS 33 "miracle" helped him win the last election.

It may or may not be relevant that the current Special Commissioner of Investigation, Richard Condon, is also a mayoral appointee, and reports only to the chancellor and to the commissioner of Investigation, who is herself a mayoral appointee. (The 1990 executive order that created the Office of the Special Commissioner called for its independence from the then-governing body, the School Board).[2] Condon has, to our knowledge, investigated few cheating allegations in recent years, and has released reports on only a small number, 6 to 8 percent, of substantiated reports of malfeasance to the public.[3] He reports on substantiated allegations only to the chancellor and the commissioner of investigation, although his mandate calls for regular reporting to the Board of Education (now renamed the Panel for Educational Policy) and an annual report following up on past allegations.

In one of the few incidents of cheating investigated by the Special Commissioner in recent years, an assistant principal at the High School for Contemporary Arts in the Bronx was found to have erased incorrect answers on students' Regents exams and replaced them with correct ones. The school had received an "A" on its recent report card, based in large part on its Regents results, and yet the DOE refused to change that grade, as its spokesperson said that the school had "performed so well by other measures that it would retain its grade even after an adjustment based on Mr. Condon's findings."[4]

An even more telling indicator of the DOE's institutional attitude towards cheating was its response to the revelation by the *New York Daily News* that the principal at Middle School 8 in Queens, John Murphy, was accused by several teachers of browbeating them into inflating grades in order to get a higher grade on the school's DOE report card. According to Melissa Weber, an eighth-grade social studies teacher, the teachers were told by Murphy, "that we could not fail a child under any circumstances." The *Daily News* reported that "Weber said she found out the hard way how important that was to Murphy after she failed five of her 120 students last year . . . 'I was called into his office and asked how dare I not follow a directive,' Weber recounted. 'He explained to me that I had to change them . . . I was afraid that I was going be fired if I didn't.'"

The *Daily News* story did not temper the enthusiasm of the DOE for its principal. According to Department of Education spokesperson David Cantor, "Under Principal Murphy, (MS) 8 has improved from a 'D' to a 'B,' and the school just came off the state's list of failing schools." What is the message about cheating sent by the leadership of the New York City school system when a principal, accused of strong-arming teachers to inflate grades, is praised by the department's public relations spokesperson for his "success in raising test scores?"

The fortunes of adults working in the city school system—from the mayor on down—are also bolstered by claims of higher graduation rates. But it is increasingly evident that the DOE's assertions that many more students are now graduating on time have at least partly been fueled by a bit of institutional cheating called "credit recovery" or "seat time." Students who fail a course required for graduation are given an opportunity to make up for their poor performance by showing up for a few Saturday sessions or by turning in a "project." With the open encouragement of the DOE, high school principals have used this questionable practices to pad their four-year graduation statistics (which also affect the grade the school gets on the DOE report card and can lead to the principals receiving hefty cash bonuses). Though technically legal, the practice of credit recovery has been so abused that it has become another example of cheating for the purpose of advancing the political and financial interests of the adults in the system.

Mayor Bloomberg has often boasted that one of the greatest accomplishments of mayoral control was that it enabled him to end forever the practice of "social promotion" in the elementary school grades. But it is now clear that between gimmicks like "credit recovery" and principals bullying teachers not to fail students, Bloomberg's schools are practicing a massive form of "social promotion" in the twelfth grade. Pumping up graduation rates is great for the mayor and chancellor and some principals, but unfortunately does little for the students, as evidenced by their recent poor results on City University of New York placement tests at the community colleges. With some three quarters of these "high school graduates" failing these basic exams, we witness the true cost of this new form of institutional cheating.

Ironically—at least in the area of testing—there was greater accountability under the old Board of Education than under mayoral control. Before test documents were destroyed, the Board routinely conducted several levels of analysis to detect cheating. Robert Tobias, former director of testing and assessment for the BOE, provided us with the following summary of the Board's procedures to screen for possible cheating:

> One was an erasure analysis that identified classes and schools with a high incidence of answers that were erased and changed from wrong to right. A second was a gains analysis that identified schools where students showed extremely high increases in test scores over the previous year. The third was an item analysis that detected unusual scoring patterns, such as large numbers of students who answered difficult questions correctly but easy questions incorrectly. In addition to these forensic analyses, we collected information on allegations of cheating from District Assessment Liaisons and other informants.
>
> When this information raised credible suspicion, we placed the respective test answer documents in secure storage, referred the matter to the Office of Special Investigations, and did not destroy the test documents until the investigation was completed. In other instances, we were directed to send the test documents to the State Education Department or the Special Investigator for the NYC Public Schools to facilitate investigations of cheating allegations referred directly to them. These procedures were in place when I retired from the public schools in Nov. 2001.

The practices described by Robert Tobias were just one layer of the safeguards known before the advent of mayoral control—safeguards that seem to have vanished.

It was also the practice of the old Board of Education to dispatch district administrators to each school on test days to oversee procedures. They would check on whether the tests were stored in a secure place in unopened cartons, observe the opening of the cartons and removal of the shrink wrap on the exams, and monitor the distribution and collection of the test materials. Finally they would oversee the delivery of the completed test papers to the district office.

This was not exactly an iron-clad system, as proven by a number of incidents of cheating that took place over the years, but it was a far higher level of security than the system that is in place today. The dissolution of the district and regional office staffs as part of the Bloomberg reforms has had the effect of eliminating even this minimal level of oversight.

Some years ago, when confronted with a computer analysis that disclosed probable cheating, the head of one American big city school system, at grave political risk to himself and the mayor who appointed him, decided to retest 120 of the classrooms, a mix of suspected cheaters and a control group. As predicted, pupils in the classrooms where cheating was suspected did a lot worse the second time around, and those in the control classes replicated their original results. A number of teachers lost their jobs.

The incident was recounted in the best-selling book *Freakonomics,* and involved the then-chief executive officer of the Chicago school system, Arne Duncan, now President Obama's Secretary of Education. It is to be hoped that as the nation's number-one education leader Secretary Duncan maintains these standards and requires school districts and states to strengthen their oversight.

As we completed this essay, we noted an article in *The New York Post* of March 12, 2009, that seemed like déjà vu all over again. The paper reported that at MS 234 in Washington Heights, teachers were awarded $3,000 bonuses for their increased scores, as "the percentage of students meeting math standards jumped to 71 percent from 39 percent the year before," according to the *Post*.[5] A 32 percentage point gain in proficiency is almost as unprecedented as were PS 33's gains in the 2005 election year. To our knowledge, no attempt has been made by the Special Investigator or those at the DOE to investigate these claims.

With more stories of "miracle" results sure to come in this election year, the public should insist on some means of ensuring that such miracles are real, before New Yorkers again celebrate what might be nothing more than a grand deception.

NOTES

1. "Fort Lee School Officials Investigating Possible Grade Manipulation," *Associated Press,* March 3, 2009.

2. Executive Order No. 11, Office of the Mayor, June 28, 1990, "Deputy Commissioner

of Investigation for the City School District of the City of New York" available at: http://parentadvocates.org/nicemedia/documents/ExecutiveOrder.pdf.

3. *See* http://www.nycsci.org/public/Executive%20Order.pdf. See also Leonie Haimson, "What corruption is the Special Investigator keeping from us, and why?" NYC Public School Parents blog, December 8, 2008, http://nycpublicschool parents.blogspot.com/2008/12/what-corruption-is-special-investigator.html, and Elizabeth Green, "When the DOE Is Investigated, Who Should Hear About It?" Gotham Schools, December 22, 2008; http://gothamschools.org/2008/12/22/when-the-doe-is-investigated-who-should-hear-about-it/.

4. Elissa Gootman, "School Official to be Fired After Cheating is Found," *The New York Times,* December 3, 2008.

5. Carl Campanile, "NY Teachers Who Share in $uccess," *New York Post,* March 12, 2009.

Student Civil Rights

- Udi Ofer

During the past seven years, public school parents, students, and educators have clashed with Mayor Bloomberg on numerous civil rights issues. These disputes have raised important questions about whether the Bloomberg administration has abdicated its responsibility to provide a sound education to all students, regardless of race, ethnicity, religion, gender, socioeconomic status, or sexual orientation.

This chapter will focus on three civil rights challenges faced by students and parents during Mayor Bloomberg and Chancellor Klein's tenure: the over-policing of schools and its contribution to the so-called "school to prison pipeline"; overaggressive military recruitment in schools; and bias-based harassment in schools. Moreover, it examines the impact that the 2002 changes to New York City's school governance structure has had on the ability of parents, educators, and even the City Council to respond to civil rights problems that arise in the schools.

Over-Policing and the School to Prison Pipeline

On January 17, 2008, Dennis Rivera, a 5-year-old kindergarten student at PS 81 in Queens, threw a temper tantrum. According to the DOE, Dennis was taken to the principal's office, where he knocked several items off a desk. In response, School Safety Agents—police personnel who are assigned to schools with the authority to stop, search, and arrest students—handcuffed Dennis's hands behind his back and hauled him off to a psychiatric ward.[1]

Dennis's case is shocking, yet unfortunately not unique. In March 2007, School Safety Agents handcuffed and arrested thirteen-year-old Chelsea Fraser in front of her classmates at her Dyker Heights school. Her crime? She wrote the word "okay" on her desk.[2]

Also in 2007, Mark Federman, the principal at East Side Community High School in Manhattan, was arrested for pleading with the police not to escort a handcuffed honor roll student out of the school's front door in front of her classmates.[3]

The above examples—and they are just a few of many such incidents that have occurred in recent years—are clear indicators of a broken school policing system.

They are also the product of years of education and public safety policies that have taken school discipline away from educators and handed them overto the Police Department, with damaging consequences to the educational environment and students' adolescent development.[4]

Emergence of Police Tactics in City Schools

In 1998, Mayor Giuliani transferred school security responsibilities from the Board of Education to the NYPD, amidst promises that School Safety Agents would not arrest students.[5] Since the transfer, and long after Mayor Giuliani's departure, the handling of minor discipline matters in the city's neediest schools is now resulting in increased numbers of serious confrontations with police personnel, sometimes followed by students being arrested, summoned to court, and sent to jail.[6]

A significant contributor to such new aggressive policing tactics is the dramatic increase in the number of police personnel patrolling school hallways. The number of School Safety Agents in city schools has increased by 64 percent since 1998—from 3,200 to 5,246—with the growth most rapid under Mayor Bloomberg, making the NYPD's School Safety Division the fifth largest police force in the country. Houston, with a population of 2.2 million, has a smaller police force than New York City schools, which have a population of just over 1 million students.

TABLE 1: Police Officers in Major Cities vs. Police Personnel in NYC Schools

City	Number
BOSTON	2,056
LAS VEGAS	2,231
DETROIT	3,164
WASHINGTON, DC	3,799
NYPD SCHOOL SAFETY DIVISION	5,200

Source: ACLU/NYCLU analysis of data from Department of Justice, Federal Bureau of Investigations, "Crime in the United States," Table 78

The DOE now spends 65 percent more per year—an additional $88 million this year alone—than it did in 2002 on school safety, despite the fact that enrollment has decreased over the same period.

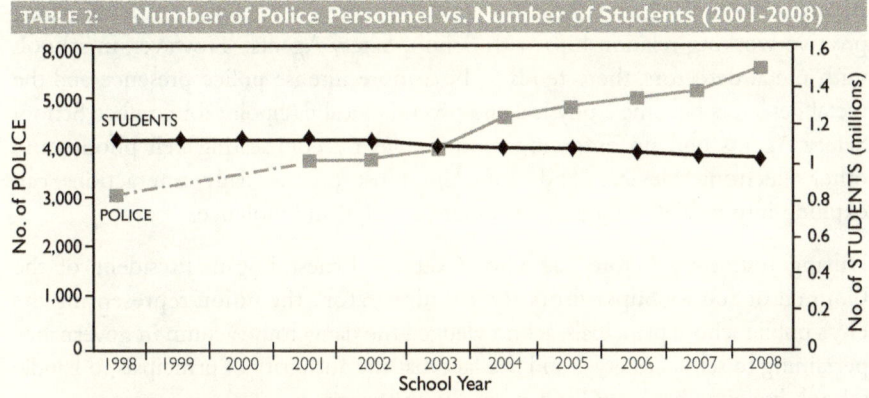

TABLE 2: Number of Police Personnel vs. Number of Students (2001-2008)

Note: Police personnel data were not available for 1999 and 2000.
Sources: Annual Mayor's Management Reports, correspondence with NYPD, City Council hearings, and news articles.
© Annenberg Institute for School Reform

Along with the steep increase in the number of police personnel, there has also been a significant increase in the number of students receiving superintendent suspensions, which are out-of-school suspensions for longer than five days. From 2000 to 2005, superintendent suspensions increased by 76 percent.

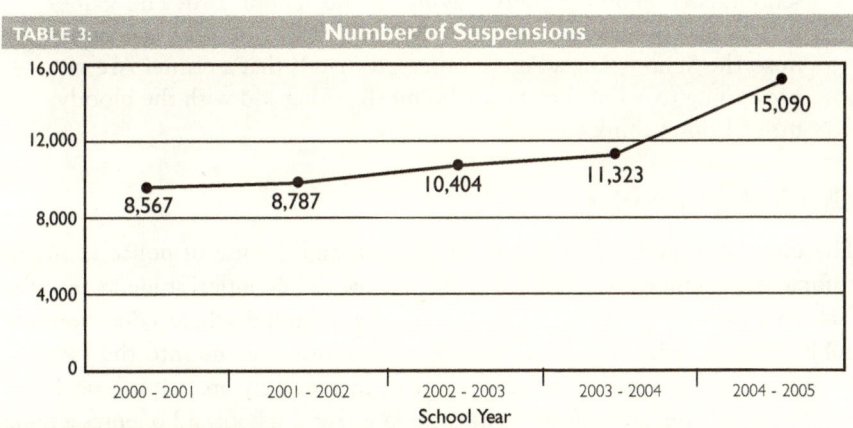

TABLE 3: Number of Suspensions

Source: NYC Department of Education

No Governance Structure Regulating Police Activities in Schools

Coupled with the dramatic increase in the number of police personnel is the lack of an official set of rules that govern the police's responsibilities and tactics in the schools. The relationship between the NYPD and the DOE in matters of school safety was initially defined in a 1998 Memorandum of Understanding. Yet the 1998 MOU expired in 2002 and has not been renewed.[7]

With no clear written policy detailing the relationship between School Safety Agents and the larger school community, their interactions with students vary widely.

In many schools—generally schools *without* metal detectors—students report positive working relationships with School Safety Agents. However, in schools with metal detectors, there tends to be a more intense police presence and the metal detectors become a physical and psychological flashpoint for conflict. School Safety Agents end up enforcing school rules by confiscating cell phones and other electronic devices, and even the most prosaic daily interactions can explode into power struggles, misunderstandings, and violence.

During testimony before the City Council, Ernest Logan, President of the Council of School Supervisors and Administrators, the union representing the city's public school principals, acknowledged the dangerous vacuum in governance pertaining to school safety—and the fact that the authority of principals to handle school discipline has been fundamentally undermined:

> Many of you have said that you have heard confusion here today at the City Council when people were asking questions about the DOE and the Police Department. Well, if you have confusion here at the City Council, imagine the confusion in 1,400 schools of how this is supposed to work.
>
> …Every incident is unique, but I am truly troubled by the fact that we are criminalizing our children…I know there is a principal of a school, two second graders playing in the school yard. The game gets heated, Jonnie hits Michael, Michael winds up with a bloody nose, the School Safety Agent observed that. Is that a crime? Are we now going to arrest the child who hit the other kid with the bloody nose? I don't think so.[8]

Police Feeding the Pipeline

The increase in police presence in the schools and the use of police tactics to enforce even minor non-criminal violations has fed countless students into the "school to prison pipeline," an alarming national trend where education and public safety policies are pushing youth out of classrooms and into the juvenile justice system. Schools across the country increasingly are relying on harsh discipline and even law enforcement to address trivial schoolyard offenses among even the youngest students.[9] Children of color and children with disabilities bear the brunt of these disturbing trends.[10]

In New York City, Mayor Bloomberg has expanded on the school-policing program begun by Mayor Giuliani, bringing the "broken windows" practice of policing—cracking down heavily on minor quality of life violators and punishing them to the fullest extent of the law—into the schools. In schools with metal detectors, which have proliferated in recent years, students are disproportionately poor, black, and Latino, and they are more often confronted by police personnel in school for "non-criminal" incidents than their peers citywide, often leading to suspension and sometimes arrest. In these schools, misbehavior that a generation ago was treated as an internal disciplinary matter is now being handled by the police.

Students, parents, and education advocates have repeatedly attempted to open a dialogue with Mayor Bloomberg or Chancellor Klein about school policing practices, but to no avail. In frustration, numerous organizations—including the Drum Major Institute and New York University's Wagner School for Public Service—have released reports critical of school safety practices in an attempt to educate the public and policymakers about this important civil rights issue.[11]

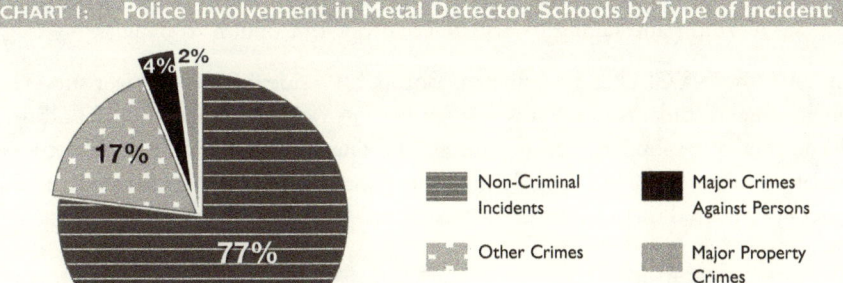

CHART 1: Police Involvement in Metal Detector Schools by Type of Incident

- Non-Criminal Incidents
- Major Crimes Against Persons
- Other Crimes
- Major Property Crimes

Source: ACLU/NYCLU analysis of 2004-2005 annual School Reports

In 2007, more than a dozen organizations came together to launch the Student Safety Coalition to combat the school to prison pipeline in New York City and its disproportionate impact on youth of color. Made up of national and local civil rights, education, and community-based organizations, the coalition drafted the Student Safety Act, which would extend the jurisdiction of the Civilian Complaint Review Board to cover complaints of misconduct levied against School Safety Agents and require quarterly reporting by the DOE and NYPD on school safety issues, including incidents leading to the arrest, expulsion, or suspension of students.[12]

In August 2008, the bill was introduced with the co-sponsorship of a majority of City Council members. Unfortunately, despite its overwhelming support, the legislation is yet to receive a single hearing in the City Council.

Unchecked Military Recruitment Activities in Schools

The passage of the federal No Child Left Behind Act of 2001 (NCLB) changed the landscape of military recruitment activities in public high schools across the nation, forcing schools to open their doors to recruiters and giving the military personal information on millions of students.[13]

While a military career may be a positive option for many students, enlistment is a life-changing decision that should be made based on sound information and in consultation with parents, rather than aggressive tactics or manipulation. To ensure that children are not inappropriately targeted by the military, school districts throughout the country have adopted policies regulating military recruiters' access to schools and enhancing the privacy protections of students.

In New York City, educators, students, and parents have complained that the DOE has failed to protect students from the military's heavy-handed recruitment tactics, particularly of poor children and children of color. They cite numerous examples of the DOE's inadequate protections, such as allowing military recruiters to take up precious class time in schools that almost never see a college recruiter and failing to distribute an opt-out option to parents.

In 2007, the NYCLU and Manhattan Borough President Scott Stringer surveyed one thousand students in schools frequently visited by the military and found that 40 percent of respondents did not receive a military recruitment opt-out form—a violation of the No Child Left Behind Act. More than one in five respondents (21 percent) reported that class time had been used by military recruiters.[14]

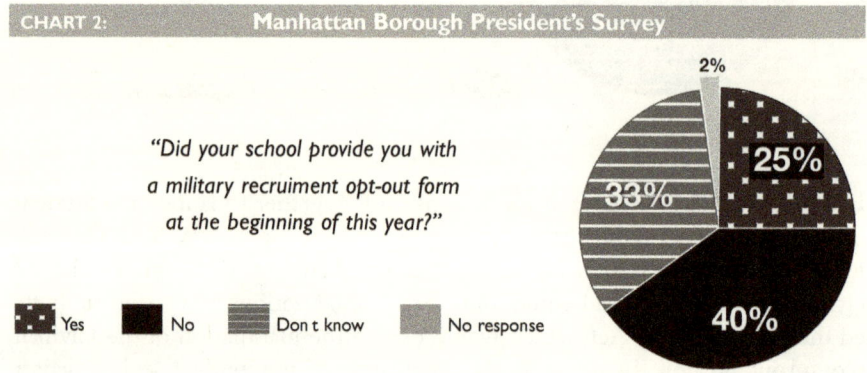

CHART 2: Manhattan Borough President's Survey

"Did your school provide you with a military recruitment opt-out form at the beginning of this year?"

2%
25%
33%
40%

Yes No Don t know No response

Rather than respond to parents' and students' requests for greater privacy protections, in September 2008 the DOE actually made it easier for the military to obtain student information by centralizing and streamlining the information-gathering process and providing recruiters with the contact information for all eleventh- and twelfth-grade public school students who had not signed opt-out forms. Whereas in the past military recruiters had to obtain information from each individual high school, now the central DOE had become a one-stop repository of information for the military. Acting as it has on other matters pertaining to students' civil rights, the DOE enacted this major policy change without any parent or public input.[15]

On November 24, 2008, Congressman Charles Rangel sent a letter to Chancellor Klein expressing concern that the DOE was not sufficiently protecting students from aggressive military recruiters. The letter was co-signed by twenty-six elected officials, including nine members of Congress, the Public Advocate, the

Bronx and Manhattan Borough Presidents, six state Senate and Assembly members, and nine City Council members. These elected officials asked Klein to allow parents, students, and educators to work together to develop a better policy to meet NCLB's recruitment requirements, and they provided the Chancellor with a detailed list of recommendations that would comply with federal law while protecting students' privacy rights.[16]

While Chancellor Klein acknowledged receipt of the letter, he did not respond to any of the recommendations made by Congressman Rangel and the twenty-six other elected officials.

Bias-Based Harassment in Schools

Harassment and bullying routinely occur in public schools throughout New York City. Students are harassed and even assaulted based on their actual or perceived race, national origin, ethnicity, religion, disability, sexual orientation, and gender.

Osama al-Najjar, a 16-year-old student at Tottenville High School in Staten Island, plunged into a deep depression and tried to commit suicide because he was incessantly referred to as Osama bin Laden. His parents claim their son was constantly harassed by teachers while school officials did nothing.[17]

Sikh student Harpal Singh Vacher, a freshman at Newtown High School in Elmhurst, was attacked and wrestled to the ground by another student, who forcefully cut off his waist-length hair. In accordance with the Sikh religion, his hair had never before been cut.[18]

Students who are routinely harassed and bullied often struggle to develop the self-confidence and social skills needed to succeed in life. They become more likely to skip school or perform poorly in class. In some cases, they become unable to cope with school altogether and drop out. Bullied and harassed students are also more likely to engage in high-risk behaviors, such as abusing drugs and alcohol.

According to the DOE's School Environment Survey Report for 2006–2007, 76 percent of sixth- to twelfth-grade students reported seeing students "threaten or bully other students at school."[19]

Despite this widespread phenomenon, Mayor Bloomberg has refused to address fully the problem of bias-based harassment in our schools and has indeed actively impeded city government efforts to address it. On June 29, 2004, the City Council passed the Dignity for All Schools Act (DASA) in an attempt to create a harassment-free environment in schools. The act requires school officials to record and track harassment incidents and to publish an annual summary of all cases. It also requires all school staff to receive regular training on how to prevent and respond to harassment.[20]

Mayor Bloomberg vetoed the legislation, arguing that harassment was already prohibited and that the legislation exceeded the council's authority. The council overrode his veto by a vote of 43 to 3, but Mayor Bloomberg has refused to implement DASA, arguing that the City Council—and thus city law—has no jurisdiction over education policy. As a result, students throughout the city continue to be degraded and hurt by their peers.

Only recently, after several organized protests by a number of community groups, has the DOE taken any steps to address this severe problem—while still refusing fully to implement DASA. On September 3, 2008, the DOE issued Chancellor's Regulation A-832 to prohibit harassment and bullying in schools. The new regulation came after two high-profile attacks on Sikh students in Queens. It was a step forward for the DOE, finally prohibiting bias-based harassment, and establishing a process to bring and investigate complaints of such harassment.[21] But the regulation falls short of full enforcement of DASA by failing to prohibit bias-based harassment by all individuals in schools; failing to require annual reporting on the number and nature of bias-based incidents; and failing to mandate regular trainings.[22]

Mayor Bloomberg has refused to address fully the pervasive problem of bias-based harassment in the schools. His failure leaves too many teachers and administrators ill-equipped to recognize and prevent this widespread phenomenon and leaves too many students at the mercy of bullies.

Unilateral Executive Authority

The changes made by the state legislature in 2002 to New York City's school governance structure have created a system that has centralized control over educational policies in the hands of a few people. Today's governance system is significantly less accountable to the public and far less approachable than the system in place before it. What in the past was a sprawling bureaucracy is now a staggering consolidation of power that excludes outsiders, including parents, educators, and even local lawmakers, from most meaningful participation. The system in place today has also made it extremely difficult for parents to protect their children's civil rights.

The DOE has repeatedly taken the position that it is answerable to no one but the chancellor and mayor, including city laws and the City Council. The DOE has denied or ignored requests made under the Freedom of Information Law and claimed that it is not subject to other open government statutes, or acts of the City Council.

For example, when advocates asked that the DOE open its new chancellor's regulation on bias-based harassment to the thirty-day public notice and comment period mandated for regulations by the City Administrative Procedures Act

(CAPA), the DOE's general counsel told the NYCLU that the DOE was not subject to the act. Hence newly issued chancellor's regulations are not subjected to public hearing or comment.

The contention that the DOE is an anomalous agency, unique in both city and state government, is startling. CAPA is a local statute with counterparts at the state and federal levels. It ensures that city agencies establish uniform standards of conduct, keep the public informed of agency actions, and allow for public participation in rulemaking. This is provided through mandated thirty or forty-five day public notice and comment periods before a new rule or regulation can take effect. Even the NYPD is subject to CAPA. In 2007, it opened for public comment proposed changes to parade permit regulations, and public participation affected the outcome of the regulations.

The New York City DOE cannot continue to act as its own autonomous agency, even if mayoral control is extended by the state legislature. Regardless of whether the DOE is headed by a chancellor who is appointed by the mayor or by a chancellor who is appointed by an independent board, the DOE must be subject to the same open-government laws that govern other city agencies.

Conclusion

The above snapshots of civil rights battles that have taken place during Mayor Bloomberg's tenure reflect poorly on his administration's commitment to upholding the basic rights of all students—regardless of race, religion, nationality, gender, socioeconomic status, or sexual orientation. In all of these instances, elected officials, parents, and advocates have urged the Bloomberg administration to recognize the need to protect students' civil rights. Yet Mayor Bloomberg and Chancellor Klein continue to act with deliberate indifference to the threats posed to students' safety and civil rights in New York City public schools.

NOTES

1. Carrie Melago, "5-year-old Boy Handcuffed in School, Taken to Hospital for Misbehaving," *Daily News*, January 25, 2008.

2. Tanya Rivera, "13-Year-Old Arrested In School For Writing On Desk," WCBS, April 5, 2007.

3. Jennifer Medina, "Police Arrest a Student, Then Her Principal, Too," *The New York Times*, October 10, 2007.

4. See Kathleen Nolan, "The Impact of Order-Maintenance Policing on an Urban School Environment: An Ethnogrphic Portrait," Voices in Urban Education, Annenberg Institute for School Reform (Spring 2008); see also "Youth Researchers for a New Education System, The YRNES Report," 2008.

5. "Board of Ed Approves NYPD School Safety Plan," Associated Press, September 16, 1998.

6. See "Criminalizing the Classroom: the Over-Policing of New York City Schools," New York Civil Liberties Union and American Civil Liberties Union (March 2007). See also Bob Herbert, "School to Prison Pipeline," *The New York Times,* June 9, 2007.

7. See Testimony by Kathleen Grimm, Deputy Chancellor for Finance and Administration, NYC DOE, and James Secreto, Assistant Chief, Commanding Officer, School Safety Division, New York City Police Department, during City Council Hearing by the Committees on Education, Public Safety, and Juvenile Justice, October 10, 2007.

8. Testimony by Ernest Logan, City Council Hearing by the Committees on Education, Public Safety, and Juvenile Justice, October 10, 2007.

9. See Johanna Wald and Daniel Losen, "Defining and Redirecting a School-to-Prison Pipeline," Framing Paper for the *School-to-Prison Pipeline* Research Conference (May 2003) (citing US DOE, Office of Special Education Programs, Data Analysis Systems (DANS)); see also "Education on Lockdown: The Schoolhouse to Jailhouse Track At-A-Glance," The Advancement Project (March 2005), p.15, http://www.advancementproject.org//reports/FINALEOLrep. pdf.

10. See Russ Skiba, "Zero Tolerance: The Assumptions and the Facts," Indiana Youth Services Association, Education Policy Briefs, Vol. 2, No. 1 (Summer, 2004); see also "Education on Lockdown," p. 18.

11. See "A Look at the Impact Schools," Drum Major Institute for Public Policy (June 2005); Kevin P. Brady, Sharon Balmer, and Deinya Phenix, "School-Police Partnership Effectiveness in Urban Schools: An Analysis of New York City's Impact Schools Initiative," Education and Urban Society (August 2007); "The Impact Schools Initiative: A Critical Assessment and Recommendation for Future Implementation," New York University Wagner School of Public Service (2006); "Policing as Education Policy," National Center for Schools and Communities (2006); "Criminalizing the Classroom: the Over-Policing of New York City Schools," New York Civil Liberties Union and American Civil Liberties Union (March 2007); "Bill of Rights," Urban Youth Collaborative (2006); "Education Not Deportation: Impacts of New York City School Safety Policies on South Asian Immigrant Youth," DRUM–Desis Rising Up and Moving (June 2006); "Teachers Talk: School Culture, Safety, and Human Rights," NESRI and Teachers Unite (October 2008).

12. Additional information on the Student Safety Act is available at http://www.nyclu.org/schooltoprison/ssa. The list of co-sponsors is available at http://www.nyccouncil.info/html/legislation/legislation_details.cfm?ID=Int%20081 6-2008&TYPE=all&YEAR=2006&SPONSORS=YES& REPORTS = YES& HISTORY=YES.

13. Title 20 of the United States Code §7908(a), codifying the military recruitment provisions contained in the No Child Left Behind Act.

14. "We Want You(th)! Confronting Unregulated Military Recruitment in New York City Public Schools," New York Civil Liberties Union and Manhattan Borough President Scott Stringer (2007), http://www.nyclu.org/node/1349.

15. Additional information on the DOE's military recruitment principal's directive that centralized DOE's military recruitment data is available at: http://www.nyclu.org/node/2042.

16. The following elected officials co-signed Congressman Rangel's letter: US Rep. Joseph Crowley, 7th District; US Rep. Gregory W. Meeks, 6th District; US Rep Jerrold Nadler, 8th District; US Rep. Edolphus Towns, 13th District; US Rep. Jose E. Serrano, 16th District; US Rep. Nydia M. Velazquez, 12th District; US Rep. Anthony D. Weiner, 9th District; US Rep. Yvette D. Clarke, 11th District; Public Advocate Betsy Gotbaum; Bronx Borough President Adolfo Carrion; Manhattan Borough President Scott M. Stringer; Sen. Bill Berkins; Sen. Eric T. Schneiderman; Sen. Jose M. Serrano; Assemblymember Adriano Espaillat; Councilmember Gale A. Brewer; Councilmember Bill de Blasio; Councilmember Inez E. Dickens; Councilmember Alan Gerson; Councilmember Robert Jackson; Councilmember Melissa Mark-Viverito; Councilmember Miguel Martinez; and Councilman Albert Vann. A copy of the letter is available at http://www.nyclu.org/node/2114.

17. Sean Alfano, "NYC Sued On Behalf Of Teen Named Osama," CBS NEWS, June 12, 2007.

18. Neha Singh and Khin Mai Aung, "A Free Ride for Bullies," *The New York Times*, September 23, 2007.

19. Report available at: http://schools.nyc.gov/OA/SchoolReports/2006-07/Survey_K277.pdf.

20. A copy of the legislation, including its legislative history, is available at: http://www.nyccouncil.info/html/legislation/legislation_details.cfm?TYPE=all&YEAR=2006&ID=Int%200188-2004&SPONSORS=YES&REPORTS=YES&HISTORY=YES&VOTE=YES&KEY=164464&FILEID=Int%200188-2004&CONSENTFLAG=0#StatedVote.

21. A copy of the regulation is available at: http://schools.nyc.gov/RulesPolicies/ChancellorsRegulations/default.htm.

22. More information on the differences between DASA and A-832 may be found at: http://www.nyclu.org/node/1965.

Special Education

- Maisie McAdoo

If a society can be judged by how it treats its most vulnerable citizens, then one way to judge a school system is by how it treats its students with special needs. These are the children who are most fragile, physically or mentally, and they are the most challenging—and expensive—to educate.

Over the last five years, it's fair to say the New York City Department of Education (DOE) has created a society more akin to despotism than enlightened governance in the realm of special education. The department has ignored mandates for student services, brushed off parents, and defied teachers. In many ways, the DOE approach to students with special needs is: sink or swim.

The department doesn't see it that way, of course. "Through our 'Children First' reforms, we have placed unprecedented focus on students with disabilities," DOE writes on its special-education web site. But the DOE's manager in charge of special education has no experience or credentials in the field. The department launched its major high-school reform, the creation of new small schools, with specific exemptions for new schools from having to accept any students who required any type of special-education classroom. And judging from meetings, appeals, due process hearings, blogs and reports, children with disabilities have not been served well and parents and teachers have grown increasingly frustrated in the years since "Children First" began.

The structure of New York City's provisions for students with special needs is defined by several clear legal mandates. When a student with a special need is evaluated, according to state criteria, she or he is issued an "Individualized Education Program" (IEP), which identifies which services the education department is legally obliged to provide. These services can extend from pull-out services for students in regular classrooms (such as occupational therapy or speech); to separate, smaller classes with specially trained teachers (such as 12:1:1, which mandates 12 students to one special-education teacher and one paraprofessional); to a special school. New York City's District 75 is a separate district charged with providing services to students with the most serious disabilities.

That's what's on paper, and that's what the law prescribes. But the reality in schools is often quite different. Under the pseudonym "Sue Denim," a second-year high school special-education teacher wrote in a blog last fall:

Most of my kids are supposed to be in a 15:1:1 environment (no more than 15 students, one teacher, and one paraprofessional). Most of their IEPs say they're supposed to be in a 12:1:1 environment, but that's just a leftover from middle school. High school students can be in a 15:1:1...but creating and updating an IEP is a sloppy process. So 15:1:1 it is. Or at least, it should be.

But by the second week of school, 12 kids turned into 17 and that second ":1" was nowhere to be found. Never mind that some of my kids are supposed to have their own dedicated para[professional], so there should be several additional professionals in the room. One would be enough. And not just for me. While I'm attending to Suli and his determined refusal to take out a notebook (or to open it if I take it out for him, or to write in it if I open it for him), nothing is being taught to Suli's classmates... *I need another adult in the room.* If I talk to my principal, I get the budget speech.

On its web site, the DOE goes on to tout its rerouting of many students with special needs into so-called "inclusion" classrooms that mix students with disabilities and students from the general population. "The number of students with disabilities in collaborative team teaching (CTT) classes, an inclusive setting, has more than doubled since the Mayor and the Chancellor announced reforms to special education in spring, 2003," the department writes, "and standardized test scores for students with disabilities have improved annually."

Inclusion is a goal that many teachers and parents support, but inclusion is not for everyone. Teachers say CTT classrooms, especially in the middle and high schools, have become dumping grounds for students who should be in separate settings, either part or all of the school day, and are too large and hard to manage. Parents have also complained that the expansion of CTT has not been met with a comparable expansion in the number of teachers qualified to offer differentiated instruction in a CTT classroom. There is also a shortage of service providers to meet the needs of all the students with IEPs now in CTT settings.

And those test scores? They have gone up a little, but pretty much in tandem with the scores of general-education students across the city, as schools have ratcheted up the time they spend preparing for the tests.

When test scores for third- through eighth-grade were released last June, the DOE did not include data on students with disabilities until it was pressured to do so. When the scores finally came out, the results were quite dismal, especially for middle-school students. In New York City, 9 percent of eighth-graders with IEPs met reading standards, compared with 49 percent of general-education students. In mathematics, 22 percent met standards, compared to 66 percent of general-education eighth-graders. These scores show that few students with disabilities are on track to graduate.

In fact, in 2008, New York City graduated just 22.6 percent of its students with disabilities after four years of high school. Even depressed "Big Four" upstate cities did better. Statewide, nearly twice as many (41.3 percent) of students with IEPs graduated on time. Looking at five-year rates, perhaps a better measure for special education, the same disparity applies. The city graduated 24 percent of its students with disabilities after five years, the latest data show, while statewide, districts average 47 percent after five years. Meanwhile, 22 percent of city students with disabilities drop out within four years, compared with 12 percent in the rest of the state.

Why are the city figures so low? Specific policies put in place by the Bloomberg/Klein administration have exacerbated the problems for this vulnerable population, as several published reports have documented.

• In April 2003, at the start of "Children First," the Chancellor consolidated thirty-seven district- and borough-based Committees on Special Education into the ten new administrative regions and eliminated nearly one thousand school-based education evaluator positions and all special-education supervisors. The rather thin rationale was to streamline administration and shift more teachers to classrooms. But with schools' evaluation and case-management capacity gone, there was a 35 percent drop in referrals and a 36 percent decline in evaluations the next year, according to Public Advocate Betsy Gotbaum.[1] As a result, thousands of students were left without evaluations or their mandated services for more than a year.

• The problems persisted. State Comptroller Thomas DiNapoli, in a June 2008 report, found that the number of students awaiting special-education evaluations for more than thirty school days nearly doubled after the 2003 reorganization.[2] More than half of all students receiving new special-education placements during the 2006–2007 school year waited longer than the federally mandated sixty school days. Meanwhile, the number of unfilled recommendations for related services, such as speech or physical therapy, more than doubled, from 28,624 in June 2003 to 64,897 in June 2007. Delays remained "at historically high levels," the Comptroller wrote. "DOE must make greater efforts to ensure that children with special education needs receive recommended services on a timely basis."

• Meanwhile, the city's new small high schools, which often received extra money and attention were excluding students with disabilities. And according to a 2006 report by Parents for Inclusive Education (PIE), there was little information or help with placements of any kind for special-needs high-school students.[3] The report said only 7.5 percent of students in any small high schools received special-education services compared with 10.7 percent of high school students citywide. Students who spend most of their day in general-education classrooms but are supposed to receive Special Education Teacher Support Services (SETSS) part time help were not getting that help in the small schools, PIE said. Students with more serious disabilities were having an even tougher time.

• Public Advocate Gotbaum surveyed school psychologists, who had assumed the responsibilities of education evaluators. She found the vast majority (94 percent) said they spend more time on paperwork than on serving students and families; more than 71 percent said the IEPs they draft for students with special needs are less effective because they do not have time to consult with the children's teachers or parents.[4]

• Budget shortfalls have worsened the situation. This fall, a cost-cutting move by the DOE resulted in two hundred fewer special education buses and many students missed classes or services. In January, Chancellor Klein admitted to the Panel for Education Policy that nearly one-quarter of students mandated for occupational therapy were not receiving it, and one-sixth of those mandated for physical therapy weren't getting that either. (The situation was better for those requiring speech therapy and counseling.)

"These are desperate times," said Carmen Alvarez, teachers' union vice president for special education, summarizing these developments. "One more round of this Chancellor will push it over the edge. This is really a lost generation of kids."

Students with disabilities can, and often do, perform at much higher levels in settings where they are receiving the supports due them. In the more prosperous "low-needs" districts throughout the state—mainly suburban, middle-class areas—74 percent of students with disabilities graduate on time, meeting the same state standards and requirements that just 23 percent of New York City's disabled students do. The difference has to do partly with social class and the disadvantages of poverty, but also with the provision, or lack, of adequate services. Students with special needs who receive speech therapy, occupational or physical therapy, smaller classes, one-on-one tutoring, or the help of a health paraprofessional are much more likely to succeed. Those who are left waiting for services for months at a time are not.

What brought about this failure? It is more than neglect, or the inevitable delays in an overburdened system. The problem is a structural one, having to do with the way this chancellor and mayor went about remaking the system.

While federal law requires that children with disabilities get appropriate services, the administration and oversight of special education rests with the local school system. In the case of New York City, the DOE management philosophy seems to be on a collision course with the needs of students with disabilities. The reorganizations of 2003 and 2007, which removed the administrative superstructure of school districts and made principals, in the DOE's phraseology, the "CEO's of their own schools," left the day-to-day administration and oversight of special education in the schools entirely to principals.

Many principals know little about special education. Yet under the new regime they are "empowered" to change student IEPs, allocate money (or not) for related services, close or create special-education classrooms, and evaluate the psychologists who are saddled with all the compliance paperwork. The monitoring and oversight by district supervisors that has traditionally ensured schools' compliance with special-education mandates has been swept away.

In addition, the Fair Student Funding budgeting system that is part of the new management paradigm is essentially a "block grant" approach. The per-student funding formula gives schools additional funds for their students with special needs, but principals are free to spend them as they choose. Many do not fully fund the paraprofessionals, specially-trained teachers and support staff, services, or classes these students need. In times of hardship they face great pressures to spend their budget allocations on programs that benefit the majority of kids and to focus on boosting overall test scores. And they have the DOE's tacit blessing for these priorities.

The painful irony is that a system whose watchword is "accountability" now fails to provide any where special education is concerned. "There's no sheriff in town," as UFT's Alvarez said. Dismantling the bureaucratic apparatus of special education in the name of school "empowerment" has left vulnerable kids alone in the deep end.

Late last spring, the Council of the Great City Schools, in a report prepared for the DOE, found this lack of accountability particularly troubling in District 75, the longstanding special-education district, which for years had been viewed as doing a thorough and reliable job for the city's most impaired students. "(Our) team could not find anything in the accountability system pertaining to incentives or sanctions for the achievement of students with disabilities," the Council wrote.

> This omission extended to the lack of extra credit in the accountability system for the use of differentiated instruction, collaborative team teaching and other inclusive models of instruction, positive behavior interventions and supports, and response to intervention practices with research-based interventions for students falling behind their peers, progress monitoring, and data-driven decision-making."[5]

This current status of special education, and the vulnerable population it serves, tells us a lot about the Klein/Bloomberg school reforms. The DOE paints a rosy picture of overall improvements in student performance, but look under the surface, disaggregate the data, ask some pointed questions, and the reality is that thousands of children are being ignored or left behind, despite the sunny slogans.

NOTES

1. "Crisis in Special Education: Gotbaum Charges DOE Created Backlog of Evaluations," Press release, Office of the Public Advocate, February 9, 2004.

2. "Waiting for Special Education," Office of the State Comptroller, Report 3-2009, June 2008.

3. "Small Schools, Few Choices: How New York City's High School Reform Effort Left Students With Disabilities Behind," Parents for Inclusive Education/New York Lawyers for the Public Interest, October 2006.

4. "Overworked, Underutilized: How the Department of Education's Reorganizations of Special Education Turned School Psychologists from Mental Health Professionals into Paper Pushers," Office of the Public Advocate, November 2008.

5. "Improving Special Education in New York City's District 75: Report of the Strategic Support Team of the Council of the Great City Schools," prepared for the New York City Department of Education by the Council of Great City Schools, June 2008, p. 54.

English Language Learners

- Deycy Avitia

N early 50 percent of New York City's student population comes from homes where a language other than English is spoken at home and almost 150,000 students (14 percent) of them are in the process of learning English and are classified as English Language Learners (ELLs). Another 12 percent of students once received ELL services.[1] ELLs face multiple challenges. Not only do they struggle as all students do with the challenges of learning and school social life; ELL students have to learn and cope in a foreign language—English— as well, in a new and unfamiliar environment.

New York City's ELLs are a diverse group. They speak many languages and represent many cultures. One out of ten ELLs have interrupted formal education and over 13 percent are also classified as needing special education. Students learning English are twice as likely to live in poverty as their English-speaking peers and are more likely to attend "linguistically segregated" schools where more than a third of students are ELLs.[2] Not surprisingly, these students are at far greater risk of dropping out of high school. Unfortunately, our school system has not succeeded in improving outcomes for most ELL students, especially students who arrive in eighth grade or later.

The DOE has focused its efforts on improving ELL education in elementary schools, and this group has shown some promising gains in recent years. The percentage of ELL fourth-graders meeting state English Language Arts (ELA) standards has jumped by nearly 30 points in five years, rising from just 4.3 percent in 2003 to 29.4 percent in 2008. Yet the share of eighth-grade ELL students meeting ELA standards has increased far less, from 0.7 percent to 5.2 percent in 2008, meaning that among ELL eighth-graders, only about one out of twenty meet standards, compared to 43 percent of native English speakers.

Unfortunately, ELL results in New York City on the national assessments known as the NAEPs have been less impressive still. Between 2003 and 2007, there was no significant gain in reading among fourth- or eighth-grade ELL students on these exams, and no significant gain in eighth-grade mathematics. The only area in which ELL students in New York City have made significant improvements has been in fourth-grade mathematics.[3] The NAEPs are considered the "gold standard" among assessments, providing the most reliable gauge of student achievement.

In a recent report, the DOE blamed the evident lack of progress among ELL middle-school students on the fact that almost 40 percent of ELL eighth-graders are either newly arrived, have an interrupted formal education, or require special education services.[4] Unfortunately, the DOE has not done enough to provide the types of support needed to help middle-school and high-school students learning English, particularly those who are at the highest risk of dropping out, like students with interrupted formal education and immigrant youth.

About a third of immigrant children join the public school system when they are teenagers. Enrolling in middle or high school without speaking English is like trying to mount a moving train, as success in upper-level classes requires greater language comprehension and subject mastery than in elementary school. By the eleventh grade, nearly half of ELLs who were in school two years earlier have disappeared—they have either dropped out or been discharged to GED programs. Barely a quarter of ELL students graduate from New York City high schools in four years–less than half the rate of English-proficient students.

According to state data, the ELL graduation rate in New York City actually declined from 27 percent for the class of 2005 to 23 percent for the class of 2007. The gap in the graduation rate between ELLs and other New York City students has significantly widened. Even worse, only one-tenth of ELL students in recent years have graduated high school with a Regents diploma.[5] Starting with the 2008–2009 school year, all students, including ELLs, are supposed to earn the tougher Regents diploma to graduate. The new Regents diploma requirement threatens to depress even further the already shockingly low graduation rate of this population.

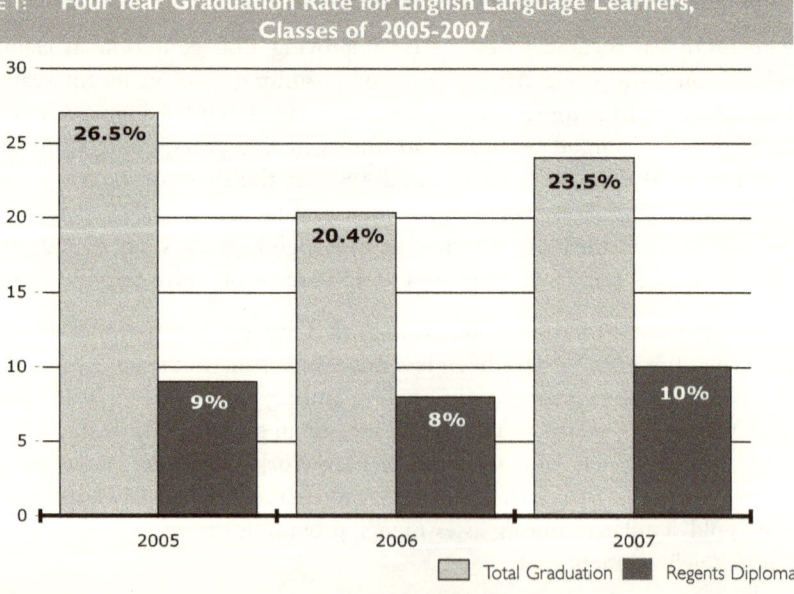

TABLE I: Four Year Graduation Rate for English Language Learners, Classes of 2005-2007

Mayor Bloomberg and Chancellor Klein claim that charter schools have brought significant opportunities to New York City students, but charter schools educate a far lower population of ELLs than the school system as a whole. While ELL students make up 15 percent of enrollment in the New York City public school system, they represent only about 5 percent of the charter school population.[6] Charter schools tend to attract and recruit "easier-to-teach" students. The charter school enrollment process is difficult for those who do not speak English, and few charter schools offer ELL or bilingual classes. With the increase of charter schools and small schools, many of which also do not have the capacity to serve ELL students, ELLs and other students have become concentrated in large schools that might not have the capacity to serve a growing ELL population.

The state and the city must provide adequate funding and resources to support ELL students and ensure that quality programs and services are available throughout our schools. Experts say that there are several elements necessary to provide a sound basic education to ELL students, including:

- Extended hours, Saturday instruction, and academic tutoring;

- Emotional supports, including guidance counseling, mentoring, and dropout-prevention programs, particularly in high school;

- Enhanced parent engagement, family outreach, and community partnerships;

- Lower class sizes, of about 15 students to one teacher, for intensive instruction; especially small classes, of about 10:1, for students with interrupted formal education;

- Trained ESL and bilingual teachers.

Yet few ELL students receive these services. One study estimates that over 7,500 additional bilingual and ESL teachers are needed to significantly improve achievement in the ELL population.[7] Class sizes remain extremely high in many middle and high schools across the city with large ELL populations.

ELL students in New York City are not receiving the extra support and attention they require. Hence, despite the fact that we know how to achieve success with this population, they continue to perform well below their English-proficient peers and to be more readily lost to the system. While we recognize some important progress that has been made with elementary school ELLs, it's time for the mayor and the chancellor to step up their efforts, invest in quality services for ELLs, and improve outcomes for ELL students.

NOTES

1. "Diverse Learners on the Road to Success: The Performance of New York City's English Language Learners," New York City Department of Education, Office of English Language Learners, March 2009, p.4.

2. "Getting it Right: Ensuring a Quality Education for English Language Learners in New York," The New York Immigration Coalition, 2008.

3. See the NAEP 2007 results for New York City in "The Nation's Report Card: Trial Urban Districts Assesssments, National Assessment of Educational Progress (NAEP)," http://nationsreportcard.gov/tuda.asp.

4. "Diverse Learners on the Road to Success," p.11.

5. Regents figures from the NYCDOE Research and Policy Support Group, quoted in "Looming Crisis or Historic Opportunity? Meeting the Challenge of the Regents Graduation Standards," NYC Coalition for Educational Justice (February 2009), http://www.annenberginstitute.org/pdf/RegentsDiploma.pdf.

6. Testimony by Eric Nadelstern, Chief Schools Officer, New York City Department of Education, during City Council Hearing, "Charter School Expansion in New York City," by the Education Committee, April 6, 2009.

7. New York State Education Department, "Teacher Supply and Demand in NYS in 2005–2006," Second Annual Report (2007), p. 27.

| Wrong on Curriculum,
| Wrong on Pedagogy

- Sol Stern

I was one of the early enthusiasts of mayoral control of the New York City schools. My hope was that a tough, goals-oriented mayor, knowing that the electorate would hold him accountable for the performance of the schools, might finally cut through the system's bureaucratic inertia and create powerful new incentives for excellence in the classroom. Plus, I thought that since Mayor Bloomberg and his new chancellor, Joel Klein, had no allegiance to either side of the "curriculum wars" or the "reading wars," they would make pragmatic instructional decisions based on what worked best in the classroom.

That hope still seemed very much alive when Mayor Bloomberg delivered a no-excuses education speech on Martin Luther King Day, January 20, 2003. Six months after the mayor officially took control of the schools, he unveiled his long-awaited plan for overhauling the system. Breaking with fifty years of education industry rhetoric about "insufficient funding" of public education, Bloomberg said that $12 billion was more than enough to provide decent schools for the city's 1.1 million schoolchildren. He promised to push more money into classrooms by dismantling the system's costly "Byzantine administrative fiefdoms." Even more significantly, he said that reading and writing instruction in the early grades would now "employ strategies proven to work," including "a daily focus on phonics"—an all but explicit rejection of progressive educators' philosophical commitment to the failed "whole language" method of teaching reading in which young children try to guess at words that they can't decode through context clues.

In his speech, Mayor Bloomberg noted that schools had enjoyed too much autonomy, bringing about "a baffling profusion of approaches to teaching the three Rs throughout the city." The new blueprint, called "Children First," was designed explicitly as an imperial system, with all roads leading directly to City Hall. Bloomberg said that the "experience of other urban school districts shows that a standardized approach to reading, writing, and math is the best way to raise student performance across the board, in all subjects." Thus the old discredited system would give way to "one unified, focused, streamlined chain of command." The mayor also revealed that "the Chancellor's office will dictate the curriculum and pedagogical methods." Despite the ominous allusion to dictatorship, I was pleased, particularly by the focus on the proven phonics approach to reading.

Just one week later, the Department of Education (DOE) announced that "balanced literacy," an approach to reading instruction that incorporates whole language with a dollop of incidental phonics drills, would now be mandatory in one thousand city schools, with only two hundred "high-performing" schools granted waivers to opt out of it. *Month by Month Phonics,* a reading program authored by Patricia Cunningham and Dorothy Hall, would be the supplemental "phonics" portion of the core balanced literacy reading program. It was soon revealed that school officials chose balanced literacy and *Month by Month Phonics* over the heated objections of seven of the nation's foremost reading researchers, who had sent Bloomberg, Klein, and the new Deputy Chancellor for Teaching and Learning, Diana Lam, a memo blasting this pedagogical approach as "woefully inadequate" and lacking "the ingredients of a systematic phonics program." Several of the researchers had been members of the National Reading Panel (created by the U.S. Congress) which had recently concluded, based on a review of three decades of scientific reading research, that a systematic and explicit phonics-based instructional approach is essential for teaching reading to beginners. If my assumption that the mayor would approach instructional issues in a pragmatic manner was right, this cautionary memo should have set off alarms at City Hall and caused some reconsideration.

A cursory reading of the easily available paperback of *Month by Month Phonics* reveals that it is not a core phonics program at all. Right from the outset, the authors themselves make it clear that they're not enthusiastic about explicitly teaching phonics as the National Reading Panel recommended. Phonics "is an important part of beginning literary instruction," they concede. But they immediately qualify that concession. "Children who are taught phonics only until they 'get it' don't suddenly get transformed into eager, meaning-seeking, strategic readers."

So how did the mayor's Martin Luther King Day promise to put a strong phonics program into almost every school morph into the very opposite? The mayor was a successful businessman; his schools chancellor was a former federal prosecutor who had recently served as CEO of a publishing conglomerate. They had moved quickly and decisively on the Management-101 part of the school system's overhaul. Dismantling the musty old Board of Education bureaucracy piece by piece, Bloomberg and Klein recruited a cadre of corporate-sector whiz kids to run school divisions such as transportation, food services, school construction, and maintenance.

But in the area of classroom instruction, Bloomberg and Klein clearly felt less confident. Looking for guidance from experts, they made the mistake of deferring to the system's progressive-ed old guard. A telling early decision was Klein's hiring of Diana Lam as deputy chancellor for instruction. On the classroom side, Lam emerged as something like a co-chancellor—her salary of

$250,000 was the same as Klein's. Lam arrived from the Providence, Rhode Island, superintendent's job—her fourth such post—with a reputation for quickly raising test scores and then moving on to bigger districts.

The "balanced-literacy" reading program that Lam and most other progressive educators favored actually had little positive effect on Providence's disadvantaged students. Yet Lam arrived in New York determined to carry on the experiment in virtually all of Gotham's poor and minority schools. Lam's progressive-ed ideology was also evident in her recommendations for the ten new regional superintendents (sometimes referred to as "super" superintendents). One couldn't help noticing the extraordinary degree of ideological affinity and the intertwined career connections among the ten who were selected. Six had a past relationship with District 2, the most progressive district in the city, where balanced literacy and non-traditional math reigned for years. Another point of intersection for some of the superintendents was the Reading and Writing Project of Columbia University's Teachers College. The project's director, Lucy Calkins, was one of the leading lights of progressive-education pedagogy in America.

Under Diana Lam, Lucy Calkins' influence grew exponentially. She was present at the press conference that announced balanced literacy with the *Month by Month Phonics* supplement as the standard reading program, and school officials pointed her out to reporters as an allegedly independent academic expert who could testify to the program's effectiveness. After the seven top reading specialists sent their letter to Bloomberg, Klein, and Lam criticizing *Month by Month Phonics* as inadequate Calkins then drafted a counter-letter, signed by more than one hundred education-school professors, that effusively praised the program. Though few of the signers had ever even looked at the program, and fewer still were reading specialists, they confidently asserted that it "has a strong track record in both New York City's high-achieving schools and in schools that serve our high-need areas." In fact, it had no research-validated track record at all.

When you consider Calkins's simultaneous status as a beneficiary of Department of Education contracts on reading and writing instruction, an advocate and political organizer for the same Department of Education leadership, and a supposedly objective university professor, there was clearly the appearance of conflict of interest. Nevertheless, Lucy Calkins is a true believer in the power of her own ideas. When I interviewed her at the time of the dust up over the mandated citywide reading program, she was articulate in defense of those ideal classrooms where young children naturally find their way to literacy without boring, scripted phonics drills.

Ironically, the old, supposedly "dysfunctional" Board of Education had implemented at least one reading program that had actually succeeded in raising academic achievement among the city's disadvantaged students. Former Chancellor Rudy Crew had created a "Chancellor's District" to tackle the problems of the city's lowest performing schools and selected a program called *Success for All* as its reading program. *Success for All* is one of the few comprehensive and core reading curriculums approved by the U.S. Department of Education. But one of Diana Lam's first official acts was to dismantle the Chancellor's District. And despite the $27 million that the city had invested in implementing *Success for All* over five years, Mayor Bloomberg's new education team decided to junk it without so much as a hearing. The developer of *Success for All,* Johns Hopkins reading scientist Robert Slavin, complained to me that Lam never responded to his letters and phone calls. "She decided on the first day not to listen to other voices," said Slavin.

One of the theoretical advantages of giving the mayor control of the schools was that the city's chief executive would be able to make a quick course correction when his education department underlings screwed up. In this case, Mayor Bloomberg could have admitted that Diana Lam's choice of a reading program was a blunder, gotten rid of it—and her—and started over from scratch. Instead of correcting the error, however, the mayor dug in his heels and pronounced himself pleased with his creation. "At every level, we have replaced an old school system where responsibility was diffused and confused," he said at a press conference as the 2003–2004 school year began. "There is [now] a direct link from the teacher's desk in the classroom right to the mayor's desk."

What the mayor didn't say was that this link carried messages in only one direction. In fact he was about to launch a three-year period of micromanaging teachers and principals to an extent unprecedented in American K-12 education. Agents of the chancellor (euphemistically called "coaches") were dispatched to almost all of the city's twelve hundred schools to make sure that every educator marched in lockstep and carried out the DOE's approved but scientifically unproven pedagogical approaches. There was now only one way, the Tweed way, to teach the three Rs in the schools. And the problem with this "dictatorial" approach went far beyond *Month by Month Phonics* and balanced literacy.

Starting in 2003, the DOE created a re-education program for its eighty thousand teachers, several thousand principals and assistant principals, and two thousand new math and reading coaches. Each teacher received a six-hour CD-ROM laying out the philosophy behind the new standardized pedagogical approach that he or she was expected to follow to a T. In addition, thousands of teachers also attended one-week crash courses offered at some of the local graduate education schools, many of them taught by professors who signed the February letter in support of *Month by Month Phonics.* The total cost of this re-education effort exceeded $60 million.

To examine the CD-ROM is to see the world of progressive education writ large, with all of its Romantic assumptions about how children learn. As the CD-ROM opens, Joel Klein announces: "This CD will walk you through the research upon which we based our decisions regarding our program choices." Diana Lam assured the teachers that the Department of Education was interested in an ongoing "dialogue" with them about education issues. The implication was that the DOE's search for "best practices" was an open and intellectually serious process.

But in fact, in the section of the CD-ROM that lists academic sources, there was not a single education writer who favors phonics for reading instruction or a curriculum emphasizing content knowledge. Teachers looking for references for further study didn't find the names of Reid Lyon, Jean Chall, E. D. Hirsch, Diane Ravitch, or countless other distinguished scholars who believe that all children, but particularly economically and socially disadvantaged children, desperately need instruction in basic reading skills and background content knowledge to be able to function in an increasingly complex information economy and to become productive citizens in our democracy.

Surprisingly, much of the text was dominated by the pedagogical principles of an education thinker of whom few New York teachers had ever heard: Brian Cambourne, a professor of education at Wollongong University in New South Wales and a leader of the constructivist and whole-language movement that dominates Australian public schools. In the CD Cambourne argues that children learn better in natural settings with a minimum amount of adult help. The role of the educator should be to create classroom conditions that stimulate children and most closely resemble the way adults work and learn. Thus, children should not sit in rows facing the teacher, but rather the room should be arranged with work areas where children can construct their own knowledge. So important did the DOE deem Cambourne's theories that it instructed teachers to go through a checklist to make sure their classroom practices met the professor's "conditions for learning."

"Where's the science" in support of phonics? Chancellor Klein once churlishly asked a reporter interviewing him for a story in the *New York Times*. Why Klein, a highly intelligent man, denied the existence of the robust scientific evidence in favor of phonics programs like *Success for All* and then imposed a never tested instructional approach on virtually every classroom in the city only he can answer. But having made those fateful decisions Klein and the mayor had to show significant progress in fourth-grade and eighth-grade reading. They thus pulled out all the stops to boost reading results. The city shelled out hundreds of millions of dollars in professional development for teachers. Schools had to devote 150 minutes of every school day (essentially half of available classroom time) to the reading program, and they spent countless hours on test-preparation drills. The overall education budget was increased from \$12.7 billion in 2002 to almost \$21 billion in 2009. The school day and school year were lengthened and teachers received raises totaling 43 percent. Despite this enormous effort, the city's record on reading improvement has remained shockingly mediocre.

There was finally a ten-percentage-point upward bump in fourth-grade reading on the 2005 state tests. Bloomberg and Klein seized the bully pulpit to proclaim that the fourth-grade gains proved that the new programs were "paying off" for kids. But the fourth-grade test scores proved no such thing. For starters, 2005 scores also rose significantly throughout the state. In large urban districts, such as Rochester, Syracuse, and Yonkers, they went up by even higher percentages than in New York City. Since none of these districts used the balanced literacy/*Month by Month Phonics* program (or other Klein-favored interventions), there was no logical reason to credit the Bloomberg administration for Gotham's gains. What's more, the fourth-grade scores of the city's Catholic schools also rose about 7 percentage points, keeping the same lead that they've enjoyed over the public schools for years. If the city's new literacy initiatives really were "paying off," wouldn't that gap have narrowed—especially since almost all the Catholic schools use the explicit phonics approach that Klein drove from the public schools?

There is another, unimpeachable source confirming that the Bloomberg administration's claims of spectacular progress on reading are more public relations than real. That source is the National Assessment of Education Progress, or NAEP. The NAEP has served as the federal education department's authoritative and "above politics" testing agency since 1990, with its fourth- and eighth-grade reading and mathematics tests often described as the "nation's report card" and the "gold standard" for assessing student achievement. Every two years, the NAEP tests a representative sample of students in every state, with an enhanced sample set for about a dozen of the nation's largest urban districts. The city's reading scores on the NAEP test did go up from 2002–2003, but that was before the "Children First" reforms were even announced. Since then— that is, from 2003 to 2007— both the city's fourth- and eighth-grade reading scores have remained flat on the NAEP test.

Having staked everything on a rigid top-down system in which there would be, to quote Bloomberg's 2003 Martin Luther King Day speech, "one, unified, focused, streamlined chain of command," the mayor suddenly did an about-face in 2006. Now he and Klein placed all their bets for school improvement on market-style accountability reforms, such as granting principals greater autonomy over budgets, making schools compete against one another for letter grades, and offering bonus pay to administrators and teachers who boosted student scores. (Meanwhile, Diana Lam was gone, having been brought down by a nepotism scandal.) The newly empowered principals would presumably also have the freedom to break away from top-down instructional mandates and to return to reading programs like *Success for All,* but there is little evidence that principals have exercised those rights. After three years of heavy-handed imposition of the DOE's own pedagogical choices, it would have taken a very brave principal to strike out on his or her own. Those years of draconian centralization, and the principals' perilous new vulnerability, were not likely to cultivate independence of thinking.

I discovered last year that despite the introduction of greater school autonomy, balanced literacy remains the core reading program in virtually every elementary school in the city. Officials at Tweed weren't able to identify a single school using a core phonics reading program. Worse, the DOE is still urging all the principals and the reading coaches who train teachers in how to teach reading to continue to use a revised version of its first Balanced Literacy handbook. Chancellor Klein did extend a contract to E.D. Hirsch's Core Knowledge program to pilot a phonics-based reading program in ten low-performing schools. And in a talk at the American Enterprise Institute in June 2008, Klein admitted that it was probably a mistake to mandate *Month by Month Phonics.* Despite these small concessions, Klein and Bloomberg have become so committed to market incentives and competition as the vehicle for improving schools that instructional issues have almost disappeared from their agenda.

Chancellor Klein has spoken very eloquently in the past two years about education reform as a "civil rights" issue and the need to narrow the Black-White achievement gap. But all the research on the achievement gap shows that it starts in reading in the early grades and that minority students who fall way behind by the fourth grade almost never catch up. E.D. Hirsch has also shown that disadvantaged students suffer most from our schools' lack of a content-rich curriculum that specifies in each grade exactly what knowledge all students should master. Under mayoral control, as in past education administrations, New York City schools have yet to develop such a coherent curriculum. The vacillation between extremes of control and autonomy reveal a fundamental vacuity in the Bloomberg administration when it comes to critical thinking about what works in the classroom. So long as there is no such thinking, we are not likely to see significant gains in learning for New York City children, mayoral control or no mayoral control.

Governance Law:

Mayoral Control Revisited

- Steven Sanders

Seven years ago the New York State Legislature passed sweeping legislation redesigning the New York City public school system and handing significant authority to the mayor. In so doing the legislature intended to "alter the school governance structure providing greater mayoral control and also to require that the Board of Education retain its role regarding educational policy issues and standards, including approval of any contracts that would significantly impact the provision of educational services, the budget and capital plan." Subsequent legislation adopted "a new community governance structure which would provide an opportunity for meaningful participation for both parents and the community." That legislation notably retained the thirty-two local community school districts and their local superintendents.

On June 30, 2009, this new system of governance will expire. The legislature is required to act, lest the law go out of existence and the former system be automatically reinstated.

The mayor would have New York City residents believe that the legislature has two choices: either allow the law to lapse and return to the old, discredited, pre-2002 system of governance, or continue the current law, as it has been implemented and interpreted by the mayor, unchanged. He is wrong. There is a third option. The legislature could decide to require the mayor finally to abide by the law as it was negotiated and enacted. The school system that has been constructed by this mayor and his chancellor is not the one envisioned by the 2002 law. The law intended to strengthen the hand of the mayor and chancellor, not grant him exclusive and dictatorial powers.

The legislation established "a balance of authority" between the mayor, his chancellor, and a new, redesigned Board of Education which was to "retain a meaningful role and continue to maintain jurisdiction over citywide educational policy issues and contracts." That has not happened. The mayor has treated this new Board of Education as a mere inconvenience to be either ignored or bullied into agreement and submission, certainly not an entity responsible for meaningful deliberations and decision-making. And this despite the fact that the legislature gave to the mayor a majority of the appointments to this Board.

Similarly, in negotiations prior to passage of the law, the mayor agreed to the proposition enunciated in the law that the thirty-two community school districts would remain intact with their local superintendents to govern them under the direct management of the chancellor. This reconstituted structure was to allow, and indeed promote, parent and community involvement through the newly created Community District Education Councils (CECs). But the mayor worked towards obliterating the CECs rather than governing with them. He reassigned the local superintendents to tasks outside their districts. In their place the mayor and chancellor introduced no fewer than three successive local governance structures all laden with new bureaucracy and job titles, each diminishing further local participation in school governance.

In 2002 the legislature voted on a governance structure for education in New York City that was coherent and balanced, with greatly enhanced powers given to the mayor and chancellor and an emphasis upon accountability. For the first time, the mayor would unilaterally select a chancellor to oversee the implementation of educational policy and programs. The chancellor in turn would, for the first time, have the authority to hire the thirty-two local district superintendents, who would continue to be the instructional and administrative leaders of their school districts but report and be accountable to the chancellor.

The retained, citywide Board of Education would consist of eight appointments by the mayor and the remaining five appointments made by the borough presidents. Those five appointments would be parents of school children. This newly reconfigured board would continue to have jurisdiction over all citywide education policies and significant contracts. It would not be involved in day-to-day management, but it would also not be merely advisory as the mayor now claims, although the extent to which it he has consulted with it even in this capacity is limited. At the local school district level, the CECs, which replaced the predecessor elected school boards, were to be comprised mainly of parents of district students, selected by the various Parent Associations from those district's schools. The superintendents were authorized to work with the CECs, and they were authorized to hold monthly open meetings to hear from the public and discuss educational priorities for their district and to make recommendations as well as to exercise some specific duties and oversight. Support and training, as well as needed information, were to be provided by the chancellor to the CECs on an ongoing basis.

Such was the governance structure given to the mayor by the legislature. It had a logical chain of command from the mayor down to the local level. It opened the door for public input and involvement. It created a deliberative body in which the mayor's and chancellor's policy initiatives could be reviewed, vetted, and voted upon. It created for the first time a working partnership between the mayor and the chancellor and it created much-needed accountability and cohesion, which had been missing from the system for generations.

Regrettably the mayor chose to maximize his power and autonomy at every turn and never took seriously the law's intent to create a school governance system that established "a balance of authority," nor did he "encourage real parental and community involvement,"[5] as provided by the law.

If the original spirit of the law had been more closely adhered to much of the public discontent and sense of disenfranchisement we have seen in the last seven years might have been avoided. And the nature of the debate in Albany, as the expiration of the law nears, would have been different.

New York City Schools:

Then and Now

- Deborah Meier

It's hard to focus on exactly what alarms me most about the past seven years, when the Bloomberg/Klein administration has been in charge of our schools. It is leading the nation on a path that's both seductive and dangerous, and doing so with an uncritical audience that has been hoodwinked by power and influence.

When I moved to New York City in 1966, with three school-age children, "everyone" told me that "no one sent their children to public schools"—and I should look for private options. Given that there were 1.2 million children attending the city's public schools, I knew that these "no ones" were a slightly skewed sample.

I decided to send my children to public schools, and to this day I don't know if I made the right choice—money quite aside. (We didn't have a lot.) But I was a "crusader," and I wanted to provide my children and every one else's with the kind of education that I thought I'd received in New York City's elite private schools—the kind deemed appropriate to enhance the power of the already powerful. I accepted John Dewey's idea that if in a democracy everyone was a member of the ruling class, then citizenship was our shared vocation, and it wasn't an easy one. The job of public schools as we saw it was to give us all the intellectual and social tools for a more equal citizenship.

I look back to those years and remember with pain and joy the active role I played as parent and citizen—including running for and getting elected to the local school board in District 3, on Manhattan's Upper West Side, in the early seventies. Decentralization was new, but we had a heady and often naive view of our power. We were like emerging democracies, not always wise about the use of our authority. We argued about who should make which decisions. We were reinventing the Constitution and Bill of Rights for schools and their communities.

I was meanwhile teaching Kindergarten in Central Harlem until, in 1974, an unusual superintendent offered me the opportunity to open "my own public school" in East Harlem. The district was one of the poorest and lowest-scoring districts, and Tony Alvarado wanted to break the mold. In the fall of 1974 we opened the first of the Central Park East schools with a hundred children, a faculty co-op. I was called "director," but decisions were made collectively and

I remained a classroom teacher for several years. While many insisted it wouldn't "work" in a low-income, minority neighborhood ("these children need something different"), in fact the school was so popular that we soon added a Central Park East II and a third—River East—and eventually CPESS, a secondary school, in 1985. Meanwhile the twenty-one old buildings of East Harlem's District 4 were soon housing many different styles of small schools of choice—fifty-one in all, including the now downsized neighborhood schools. Over time I was required to take on the title of principal, but with support from both Alvarado and Steve Phillips, the head of the flourishing alternative high school division, we had considerable flexibility in hiring staff, deciding on curriculum, and extending accountability to more useful authentic forms.

In the secondary school, for example, we held school reviews at least annually with external experts, who examined our students, their work, our classes, and comments from parents and the community, and made their reviews available to the public. Parents were always welcome, and our staff meetings were closed only for personnel matters. Staff met several extra hours a week to make formal decisions. We communicated with families and others weekly—providing all the "data" we could get our hands on and met face-to-face at least twice a year with each family. In 1996 I moved to Boston and started a K-8 public school in the neighborhood of Roxbury where we were able to create our own board of parents, staff, students, and members of the community. Under a union/management experiment we, along with many other schools, built our accountability system on embracing those we were directly accountable to (our own constituency), alongside a three-day quality review by the district, carried out by fellow educators. (The intrusion of the Massachusetts's "comprehensive assessment system" and the federal No Child Left Behind requirements have considerably weakened this promising system of accountability.)

Meanwhile, back in New York City—where part of my heart still belonged—our vision had spread to several hundred progressive schools where thirty years before there had been none, alongside interesting new small schools built on other innovative models. Most were in neighborhoods serving some of the poorest minority children in the city and having remarkable success. Based on a study commissioned by the state's commissioner of education, the most "radical" of these were improving graduation rates, subsequent college attendance, and retention. The high schools were based on graduation by "performance"—authentic presentations and defense by students of their work before external reviewers. It was the tip of a huge iceberg, but it was large enough to prove something: progressive schools could do as well as traditional ones (we felt we had evidence that they did better), and we needed to adapt the larger system to support such diversity.

We were, alas, struggling with the impatience of the corporate and foundation world with our pace, they were either seeking an approach that could leverage change everywhere at once or could replace the experiment in public education with a more market-friendly one. Even though private money was a very small fraction of the budgets of New York City's public schools, it carried enormous weight in the circles that mattered and over the next ten years our reforms were undermined or ignored, except in small, determined pockets. A new wave replaced it, using much of the same language, but built to place power mostly in centralized hands.

We saw school choice as a useful means for showing what could be done and a potential tool for allowing many flowers to bloom. If we couldn't all agree on a single solution, let us not fight amongst ourselves but support different routes. We thought small schools—where everyone would know what everyone was up to— would alleviate pressure for rigid systems of accountability. We didn't see, offhand, how it could do any harm—even though we were well aware that there might be small schools of choice that were mediocre at best. It wasn't a magic bullet (as we warned Bill Gates when he first began researching small schools for his foundation), but it was an open-ended approach that we believed would produce more good than harm. But when choice and smallness became a policy priority, they were required to fit into a one-size-fits-all citywide plan, thus undermining the very essence of why choice and smallness were useful.

We failed—for many reasons. We didn't count on the fact that what was sought was a faster solution—a revolution—in a labor-intensive "industry" where human minds move more slowly than the pace of change the new reformers sought. So the powers-that-be, with experience in the world of Wall Street, leaped into the puzzle to see if they could put the pieces together faster. They were fascinated by the idea that they could, literally, do it better. And why not? They were, after all, smarter. (Proof? They had higher SAT scores and graduated from "the best" colleges, or they had made a lot of money on Wall Street.) The ideology of "best and brightest"—and richest—overcame caution.

They came with a certain mind-set. Merit equals doing well on objective and standardized tests. Equity means applying the same high-stakes exams to all children, and pushing them all to achieve higher scores. Over the past ten years the Department of Education and the foundations have poured resources, energy, and the best of intentions into creating a system based upon these values.

At a time of increasing inequities in every other sphere, education alone was seen as the solution—if it rested in the right hands.

That meant, for example, that they saw small schools as a reform easily mandated from above—creating cookie-cutter look-alikes called A>B< C< D (though usually with fancy and inspiring names). They assumed that the dissatisfaction that communities, students, and teachers alike expressed over the new small schools would only be temporary. They'd get over it. No one likes change. We know better. Until, that is "we" change our mind—as the Gates Foundation did ten years later when it fell out of love with small schools.

You're too patient, they'd tell me. We can't afford patience, they insisted. What could I say? Except that a study of history suggested that only through patience could long-term change occur. Small schools and choice were ideas whose merits were substantial enough that we should not allow them to become fads, we argued back. (Some of us even suggested that integration remained a good idea.)

The emphasis on testing has spread throughout the educational system. When my children were young, the early childhood years were mostly still a time for play—imaginative games, art, music, block building, water-sand, live animals, and live plants, big and noisy rooms. (However, I once removed my son from an "unplayful" Kindergarten and took him with me to my job as a Head Start teacher.) As a Kindergarten teacher myself, preserving and extending such intellectually curious workshops for learning into first and second grade was my agenda. Eventually my agenda extended all the way through high school, at Central Park East. We made headway—slowly.

Today, in New York City, as well as other districts throughout the country, I no longer can find such Kindergartens. And pre-Kindergartens too are devoted now to prepping, with test-like skill-sheets and nary a block, live animal, or plant—not even an easel. Five-year-olds worry, not about whether they will make friends, but whether they will be held over because they haven't yet learned all their letters and phonemes. Even earlier, anxious parents are plotting how to get their four-year-olds into gifted classes, by prepping them for IQ tests that no serious scholars consider reliable—and that overwhelmingly favor white children from wealthy families (a fact that has been well known since these tests were invented a century ago). In the 1960s we fought against so-called ability grouping—tracks—in schools, and we won. Today the junior high across from my old apartment is being closed and reopened with mostly "gifted" programs. White middle-class parents can return to public schools "safely" by choosing among a wide array of selective small schools.

Today parent power and citizen and community voices have entirely disappeared. There is nothing that lies between the million families whose children attend our public schools and the system itself. There's Chancellor Klein, ruler of the King's Navy, and "the rest of us" below. With a flick of his hand, he can close neighborhood schools and turn them over to favored charter-school operators.

Even Shanker's once-feared teacher's union is weakened, forced to accept lesser evils rather than confront the power of the mayor. The famous "rubber room"—where unwanted teachers can be sent at the whim of their supervisors without any official charges filed against them—is not an institution that any union leader should accept happily, nor are the administration's experiments in bonus pay for teachers who raise test scores. But there is nothing, not even a weakened union, to defend the rights of parents and children, except impotent district advisory bodies.

While principals may have more power over hiring and firing of staff, they are more than ever under the thumb of the dictatorial chancellor, though they no longer need fear ornery parents. Yes, the squeaky wheel probably got more attention than he or she deserved in times past—but better that than no wheels at all. And a dissatisfied teacher or principal could more easily escape a difficult supervisor, by switching districts or schools.

I remember all the teacher centers that popped up around the city, where excited young men (avoiding the draft in many cases) and women were discovering the possibilities of their profession. Today there may be more time devoted to professional development, but mostly it is aimed at improving standardized test performance and training teachers and administrators to crunch numbers. The "idea" of professional development as a bottom-up movement that focuses on teaching has come and gone. I was the beneficiary of that movement—and I regret that so few of us had that chance.

I remember our groans and moans about testing, and how we fought back and got the tests postponed until third grade. Now our children are tested as young as four years old—to sort out the "gifted"and to advise teachers and parents of their child's academic status as compared to other children.

Even in the early sixties, annual school test scores were posted in all the local papers, along with stories about the high and low performers. And superintendents held sessions threatening and cajoling principals and conniving for ways to bring up scores, which usually involved special programs for those just below the median. We were simultaneously told by the test makers that this would be ineffective, that it was a form of cheating, and then told how to do it more effectively. Today, children get such pre-tests every five weeks!

I used to laugh at all the data collecting that went on, and how quickly those responsible for filling out the forms learned how to disguise unwanted truths. Like children, and bankers, we used our smarts to escape oversight. Some students passed notes and cheated on exams, some teachers no doubt closed their doors and learned to say "oops, I'm sorry" if caught exercising judgment. Principals dodged the bullets coming their way, and mayors did the same. You want better attendance data? Done. You want higher test scores? How high? Done. You want lower drop-out rates? Done. Of course, I'm exaggerating, but not a lot.

And while there is more data than ever, none of it seems any more reliable or understandable. Test data no longer comes with well-informed, psychometrically sophisticated manuals. Clever people have devised systems of reporting data, and tying it to consequences drawn from business and financial models. But I wonder, if they couldn't get it right for Wall Street, why in the world do I trust them to be smart or honest enough to get it right for public education? As long as the data serves its masters well, accuracy can wait. If Moody's gave Lehman Brothers an AAA rating two weeks before it collapsed, what makes me think Tweed's analysis is any better? Transparency is an illusive goal—best served by direct observation by those closest to the action. Everything else is gravy.

In a system designed to promote equity and democracy, I want information that can be interpreted by human judgment—my own and that of fellow citizens. I don't want to be "data-driven," but data-informed; and the informants should include real-life students, parents, and teachers.

Meanwhile, those in high places, like the Oval Office, have thoughtlessly begun to embrace the idea of moving this system to the national level—with similar sleights of hand. Quietly. Behind the scenes. Meanwhile NCLB, I fear, may soon look benign.

Its successor will come with a new name. And K–12 will only be the start. They're thinking now of starting these injurious practices at age three to four, and translating them into policies for colleges, maybe soon for PhDs. The best and brightest are looking for ways to insure that their scoring system of five-to-eighteen-year-olds has weight in the world after school—making one's test scores a gateway into all decent work or study. These are not evil men with evil designs. They are conducting the business of schooling based on a model that makes sense to them—a model that worked well for them personally, a model consistent with their marketplace ideology.

But, in fact, America's historic economic success was built on performance, not test scores. As we eliminate the "road test" and rest our success on generic forms of assessment, we may find it harder to achieve a more prosperous and equitable future. The "road test" works because it's not a secret measure of who is better than whom; it does not rank. That's what we need to invent, school by school—believable road tests.

An oligarchy of the meritorious is the new reformers' "hidden" goal. Democracy, for them, has its limits. A democracy rests on a far from infallible faith that the "people" are wise enough to make sound decisions if they are well informed. But if getting them well informed will take too much time to insure the economic future of the nation, we seem to be prepared to abandon democracy. Instead we need the opposite. We need to broaden the ways we measure "intelligent enough," not narrow them, and we need to invent ways to engage young people and their families in the exciting adventure that a good education can be. You don't have to convince would-be basketball stars that they have to practice shooting hoops, and you shouldn't need to convince engaged learners to learn. We come "wired" that way from birth.

The stories we tell have unintended consequences. It's probably no great surprise that most of the new-fangled schools being invented by people in high places—the meritocracy—are surprisingly like the ones we went to a century ago. Better technology, rearranged desks, less physical punishment, but at heart built around a traditionally-imposed, traditionally-delivered curriculum by compliant young teachers to a bored but anxious student population.

But, there are bright spots. Voices that refuse to be shut up or shut out, schools that sneakily ignore the latest fads designed to raise scores, still have recess, the arts, physical education, music, and dance, and encourage kids to talk and ask questions —including the kind that won't be on the tests.

We will try—and we will, I hope, begin to win some concessions so that New York City's children can be educated in a system dedicated to demonstrating the arts of democracy. In the long run we will confront that bottom line: that we are ill-served as a nation by a public that has not been educated to exercise good judgment about complex matters. Calculus and physics are no harder to teach than democracy, no less counterintuitive. But though we can survive with only a relatively small number of physicists and mathematicians, we cannot afford fewer than 100 percent well-educated voters.

Further Reading

Arts Education

"Arts in the Schools Report," New York City Department of Education (October 2008), http://schools.nyc.gov/offices/teach learn/arts/Documents/AnnualArtsReport08.pdf.

"Out of Tune: A Survey on NYC Students' Access to Arts Education," Betsy Gotbaum, Public Advocate, City of New York, Office of the Public Advocate (June 2008), http://pubadvocate. nyc.gov /policy/documents/ArtsEducation Report_web_.pdf.

Campaign for Fiscal Equity Decision

Campaign for Fiscal Equity, Inc., et al. v. State of New York, et al., 100 NY 2d 893, 911-12 (2003), http://cfequity.org/CFEIIdecision.pdf.

Campbell's Law

Donald T. Campbell, "Assessing the Impact of Planned Social Change,"The Public Affairs Center, Dartmouth College, December 1976, p. 49, www.wmich.edu/evalctr/pubs/ops/ops08.pdf.

Class Size

"New York City Department of Education Administration of the Early Grade Class Size Reduction Program," Report #2005–N– 2003, New York State Office of the State Comptroller, March 15, 2006, http://www.osc.state.ny.us/audits/allaudits/093006/05n3.pdf.

"Benefits of Smaller Classes," Class Size Matters fact sheet (October 2008), http://classsizematters.org/benefits_of_CSR_08.pdf.

"The Importance of Class Size in the Middle and Upper Grades," Class Size Matters fact sheet (October 2008), http://classsizematters. org/fact_sheet_on_upper_grades_CSR.pdf.

Leonie Haimson, "Smaller is Better: First-Hand Reports of Early Grade Class Size Reduction in New York City Public Schools," Educational Priorities Panel (April 2000), http://www.edpriorities.org /Pubs/Report/Report_Smaller.html.

Discharge and Graduation Rates

Jennifer L. Jennings and Leonie Haimson, "High School Discharges Revisited: Trends in New York City's Discharge Rates 2000–2007," Office of the Public Advocate, City of New York (May 2009), http://pubadvocate.nyc.gov/new_news/documents/Discharges Revisited.pdf.

"Dead Ends: The Need for More Pathways to Graduation for Overage, Under-Credited Students in New York City," Advocates for Children (December 2007), http://www.advocatesforchildren.org /pubs/dead_ends.pdf.

"Pushing Out At-Risk Students: An Analysis of High School Discharge Figures," Advocates for Children and the Public Advocate for the City of New York, November 21, 2002, http://www.advocates forchildren.org/pubs/2005/discharge.pdf.

"School Pushout: Where are we now?" Advocates for Children, Issue brief (February 2008), http://www.advocatesforchildren.org /pubs/pushout_update_2008.pdf.

Finances

"Adding up the Numbers: The Education Budget under Mayoral Control," Educational Priorities Panel, Bulletin #2, January 20, 2006, http://www.edpriorities.org/Info/CityBudget/Bulletin_2Jan06.pdf.

"The School Accountability Initiative: Totaling the Cost," Independent Budget Office, Fiscal brief (November 2008), http://www.ibo.nyc.ny.us/iboreports/SchoolAccountability111308.pdf.

George Sweeting, Independent Budget Office, testimony during New York City Council hearings by the Contracts and Education Committees on Contracting Practices of the Department of

Education, April 1, 2009, http://www.ibo.nyc.ny.us/iboreports/3109 DOEContractingtestimony.pdf.

City Comptroller William Thompson, letter to Chancellor Klein on contract overruns, April 1, 2009, posted with attachments at http://www.comptroller.nyc.gov/press/2009_releases/pr09-04-078. shtm.

Governance

"Recommendations on School Governance," Parent Commission on School Governance and Mayoral Control (March 2009), http://www.parentcommission.org/parent_commission_Final_Report.pdf.

Transcripts of New York State Assembly Hearings by the Standing Committee on Education on Governance of the New York City School District, January 29, 2009 (Queens), February 6, 2009 (Manhattan), and March 20, 2009 (Brooklyn), http://assembly.state.ny.us/mem/?ad=037.

Middle Schools

"New York City's Middle-Grade Schools: Platforms for Success or Pathways to Failure?" Campaign for Educational Justice, in collaboration with the Annenberg Institute for School Reform (January 2007), http://www.annenberginstitute.org/pdf/MiddleGrades.pdf.

"Our Children Can't Wait: A Proposal to Close the Middle Grades Achievement Gap," Campaign for Educational Justice, in collaboration with the Annenberg Institute for School Reform (January 2008),http://www.annenberginstitute.org/pdf/MiddleGrades2 .pdf.

"Stuck in the Middle: The Problem of Overage Middle School Students in New York City," Advocates for Children (July 2008), http://www.advocatesforchildren.org/Stuck%20in%20the%20Middle (final).pdf.

Military Recruitment

"We Want You(th)! Confronting Unregulated Military Recruitment in New York City Public Schools," New York Civil Liberties Union and Manhattan Borough President Scott Stringer (2007), http://www.nyclu.org/node/1349.

Parent Involvement

"The Independent Parent Survey: Views of New York City Public School Parents and Parent Leaders on Class Size, Testing, and Mayoral Control," Class Size Matters (February 2008), http://www.classsizematters.org/parent_survey_report_FINAL.pdf.

"Parents Dismissed: An Analysis of Manhattan's Community Education Councils and the New York City Department of Education's Role in Engaging Parent Leaders," Office of Manhattan Borough President (June 2006), http://www.mbpo.org/uploads/PARENTS%20DISMISSED.pdf.

School Overcrowding

"A Better Capital Plan," a report from the Manhattan Task Force on School Overcrowding, Class Size Matters, the United Federation of Teachers, and The Center for Arts Education (October, 2008), http://www.classsizematters.org/abettercapitalplan.html.

"Capital Promises: Why NYC Children Don't Have the School Buildings They Need," Educational Priorities Panel (April 2007), http://www.edpriorities.org/Pubs/Report/Capital%20Promises%20July%2007%20report.pdf.

"Castles in the Sand: Why School Overcrowding Remains a Problem in NYC," Educational Priorities Panel (April 2002), http://www.edpriorities.org/Pubs/Report/Castles%20in%20the%20Sand.pdf.

"Crowded Out: School Construction Fails to Keep Up with Manhattan Building Boom," Office of Manhattan Borough President Scott Stringer (April 2008), http://www.mbpo.org/uploads/StillCrowdedOut.pdf.

"Growing Pains: Reforming Department of Education Capital Planning to Keep Pace with New York City's Residential Construction," Policy Report of the New York City Office of the Comptroller, Office of Policy Management (May 2008), http://www.comptroller.nyc.gov/bureaus/opm/reports/05-09-08_growing_pains.pdf.

Emily Horowitz and Leonie Haimson, "How Crowded Are Our Schools? New Results from a Survey of NYC Public School Principals," Class Size Matters, October 3, 2008, http://www.classsizematters.org/principal_survey_report_10.08_final. pdf.

Small Schools

"New Century High Schools: Evaluation Findings from the Second Year," Policy Studies Associates, March 16, 2005, http://www. policystudies.com/studies/school/NCHS%20Second%20Year%20 Report.pdf

"Small Schools, Few Choices: How NYC's High School Reform Effort Left Students with Disabilities Behind," New York Lawyers for the Public Interest (October 2006), http://www.nylpi.org/images /FE/chain234siteType8/site203/client/DLC%20-%20Education %20-%20High_School_Report.pdf

"So Many Schools, So Few Options: How Mayor Bloomberg's Small High School Reforms Deny Full Access to English Language Learners," The New York Immigration Coalition and Advocates for Children of New York (November 2006), http://thenyic.org /images/ uploads/NYIC_AFC_ELL_Small_Schools_Report_11-28-06.pdf.

William Gates, "2009 Annual Letter from Bill Gates: U.S. Education" at http://www.gatesfoundation.org/annual-letter/Pages/2009-united-states-education.aspx.

Jennifer L. Jennings and Aaron Pallas, "Who Attends Small Schools?," presented at the American Educational Research Association annual conference, San Diego, CA, April 13–17, 2009.

Special Education

"Audit Report on the Monitoring and Tracking of Special Education Services For Elementary School Students by the Department of Education, MD06-073A," William C. Thompson, Jr., New York City Comptroller, City of New York, Office of the Comptroller, Bureau of Management Audit (June 29, 2007), www. comptroller.nyc.gov/bureaus/audit/PDF_FILES/MD06_073A.pdf.

"Educate! Include! Respect! A Call for School System Reform to Improve the Educational Experiences of Students with Disabilities in New York City," ARISE Coalition (April 2009), http://arisecoalition.org/Include%21%20%20Educate%21%20%20 Respect%21.pdf.

"Leaving School Empty-Handed: A Report on Education and Dropout Rates for Students Who Receive Special Education Services," Advocates for Children (June 2005), www.advocatesfor children.org/pubs/2005/spedgradrates. pdf.

"Left in the Dark: Citywide Council on Special Education Survey Finds DOE Not Informing Parents of Educational Opportunities for Children with Disabilities," Betsy Gotbaum, Public Advocate, City of New York, Office of the Public Advocate (June 2007), http://pubadvocate.nyc.gov/policy/documents/CCSEREPORT FINALWEB.pdf.

"Mixed Signals: 311 Fails to Provide Consistent Information to Parents of Children with Special Needs," Betsy Gotbaum, Public Advocate, City of New York, Office of the Public Advocate (June 2008), http://www.pubadvocate.nyc.gov/policy/documents/311-specialedReport-WEBFINAL.pdf.

"Overworked, Underutilized: How the Department of Education's Reorganizations of Special Education Turned School Psychologists From Mental Health Professionals Into Paper Pushers," Betsy Gotbaum, Public Advocate, City of New York, Office of the Public Advocate (November 2008), http://www.pubadvocate.nyc.gov/policy/documents/SchoolPsychologistsWebFinal.pdf.

"Transitioning to Nowhere: An Analysis of the Planning and Provision of Transition Services to Students with Disabilities in NYC," Advocates for Children (September 2007), http://www.advocatesforchildren.org/pubs/Transitioning_to_nowhere_ final_report.pdf.

"Waiting for Special Education," Report 3–2009, Thomas D. Napoli, Comptroller, State of New York, Office of the Comptroller (June 2008), http://www.osc.state.ny.us/osdc/rpt3-2009.pdf.

Thomas Hehir, et al., "Comprehensive Management Review and Evaluation of Special Education," submitted to the New York City Department of Education, September 20, 2005), http://schools.nyc.gov/NR/rdonlyres/BB43599E-F0AE-48E2-B657-5E392 D3968D9/0/FinalHehirReport092005.pdf.

Student Civil Rights and the School to Prison Pipeline

"Criminalizing the Classroom: The Over-Policing of New York City Schools," New York Civil Liberties Union and the American Civil Liberties Union (March 2007), http://www.nyclu.org/pdfs/criminalizing_the_classroom_report.pdf.

"Deprived of Dignity: Degrading Treatment and Abusive Discipline in New York City & Los Angeles Public Schools," National Economic & Social Rights Initiative (March 2007), http://www.nesri.org/programs/dignity_report.html.

Testing

"The Nation's Report Card," National Assessment of Educational Progress (NAEP), http://nationsreportcard.gov.

James F. Brennan, "New York City Public School Achievement Before and After Mayoral Control," January 28, 2009, http://www.assembly.state.ny.us/member_files/044/20090128.

Joshua Feinman, Ph.D., "High Stakes, but Low Validity? A Case Study of Standardized Tests and Admissions into New York City Specialized High Schools," Education Policy Research Unit, Arizona State University, October 2008, http://epicpolicy.org/publication/high-stakes-but-low-validity.

Daniel Koretz, *Measuring Up: What Educational Testing Really Tells Us* (Cambridge: Harvard, 2008).

Recommended Blogs

NYC Public School Parents: http://nycpublicschoolparents.blogspot.com.

Aaron Pallas at Gotham Schools: http://gothamschools.org/author/aaron-pallas.

Eduwonkette (Jennifer L. Jennings), archived at Edweek: http://blogs.edweek.org/edweek/eduwonkette.

Bridging Differences (Deborah Meier, Diane Ravitch): http://blogs.edweek.org/edweek/Bridging-Differences.

www.ingramcontent.com/pod-product-compliance
Lightning Source LLC
Chambersburg PA
CBHW021102090426
42738CB00006B/473